THE RISE AND FALL OF AMERICAN SOCIALISM

ELISE WHITWORTH

Restoring Faith, Family & Freedom, LLC
Dahlonega, GA
www.elisewhitworth.com

Revised Reprint of First Edition "Fruit Loons: The Rise and Fall of American Socialism"

DEDICATED TO

Henry Lewis and Lucy Whitworth
(Dad and Mom)

Restoring Faith, Family & Freedom, LLC
191 Sequoyah Place
Dahlonega, GA 30533

www.elisewhitworth.com
elisewhitworth@gmail.com

Printed in the United States of America
ISBN: 978-1530010639

Royalty Free Clip Art and Illustrations from:
www.iclipart.com
www.clipart.com
www.clipartof.com

Note: Clipart captions and figure descriptions are mine unless the caption is part of the clipart's original cartoon caption line (for example: Figure 9).

Fruit Tree and fruit text content and structure are author's original work.

TABLE OF CONTENTS

CHARTS

KEY ILLUSTRATIONS

ABOUT THE AUTHOR

Elise Whitworth is a native Georgian who entered ministry in 1976 as an adult educator and writer. To broaden her perspective and education, she worked her way through college and graduate schools, earning a BA in psychology, M.Ed. in adult education, a M.Div., and a doctorate in religious education. During her educational pursuits, she lived and worked in England for a year, and returned to the USA to help launch adult training centers and a master's level institute of strategic Christian leadership.

Believing in contributing to society beyond the classroom, she served in a safe house for victims of domestic violence, a volunteer police chaplain, and pastored several churches in South Georgia. She currently serves as Wing chaplain with Georgia Wing CAP- U. S. Air Force Auxiliary and was awarded the National Chaplain of the Year Award in 2009, and the National Squadron Chaplain of the Year Award in 2012.

Elise stands in support of American families and individual freedom while firmly believing that if we assume our responsibilities as citizens of this great nation, we can and will exile socialism and continue to restore sanity to America. A major part of this restoration is to pass the torch of faith, family and freedom to the next generation.

FORWARD

I acknowledge the following with a grateful heart and special thanks- first, to God in whom is our hope and strength, and secondly, to my friend and copy editor, and a host of other faithful prayer warriors, without all of whom this book would not have come to fruition.

The contents of this book will hopefully challenge people to read, dig deep, pray, think, expand their horizons, and laugh. 'A picture is worth a thousand words'- so a few graphics and charts for more complex information are included (K.I.S.S.).[1] The basic writing strategy is to not bore, depress, or scare people to death, but tell the truth, stir in generous portions of love, and salt with humor. This was God's plan for this book, and God's thoughts really are higher than our thoughts (great news for Christians- not so much for Secular Humanists, Socialists, Progressives and atheists).

Let's break a few formal English composition rules and be fireside chatty; and just for the sheer fun of it, occasionally throw Strunk & White's *Elements of Style* under the bus and make up a few words along the way. It took several months to start writing this book because I was purposely avoiding writing about some of the serious stuff that makes us want to cry, chop wood, or run to the nearest government office, school board, city council, or church screaming, "What were you thinking when you...???" Use your memory to finish the sentence folks; I know you have thought about doing that. Perhaps we are avoiding the risk of confronting the unnerving sight of a spinning head or enduring the arrogant talking bobble head who tries to justify insanity or theft. Deep down, maybe we realize it is like talking to a fencepost—but even a fencepost has to yield to a force of nature. With God, all things are possible. P.S. Not all politicians are created alike- there are the rare few who are true, honest Statesmen who believe in upholding the *Constitution*; thank you for "serving" with integrity.

Warning- this is a politically incorrect book, but I double-dog dare you to read it anyway. After all, we need to stop taking ourselves so seriously and check the super-sensitive ego at the door (or, better yet, immediately call a counselor and get help). Chill, kick back, enjoy the candor and honesty, and risk laughing at ourselves (to keep from cry-ing). America is at a critical juncture (i.e., to be free or not to be free) and this is not the time to hold back and short change those who want the truth or are brave enough to face the truth.

It will be tempting to skip over the first nine chapters on America's history regarding the constitution and American liberties and go directly to the solutions section (Chapters 10 through 13). However, having an understanding of the root of our problems in America is essential if we want to stand boldly in the face of tyranny and shouting with authority and conviction, "ENOUGH."

If we are going to restore sanity to America, we must realize that we have missed or overlooked important pieces of the Progressive puzzle because of American Socialist's control of our public education and mainstream media that leans more in in favor of socialism. Knowing the subtle (or not so subtle) contrasts between the nature of American liberty versus the enemies of those liberties such as Socialism, understanding Progressive language and the twisted meanings of liberal lingo, and having an understanding of the root of our problems in America is critical. Knowledge is power, which explains why bureaucrats have systematically dumbed down the public education system to weaken the heart and soul of America. A concerned American mother, wife, grandparent, businesswoman and my close friend, who has asked to remain anonymous, expressed it this way:

> "I have attributed the rapid decline of all aspects of our culture to the unchecked desire of each generation to shrug off restrictions of the previous generation. Never would I have believed that this is because of a concerted calculated effort to manipulate our thinking by crippling our capacity to learn and by promoting relaxation of our moral values to the point that we are not even aware of how good we have it in this country and why we have it. I am heartsick to learn that each generation's thinking has been manipulated by Americans who have been taught to hate this country and are unable to see that the uniqueness of our Constitution ultimately allows for wrongs to be righted."

So be prepared to read some inconvenient truth, PRAY and be challenged to *think*. At the end of each chapter, there will be a *21st Century Truth or Consequence Question*, and a *Dig Deeper* section suggesting in-depth resources to read or view. So let's shake a few trees and see what falls out.

Elise Whitworth

INTRODUCTION TO REALITY

"For you...have been called to liberty."[2]

The Rise and Fall of American Socialism is about revealing, confronting and dismantling the forces that have systematically undermined America's faith, families, and freedom. The intent of this book is to provide an overview of America's original roots, the intrusion of socialism, the underlying worldviews that feed the Socialist Machine in America, the end game of socialism, and how Americans can be a vital part of reversing the curse of socialism. A number of graphic trees will portray the roots and corresponding fruit produced by some major worldviews and philosophical movements. There will be good trees with healing power in their leaves, and other trees that produce poisonous fruit. If we understand the root of our problems in America, we can stop the implosion of our families and freedom by refusing to cultivate and feed on poisonous fruit. We have a fighting chance of survival as one nation under God and as a thriving and prosperous democratic republic capable of facilitating true God-honoring liberty around the world if we will embrace God's truth and way and actively seek to restore liberty according to God's design.

If *The Rise and Fall of American Socialism* is not what you expected, then we have something in common—neither did I. I experienced the agony of reading hundreds of non-fiction research works, some of which delved deep into the abyss of socialism, Marxism, and Darwinism, and others that were downright boring but necessary to consume. Had it not been for prayer warriors, supportive friends, a strong biblical foundation and faith in God, and great books from men and women of courage and integrity who spoke truth—depression would have consumed my time and energy.

After reading about the ungodly and inhumane horrors committed by crazed lunatics who enslaved others in their web of deceit and pit of darkness, I was left with one thought. God help us if we continue to feed at the trough of social Darwinism, cower behind the curtain of political correctness, and avoid facing our moral and ethical deviance cloaked as humanistic social justice while demanding our rights and habitually avoiding personal responsibility.

Before we have a yawn-fest, let's talk about all-knowing *extremist loons*. We can have a lot of fun with this group simply because they make it so easy to spot the absurdity of what they consider to be their great moments and historical attempts to fix society while thinking in their minds- 'move over God, I've got this one.' To be a member of the *extremist loon* gang, one must fake intelligence, pretend to care about others, worship at the altar of self, have the ability to lift one's nose in an upward motion or raise an eyebrow to display arrogance, lack real logical thinking skills, and be a robotic talking head for the socialism. They also have mental convulsions when hearing the words accountability, conservative, *U.S. Constitution*, Israel, God, or Christianity while secretly or overtly campaigning to erase any sign of God from public view and outlawing godly morality. They are extremely loyal to socialism and want to turn America into some sort of fantasy utopia.

Figure 1: The All-Knowing Extremist Loon

Extremist loons think their plans are the only solution, are overly sensitive and paranoid, won't stop talking long enough to listen, can change like a chameleon to fit any circumstance (displaying schizophrenic symptoms while hoping no one will notice), insist they are the ruling elite, and think we are too stupid to figure out what their real agenda is. They also become deaf at inconvenient moments, and consider themselves citizens of the world at the expense of American liberties and sovereignty while prostituting the *Constitution of the United States of America* and bowing to leaders who hate America. As you may have noticed, I have not mentioned any names because you are smart enough to figure it out. If it waddles and quacks like a duck, and hangs out with other ducks, then it is a....

Figure 2: This really is a duck, unless...

someone has paid a lawyer, politician, or newsperson to convince us that it is a turkey, as we wonder, "Who's the turkey now?"

I would be negligent if I did not acknowledge the beauty and grace of the great North American Loon who is an aquatic bird known for its unique yodeling sound and expert diving ability. In no way is my use of the term *extremist loons* a reflection on this great American bird, but is simply a metaphor for those creatures who seek to undermine America and her constitution and have little regard for individual freedom, faith, and American families while shoving their absurd agendas down our throats. Loon means *absurd* or *crazy,* therefore, *extremist loons* refers to the absurdities and insane extremist goals produced by American Socialists and Progressives.

About twenty years ago, I began to realize that something was not right with this American Dream picture. You may vaguely remember this picture—it was when folks could leave their door open and take a walk in their neighborhood without fear of harm, the *Constitution* as the law of the land was respected, children could be children, and families were strong in their resolve to stick together during the good and bad times. Gradually, faith, hope, and love seemed to waver, and struggle for survival and being a God-fearing person ceased to be acceptable to the point where one is compelled to practice self-censorship for the sake of political correctness. Teenage high school students are not permitted to erect crosses on school grounds as a memorial to their deceased classmates, and bereaved families of soldiers and law enforcement officers lost in battle overseas or on American soil have to defend their constitutional right to show respect according to their faith in public and in peace.

As the American Dream began to fade, I wanted to discover what happened and what was at the root of this downward spiral. How and when did freedom begin to dwindle? What worldviews, philosophies, or political agendas were undermining the original intent of America's *Constitution*? What forces were provoking fear and chaos and choking the life out of the Spirit of Liberty Tree? I soon discovered I could not hope to join the movement to restore America's faith, hope, and love until these revived in me first. So began my journey of scripture meditation, prayer, confession, repentance, fellowship, diligent research, logical thinking, responsible citizenship, and active service.

There is one thing that drives pseudo-intellectuals crazy, and that is good old-fashioned *common sense* and *simple truth*. If you have not guessed it by now, I am a Bible believing, U.S. *Constitution* carrying, pro-Israel supporter, and conservative American. I unashamedly love God and my country and still believe that America is great and is the only place on earth where evidence of life, liberty, and the pursuit of happiness is still alive, although, admittedly gasping for air at this point in her history.

There has been and continues to be an agenda in play to turn America into a two-class society- the very rich ruling elite and the poor, thus eliminating the thorn in the side of the ruling elite, that is, the hard working middle class. I refuse to remain silent while *extremist loons* dismantle and pervert our liberties and heritage. So join me as we begin with common sense and have an honest reality check by telling the simple truth.

Part of me honestly wants to suggest that if American faith, family and freedom as defined by God in the Holy Scriptures, and as protected by the original intent of the *U.S. Constitution* offends you so much that you feel compelled to fundamentally transform it, please move to someplace else like North Korea, Cuba, Iran, or Russia. As for me, I choose mercy, grace, and love, realizing that we all have had some part in dismantling portions of our liberties, whether it has been through overt activism, covert compromise, or passive neglect, and we have failed to realize that we have fallen asleep at the wheel.

Let us pray that we *all* wake up, embrace God's eternal truth, and choose life for everyone--including the unborn. "Lord, help us to 'humble ourselves and pray, turn from our destructive ways and seek your face that we may be forgiven and our land healed,'[3] and purged of all forces that seek to undermine God-given liberties and destroy our families and country. Help us to remember, 'where the Spirit of the Lord is, there is liberty.'[4] May the true spirit of thankfulness and humility find a permanent place in our hearts, and may we never forget the unwavering fortitude of our founding fathers and mothers who followed your guidance and paved the way for America to grow, prosper, and become the standard-bearer of God-honoring liberties. Grant us the courage to stand in the gap as faithful guardians of faith, family, and freedom. According to your grace and mercy Lord, restore her purpose as 'a light to the world and a city set on a hill that cannot be hidden.'[5]

We have very little time left to restore the American Dream and save our families—and this decade may be our last opportunity to turn the tide so that Americans may once again fulfill their purpose and restore their position as the honorable champions of the true spirit of liberty, justice and peace. Therefore, those who are of sound mind and body declare that as socialism has risen in this country masquerading as liberalism or progressivism, so shall it fall from its high places in the 21st century if we will pray and fulfill our duty as responsible citizens.[6] It is time to be courageous and root out the plans and programs of *extremist loons*, reclaim the land, throw out the rotten fruit, and replant seeds of true faith, hope, and charity in America's heart, soul and social institutions.

21ˢᵗ Century Truth or Consequence Question: *Am I ready to roll up my sleeves and work toward restoring and maintaining all my freedoms and God-given unalienable rights in America?[7]*

Dig Deeper

1. *The Constitution of the United States of America*
2. *The Declaration of Independence*
3. *The Book of Proverbs*

CHAPTER 1
THEN THERE WAS HAL

"...a tree is known by its fruit."[8]

When the first IPad came out, I thought $798+ was a bit pricey for a whoopi cushion or a pirate's eye patch, until I discovered it was one of those computer gadgets. Anyone would have thought the same thing whose first portable computer was an Osborne 1 that looked like a sewing machine, weighed 24.5 lbs., touted a grand memory of 64K RAM processing at turtle speed, used floppy disks for data storage, and sold for $1795.

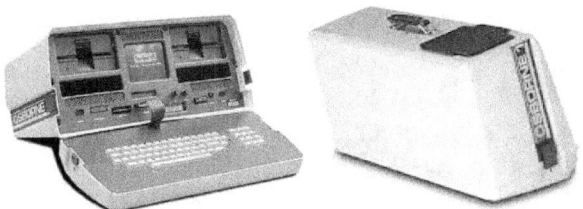

Figure 3: 1981 Osborn 1 Portable Computer[9]

Dad and I found this little jewel at a technology fair, and I was so excited when he purchased this creature from outer space that I immediately signed up for a basic computing course. When the instructor began talking about all those 1001100111000101's and other techy stuff, I dropped the class. It was much easier for me to sit like a zombie for hours in front of this alien creature, pressing F-function and alpha/numeric keys while following the archaic operations manual until I achieved success. The first function I learned was ON, the second SAVE (to prevent panic), and third EXIT (to maintain sanity)—after a few days of this, I felt like I had conquered the world.

To my father's delight, I even figured out how to load and operate a complex accounting program—little did I suspect that his plan for me was to keep the books on an estate of which he was executor. I continued developing bookkeeping and tax preparation skills which led to a viable income for me as a freelance bookkeeper while in the early stages of ministry work and continuing education. I discovered through my Osborne experience that teachers could talk until they were blue in the face, and I still would not grasp the maze of their concepts—I had become a hands-on, self-directed learner when it came to the complex. Thanks Mom and Dad for the analytical and creativity genes.

The computer industry claimed that computers would save time and money, increase productivity, and make life easier. As most of us discovered, sometimes computers consume more time than they save, and plunging for a $1000 or more computer every two+ years (due to constantly changing software requiring more speed and space with each "improved" version that forces incompatibility issues with the hardware) becomes a source of constant irritation. If any life or non-life form has spent time hanging out with computers (be it man, monkey or robot), this may sound familiar—"I have a love-hate relationship with computers." Imagine for a moment, the first space chimp that sat in front of a computer panel thinking, "Where's the swinging tire?" I am sure a few freaky jungle sounds and gymnastic chimp maneuvers filled the room in that first encounter after mistaking the joystick for a banana and the big red button for an apple.

In late 2007, I had a "2001: Space Odyssey" HAL[10]-moment with my computer and a few foreign tech support persons. After four hours of jumping through repetitious tech hoops while letting off a few screech-owl sounds in the last hour via cellphone, and several days trying to fix HAL, I surrendered my computer to the garbage dump and determined never to buy that particular brand again. When I recently heard a computer expert shouting, "I HATE COMPUTERS," I knew I was not crazy and alone in this techno jungle.

As I am sitting here having a spaghetti-on-the-wall moment to see what sticks, I remembered why I love America. America is the only place on earth where people can live freely as individuals and be all they can become, raise a family in peace, shop-'til-we-drop, speak our mind, and vote the bums out.

16

As illustrated in my stroll down memory lane, America is still a land of opportunity where people can exercise their ingenuity, creativity, and work ethic. A few original American ideas and inventions included mail order, telephone, bifocals, cotton gin, cupcake, electric stove, and the light bulb. It is still somewhat possible to make a decent living through gainful employment, providing a service, creating a new product, or owning a business. Granted, sometimes we have to start at the bottom and work our way up doing jobs we don't particularly fancy at wages we are not keen on, but that is a big part of taking personal responsibility for providing for our own basic needs or supporting a family. "I have been young, and *now* am old; yet I have not seen the righteous forsaken, nor his descendants begging bread."[11]

This brings us to our first tree- the Spirit of Liberty Tree and the fruit it produces as illustrated on the next page. The first Liberty Tree (1765) was an elm tree in Boston serving as a rallying point for colonists and Sons of Liberty who opposed King George III's Stamp Act that taxed legal and public documents including playing cards and newspapers. The stamp tax, known as the "knowledge tax," was considered censorship that violated the colonists' right to express themselves freely. American taxpayers were forced to cover England's debt that she had accumulated during the French and Indian War.

The "Tree of Liberty," served as a symbol of individual liberty and resistance against 18th century British tyranny, censorship, and unfair taxation. When George Washington's troops trapped British Loyalists inside the city of Boston, and the Loyalists tarred and feathered American patriots under the tree and later cut it down, using it for firewood- this act only served as fuel for the colonists and the American Revolutionary War. During the war, colonists flew Liberty Tree flags to demonstrate their unwavering determination to free themselves from oppressive elitist rulers.

Once the Spirit of Liberty Tree was planted in the hearts and minds of American patriots, freedom began to flow like a river of life, and its fruit supplied the strength for liberty to thrive. Without strong families, courageous faith, and responsible exercise of freedom, liberty cannot survive, and as faith, family, and freedom flourished, each grew into a full orchard rich in fruitful progress and prosperity.

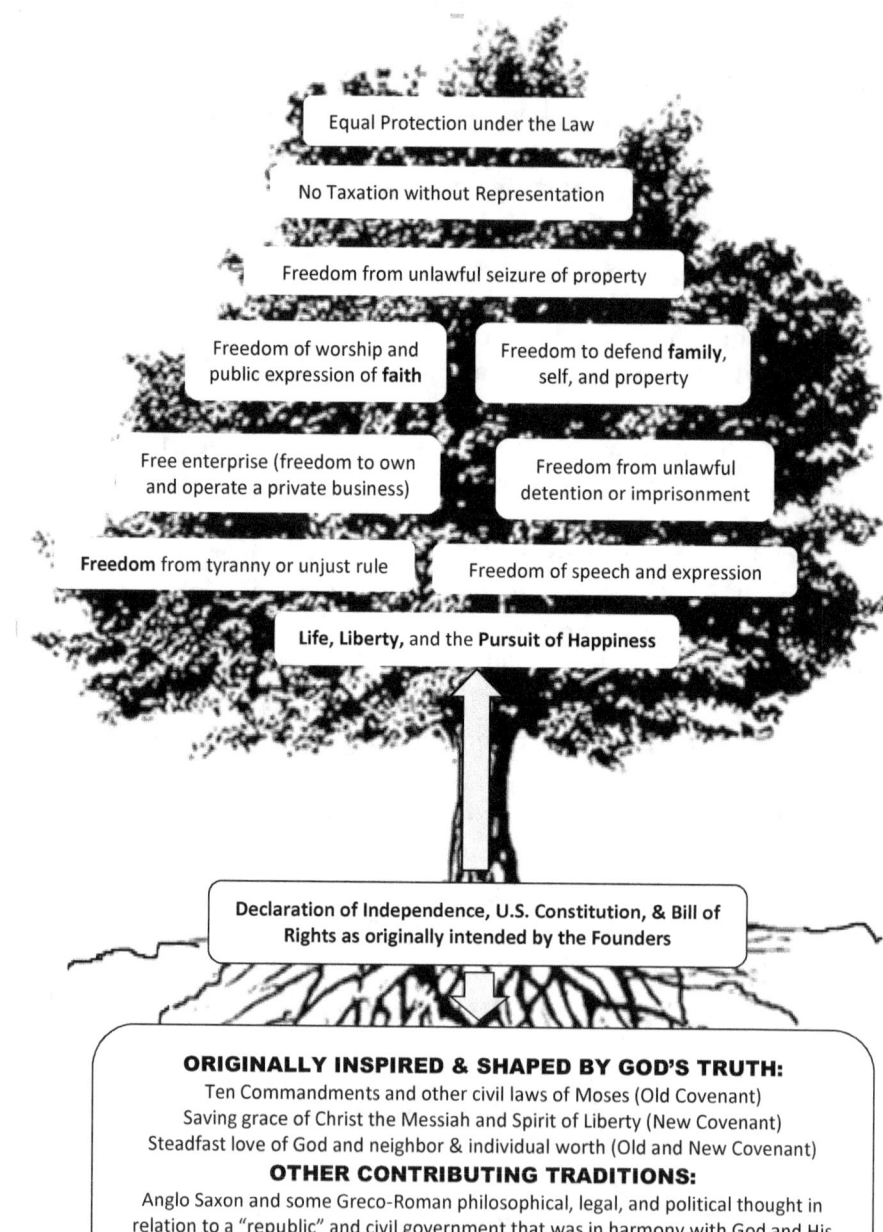

Figure 4: Spirit of Liberty Tree

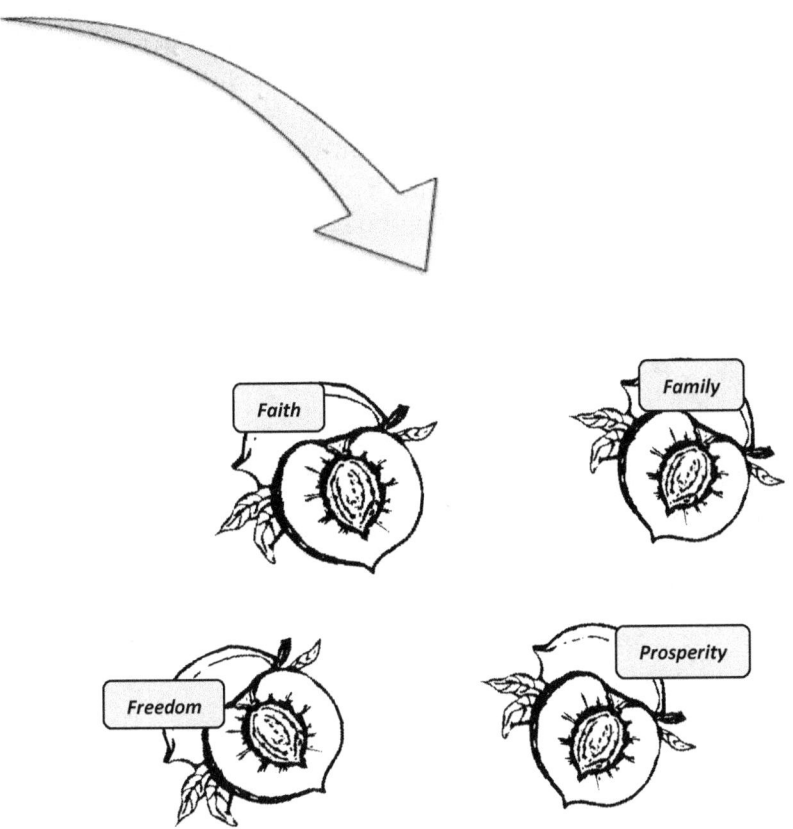

Figure 5: Fruit falling from the Spirit of Liberty Tree (courageous faith, strong famlies, responsible freedom, and prosperity)

Before delving further into important principles regarding faith, family, freedom, and prosperity in relation to liberty, which we will tackle later in this book, I want to introduce a resource section titled "Dig Deeper." Materials listed in this section cover topics discussed in the chapter and represent some of the best, well-researched resources available that hold true to the original record of history.

If we are serious about taking back the freedoms we have lost and maintaining liberty for this generation and the next, and we have not already read these materials, then I challenge everyone to turn off the TV (which I call the "idiot box" because it induces mental comas and

19

strange behavioral shifts if habitually viewed in heavy doses). In addition, unplug "twitter" devices, shut off other intrusive technology (unless you Nook- or Kindle-read books), find a quiet room, and become informed and educated. The majority of information in these resources has been purged from our school and college textbooks, and a vast number of libraries, especially within the last four decades—all part of the "political correctness" and Secular Progressive scheme of transforming America into a Socialist State. Start your own library of credible sources—better yet, why not create "Freedom Libraries" in our homes and neighborhoods, then let good news and sound wisdom spread like wild fire.

21ˢᵗ Century Truth or Consequence Question: *Look at the Spirit of Liberty Tree's "freedom fruit" again and answer the following: Which freedoms am I willing to let go of so that America can be "fundamentally transformed" and made subject to foreign laws and power in exchange for the meager privilege of calling myself a "citizen of the world"?*

Dig Deeper

1. Sandra Reid, *America: Land of Principles and Promises* (Mesa, AZ: Heritage Academy, 2011).
2. W. Cleon Skousen (1981), *The 5000 Year Leap: A Miracle that Changed the World* (Malta, IN: National Center for Constitutional Studies, 2006). www.nccs.net

CHAPTER 2
WILD TURKEYS AND GREEDY KINGS

"For you...have been called to liberty; only do not use liberty as an opportunity for the flesh, but through love serve one another."[12]

Before moving forward, let's review a few important historical events in America's infancy. The first order of business for the colonists was to form and solidify a governing instrument and body. On June 11, 1776, the Continental Congress appointed a committee to write a governing document for the thirteen states. As a knee-jerk reaction to the oppressive tyrannical rule of King George III (monarchy), the committee favored a "people's law" type structure that gravitated more towards rule without law (anarchy), placing most of the ruling power in the hands of each separate state.

The first governing instrument was the *Articles of Confederation*[13] whereby the states determined what powers the centralized government would have. Because the states would not authorize much power to the central government (called the Confederation Government), it was not able to provide sufficient supplies to the Continental Army. This resulted in starvation, disease and death for 2,000 soldiers, and 3,000 more abandoned George Washington at Valley Forge.[14]

Fast forward to the past: On two occasions, the colonists had experienced centralized planning, redistribution of wealth, and the communal or common-store system (known today as socialism, Marxism, Fascism, or Communism) which King James of England had established for a period of five years. Round One: Under the first "New World" settler's communal system at Jamestown (1607), they deposited their food and supplies into a central storehouse from which everyone could take what they needed. Because many colonists consumed more than they were willing to produce and deposit into the common storehouse, many starved to death.[15]

Instead of facing the reality that the communal system was not working, the London Trading Company dug in deeper by substituting the promise of housing in place of wages, and distributing harvested crops equally among the settlers. The biggest drawback was that the London Company had established itself as a bureaucracy, taking immediate profits for itself and equally distributing leftovers to participating colonists several years later, which is similar to what is happening in our government today. Even though land for farming and building a homestead was given to the colonists, the colonists once again consumed more than they produced and deposited, whereby the system eventually fell apart.[16] The land belonged to King James, and the London Company gave land to settlers who in turn became the indentured servants of the king. Yeah, that system really worked out well, costing the lives of over half the New World's early population.

<u>Round Two</u>: The *Mayflower* arrived at Plymouth Harbor on December 21, 1620. Since they were initially beyond the reach of the London Company's bureaucracy, and the colonists were familiar with a "republic" type of self-government, the men wrote and signed the *Mayflower Compact* before landing, voluntarily committing to loyalty and obedience to God and King James, and to whatever laws necessary to ensure the preservation and welfare of the colony.[17]

Figure 6: Signing of the Mayflower Compact by the Plymouth Pilgrims[18]

Eventually, the trading company's creeping vine of bureaucracy wrapped itself around the Plymouth Pilgrims, forcing them under the same failed communal system as Jamestown—early evidence of the *extremist loons* in operation. As a result, Plymouth plunged into a "starving time" for seven years because of the compulsory Socialist system, a system in which those who think they are entitled to handouts refuse to put forth the necessary effort to provide for their own needs and never for the needs of others.[19] The cost of a predatory bureaucracy and its entitlement recipients will always undercut the efforts of the industrious hard worker and end in a shortage of food, supplies and other life- and health-sustaining necessities for everyone (except for the ruling elite who always take what they need first).

King James and London Company- "Thanks, but no thanks!" The Pilgrims finally secured the right to keep what they produced and earned, and willingly shared the fruits of their labor with others who invested equal effort and with those too sick to participate. Because of the bountifulness of the harvest, they celebrated in a three-day feast, which became known as the First Thanksgiving and established as Thanksgiving Day in 1863 by President Lincoln.[20]

Figure 7: 17th Century Plymouth Pilgrims giving thanks to God[21]

Shortly after the Plymouth Thanksgiving feast, the memory of what was working began to fade. The pilgrims reverted to the communal system again with an added twist- the women were forced to do chores and labor for men who were not their husbands or part of their family. Their husbands had a few things to say about that plan. Once again, production dropped followed by starvation, disease and death. Governor Bradford concluded that following Plato's philosophy of taking away property and securing it for the common wealth was detrimental to the life, liberty and welfare of the colonists.[22]

Plymouth returned to their former free enterprise system that was capable of supporting the colonists, sustaining their growth and prosperity, and enabling them to pay off their debts to the London Company within nine years. Families worked together and labored harder under the free enterprise system once they had the freedom to be the first to benefit from their efforts and keep their property.[23]

The Plymouth colonists were the first freemen to establish a "General Court," which became the first American representative government system. As the colony expanded into other townships, deputies were elected to represent the people of their respective townships at the General Court where legal and practical business for the colony was conducted (1639). Plymouth became the first to lay "the foundation for religious and political freedom."[24]

Eventually, the London Company failed because King James was constantly changing the charters and boundaries, making survival as a business impossible. There were several trade companies courting the king's favor, and the king chose the winners and losers. Does this sound familiar 21st century America?

The 17th century communal system experience demonstrates the importance of knowing history.[25] Lessons learned may help us avoid repeating the same mistakes that can jeopardize our lives and future as a sovereign nation of free persons. Fast forward to today: Why are we allowing our leaders, educators and economists to play jeopardy with our individual liberty and allowing ourselves to be enslaved by socialism? Anyone with common sense would diagnose this as insanity—that is, making the same mistakes repeatedly and expecting different results. Could it be that we as a nation have forgotten to be thankful for simple things and have forsaken God's truth, wisdom, and guidance? Have we not learned history!

Now back to the American Revolution: King George III continued the previous British monarchy's imposition of oppressive regulations, economic plundering, and burdensome taxation on the colonies. On June 12, 1775, England declared martial law and confiscated properties without compensation to house British and Hessian troops. It had become obvious that the colonists would have to fight for their freedom. Patrick Henry expressed his resolve and the sentiment of other patriots when he said, "Gentlemen may cry peace, peace—but there is no peace ...Almighty God! I know not that course others may take; but as for me, give me liberty, or give me death."[26]

In response to King George III, Thomas Jefferson (1776) wrote the *Declaration of Independence* that clearly stated the colonists' grievances and their declaration of independence from British rule. This transpired shortly after the first draft of the *Articles of Confederation* and before its ratification by the thirteen states. A week after George Washington raised the first official battle flag at his camp to signify the colonists unifying to secure their freedom, Thomas Paine wrote and distributed *Common Sense*.[27]

After reading Paine's pamphlet, it was easy to see how it had served to rally the patriots under the common cause and purpose of Divine Providence to secure freedom from arbitrary power and establish a true republic that has no need of a king. The colonists definitely preferred the freedom to eat their own wild turkeys as opposed to slaving away for greedy kings in exchange for meager and insufficient provisions; having one's property and wealth gobbled up by kings and bureaucrats and starving to death was a no winner for freedom-loving patriots. Thousands of American patriots and Frenchmen died to secure liberty in America. After six years of war, final victory was won by sea at Chesapeake Bay and by land at Yorktown, Virginia. British and Hessian troops waved the white flag of surrender on October 17, 1781, and the Articles of Capitulation was signed on October 19, 1781,[28] paving the way for American sovereignty to be firmly established.

Next order of business for the colonists after the war was to solidify the unity of the colonies as a civil society under strong principles and consistent civil laws. The primary task for the founding fathers was to achieve a balance between the extremes of tyranny and anarchy to ensure liberty for everyone. To understand the mindset and heartbeat for freedom of the Founders as they confronted the task of framing a governing structure sufficient to sustain American sovereignty and secure the welfare of her people, we will uncover some important lessons they learned from ancient history.

Figure 8: Thanksgiving from the turkey's perspective

The colonists discovered what worked and what did not work. The following is a summary of some of the lessons they learned:

1. It is prudent and necessary to seek God's guidance and wisdom and thank Him for His provision and mercy.
2. Centralized planning (i.e., big government and large business monopolies favored by government) is ineffective, and their CEOs, dictators, and monarchs take more than they give.
3. No single person or entity can handle absolute power.
4. Communal systems (socialism) create counterproductive entitlement groups and eventually fail to meet the needs of each group, which leads to a revolt, thus ending with tyrannical leaders declaring martial law or war on their people.
5. There will always be people who want something for nothing.
6. A free-enterprise system better facilitates prosperity.
7. Individual ingenuity, creativity, and industriousness and people working together freely are more effective in meeting the needs of individuals and society than a socially engineered, national workforce or slaves of the aristocracy.
8. A "republic" type of self-government with mutually agreed upon laws is more effective in securing the welfare of the people.

Understanding the Founders' mindset and heartbeat for freedom as they confronted the task of framing a governing structure sufficient to sustain American sovereignty and secure the welfare of the people requires historical insight into ancient history regarding government. To begin with, the colonists had enough of the "king" thing. So, they looked to wisdom from ancient and contemporary thinkers of substance (that is, men who possessed spiritual and mental depth), integrity, high moral virtue, and champions of liberty and civil order. Thomas Paine clearly expressed the desire of the patriots to axe the "king" thing from the governing structure of the colonies when he elaborated on the historical example of the ancient Hebrew nation in *Common Sense*, so, it is here that we begin our brief journey into the ancient past.

From the time the Israelites entered Egypt until Moses led them out of Egypt (430 years[29]); they were enslaved by the oppressive rule of Pharaoh Dynasties and subjected to Egyptian polytheism.[30] The ancient Egyptian Pharaohs maintained a three-class society (the ruling priest cast, military, and servant slaves[31]), and idolatrous rituals cen-

27

tered on deification of the Pharaohs who used religion to strengthen their grip on the people like modern day cults do. The servant slaves of the Egyptian Dynasties died with their masters to continue serving them in the afterlife.

To maintain order in their mobile community after deliverance from Egyptian bondage, the Hebrews needed to establish a civil order structure and legal system to secure justice and safety. They knew that single-family or religious class monopolies (i.e., dynasties of the Pharaohs) did not work out so well, so Moses instituted a self-governing republican structure whereby God commissioned Moses as Israel's leader, counselor, and judge (equivalent to a Chief Magistrate), and appointed Aaron as Moses' assistant. After Moses, the people elected the chief magistrate. Because one man could not carry the load of hearing civil dispute cases and making decisions for three million people, Moses followed the advice of Jethro, his father-in-law, and organized the Hebrews into a more manageable civil society.

The people chose elders according to their tribes and groups of 10, 50, 100, and 1,000 families, thus creating a "Senate" of elders or representatives.[32] Disputes and legal cases not settled within family units or groups of families moved up the chain to the Senate, and Moses ruled on cases that were not resolved at the Senate level. This established the first stage of self-government; that is, the people had the responsibility and freedom to settle affairs locally amongst themselves instead of some distant centralized bureaucracy that was out of touch with individual families and local issues.

Second stage of self-governance was to establish civil boundaries and guidelines for individual responsibility and a legal accountability code. Based on past human history, it was obvious that unrestrained freedom led to all manner of mischief and chaos whereby people became slaves to unhealthy passions, self-centeredness, and greed that interfered with the welfare of the individual and other creatures (both human and animal). This truth was illustrated at the Golden Calf Party Aaron threw while Moses was at the Mount Sinai Summit meeting with the LORD God Almighty and Supreme Ruler of the Universe. The calf-incident underscored the fact that Aaron and the other Hebrews had not completely recovered from the bondage of an idolatrous culture and "were unrestrained" in their behavior.[33]

28

Therefore, to keep the Hebrew society "civil" and on track morally, God gave Moses the *Ten Commandments*[34] and other civil laws. It is important to note that these were the *Ten Commandments* and not the ten suggestions. These *docu-stones* also served as a moral code to secure the rights of individuals and families (including the weak and poor) based on God's natural and unchanging laws encoded in the conscience of every person from the beginning of human history.

"We only have a few rules around here, but we really enforce them."

Figure 9: Moses as a CEO in the 21ˢᵗ Century

The Mosaic Law Codes' main principle as it relates to the American Founders' intentions was the God-given equality, value, and dignity of each person. The human spirit, mind, and body is not designed for slavery or forced servitude, but each person is created with a specific purpose and destiny, and everyone is equipped to fulfill these by God's grace and through Divine Providence. The right to choose leaders from among their own families and tribes regardless of social standing was the recognition and exercise of each Hebrew citizen's equality, value, and dignity.[35] The only qualifications to serve as a leader were to possess wisdom, understanding, ability, integrity, a healthy fear of God, and to hate covetousness (covetousness meaning the insatiable desire for wealth).[36]

To review, the basic Hebrew governmental structure consisted of a Chief Magistrate (Moses was the first, then the people elected Joshua after Moses' death[37]), the Senate, and the Hebrew Commons (the people, all three million of them). According to the Hebrew constitution (law code), the people could alter the structure at any time.

The Ancient Hebrew Republic and Mosaic Law Codes served Israel well, and they prospered and survived as a nation approximately 500 years (from about 1490 BC to 990 BC). However, the Israelites rejected God's predominant leadership role and <u>demanded</u> a human king rule over them, thinking that if they became more like the other nations, they could obtain relief from oppressive tribes and endless wars, thus making peace a reality. As we recall from Israel's history, and as she discovered in her years of tragedy, *compromising and being like other nations did not guarantee peace and security.* I have underlined the previous statement because it still holds true today. More often than not, when compromise is **demanded**, it often diverts the course of action away from unchanging moral and ethical values and fixed principles, thus introducing moral ambiguity, violating the human conscience, and sacrificing personal integrity.

Figure 10: "Now remind me again which command was not crystal clear."

On the next page is a summary of the Mosaic Law Codes' key principles as compared to Polytheistic Law Codes.[38] It does not take a brain surgeon to sort out which code best supports liberty for a nation and life for its people. Greece and Rome, with all their cruel, petty, vindictive and perverted deities, attempted a "Republic" form of city-state government but refused to recognize the equality of persons, and as a result failed miserably. Enslaving people under tyrannical rulers may maintain order for a season but always results in immorality and crime and carries the high price of oppression and a tragic loss of liberty, limb, and life.[39]

Today, in some ways, we have become indentured slaves of the State. Think about it- the government reaches into our pockets and forcibly takes one-third or more of our hard-earned income, on the way to the grave they grab more of our money through inheritance taxes (double taxation on the same hard-earned money), and then the local government takes away our property if we fail to pay property taxes. To add insult to injury, there are "hidden taxes" in our phone and utility bills, the price of fuel, excise taxes, sales tax, permit and license fees,

ANCIENT MOSAIC CODE	ANCIENT POLYTHEISTIC CODE
☺ The unity of God enabled every person to reach his or her highest purpose and destination	☹ Polytheism was used by ruling classes to enslave their subjects and stifle individual potential
☺ Unity and equality of people based on God's eternal natural laws of liberty	☹ Dualistic belief in a two-class society of intellectual priestly rulers and common slaves
☺ Mosaic Law Code established and outlined God-given rights and responsibilities of freedom	☹ Common people were property of ruling class and had no individual rights
☺ Declaration of liberty from "the house of bondage" and servitude (1ˢᵗ commandment)	☹ Even in death, there was no liberty for the common servant slave class
☺ Ownership of private property keeps the power of government in the hands of the people	☹ Denial of private ownership of property ensures dependency on and servitude to rulers
☺ The laws and leadership of God and Moses were accepted by consent of the people	☹ Tyrannical rulers and arbitrary laws forced on the people without their consent
☺ By law, the rich and strong were not to abuse the poor and weak	☹ The rich and strong had free reign to abuse the poor and weak
☺ A check and balance system foiled tyranny and anarchy	☹ Leadership's power was unchecked and without restraint

regulatory fees, toll road fees, administrative fees, late fees, penalty fees, and the list goes on ad infinitum. Read the left column of the previous chart again and answer this question- how close are we to becoming slaves like the Hebrews were in Moses' time? Have we been subconsciously demanding a king to rule over us, and have we really considered the consequences of that demand?

The Founding Fathers studied all of the different government and legal structures and discovered what worked and what failed. They concluded that the original Hebrew Republic and Mosaic Law Code combined with numerous New Testament principles would best benefit and sustain "one nation under God, indivisible, with liberty and justice for all."[40]

21st Century Truth or Consequence Questions: Consider this local versus centralized control scenario: A polytheistic nation or the UN's global government has gained control of America, and everyone is under International Law. Who do I think will be at the top of the food chain as opposed to who will be in the Global Cafeteria line waiting to be served- me and my family or the extremist loons?

Dig Deeper

1. Mark A. Beliles and Stephen K. McDowell (1989), *America's Providential History* (Charlottesville, VA: Providence Foundation, 3rd edition, 2010).
2. Friedrich A. Hayek, *The Road to Serfdom (Abridged Edition)* (Washington, DC: The Heritage Foundation; University of Chicago Press, 1994).
3. E. C. Wines, *The Hebrew Republic* (American Presbyterian Press online at: http://www.amprpress.com/fundamental_principles.htm [be sure to follow the other tabs at bottom of page for full version]).
4. Larry Schweikart and Michael Allen (2004), *A Patriot's History of the United States* (New York: Sentinel, Penguin Group, 2007).

Figure 11: Yeah- its dinner time.

CHAPTER 3
WHERE'S THE BEEF?

"A wise man will...increase learning, and a man of understanding will attain wise counsel."[41]

Having won the right to exist as a sovereign nation, the Continental Congress became the Confederation Congress after winning independence from British monarchial rule. Many members of the Congress returned to their home states to focus on their state's welfare. Though successful during the American Revolution as a governing instrument, the *Articles of Confederation* and sparsely attended Confederation meetings proved inadequate for continued long-term maintenance of a sovereign nation.

Congressional members were in conflict with one another because of their state-centered focus; hence, the ongoing battle between federalism vs. nationalism began. To survive, the nation needed adequate support to maintain national security, form a judicial court system to ensure "justice for all," and establish a leadership body for the nation. During this time, Confederation meetings simulated a "conflict of interest" scenario like that of Turkey vs. Pilgrim (see Figure 12).

The key difference between Turkey vs. Pilgrim and the Confederation Congressmen's conflict was that the latter left their muskets at home and instead resorted to squabbling and marking of territory (early signs of political insanity). The question was how were they going to strike a balance between Federalism and Nationalism, or anarchy and tyranny and arrive at the final destination of liberty secured by a stable justice system based on unchanging principles? The Founders were determined to live in peace as free persons, so they eventually sorted out their differences to form "a more perfect union."[42]

The chart after Figure 12 summarizes the founder's initial under-standing of Federalism vs. Nationalism.[43] Even though this was an im-portant issue debated for years, there were more pressing issues to re-solve such as establishing the founding principles of the new America.

Figure 12: Conflict of Interest

FEDERALISM MODEL	NATIONALISM MODEL
Decentralized Confederation	**Sovereign Centralized State**
"…a system of parallel governments (state, local, and national) each with its specified powers, but sovereignty ultimately rested in the states and, by implication, the people them-selves."[44]	"Divided power among…three levels (state, local, and national) but with the national government retaining the ultimate authority."[45]

The *Declaration of Independence* was their starting point, and they understood that:

✓ God created government as "His divine order" for civil society
✓ God is the "Grantor" of rights and freedom, not government
✓ God sustains or removes governments at His good pleasure
✓ God's Providential Hand was upon the new America
✓ God had raised up America to be a beacon of life and freedom[46]

Unlike former monarchies, dictators, and other 21st Century Progressives, the framers of the Constitution were not a bunch of self-seeking elitists grabbing for power and money. They were a group of farmers, educators, pioneers, preachers, the rich, and the poor; most came from different churches and some from no church. They had a common bond that held them together- they all held "strong and... well-defined convictions concerning religious principles, political precepts, economic fundamentals, and long-range social goals."[47]

For 180 years prior to this point in America's history, the colonists had a standard tradition of emphasizing education in a broad range of subjects including history, philosophy, religion, literary classics, and economics. Education occurred in the home, in free local common schools, and universities established by different denominational ministers. Early colonists were the product of the Reformation which marked a time when the Bible had been translated into the common language of the people, thus planting love, peace, faith, and freedom in their minds and hearts. After the Reformation and during early colonial American history, people respected Christ.[48]

Old and New Testament biblical principles paved the way for liberty and became the key component of early American education. Prior colonial state charters, constitutions, and the *Declaration of Independence* expressed the involvement and protection of Divine Providence, a "declaration of independence from Britain and dependence on God."[49] This was evident in the first state constitution (*Fundamental Orders of Connecticut*, 1650) which stated, "...when a people are gathered together, the word of God requires that to maintain the peace and union of such a people, there should be an orderly and decent government established according to God."[50] Eight of the early colonial state charters included a statement of Christian goals and reference to God's guidance in their first charters. It is clear, therefore, that the future framers of the *Constitution* held similar convictions because they were well versed in knowledge and principles that nurtured and sustained liberty.

It is an historical fact that the Bible was highly esteemed among the colonists and leaders of early America. Because of the American Revolution, bibles were in short supply during and after the war. Having already acknowledged the value of biblical principles and the importance of keeping this knowledge flowing in colonial society, the full Continental Congress granted Robert Aitken permission to print an American edition of the Bible on his *Pennsylvania Magazine* press. The first American English edition of 1782 had the following Congressional endorsement printed on the first page: "Whereupon, Resolved That the United States in Congress assembled…recommend this edition of the Bible to the inhabitants of the United States."[51]

'In early 1970, two political science professors, Donald S. Lutz and Charles S. Hyneman, statistically analyzed over 15,000 books and documents written and/or printed between 1760 and 1805, and identified 3,154 direct quotes and documented their original source.'[52] Their findings revealed that 34% of the Founders' direct quotes came from the Bible while the remaining quotes came from other sources, with no single source being more than 9%.[53] Evidence clearly points to the fact that the colonists considered the Bible an appropriate and necessary text on liberty.

Why did the founders rely so heavily upon biblical principles? First, as revealed in the previous chapter, the Mosaic Law Code provided the principles needed to sustain a civil society. Secondly, Christ fulfilled the OT covenant, and because of humanity's inability to follow the whole law, Christ fulfilled the law, set the captive free, and proclaimed liberty for the oppressed by a single act of sacrificial love (there is 'no greater love than this that a man should lay down his life for his friends').[54] In essence, God cut a new covenant with humanity and sent the Spirit of truth to guide us into all truth.[55] The Old and New Covenant's principle of loving God and neighbor[56] provided a solid foundation for the free flow of liberty, securing freedom for all the colonists from coercive restraint. In comparison to law codes of other nations, the original Mosaic civil and moral laws and new covenant's royal law of love[57] and liberty were consistent and did not change according to cultural trends.

Please step away from that Progressive panic button if you suddenly have the urge to push it. I am not suggesting that we establish a

Theocracy or "church-run" State in America before the Messiah returns. There is no human being able to handle that much power as sole chief ruler of any state or nation. Remember the Waco, Texas slaughter, Tom Jones' Guyana mass suicide incident, and the power grab that is currently in full swing whereby the ruling elite are trying to consolidate power and work around what they view as that pesky consent-of-the-people and State sovereignty rule in the *Constitution*.

In contrast, the law codes of anti-God nations changed according to the whims of the ruling elite who constantly instituted arbitrary laws to enslave and maintain control of their people. As a nation becomes increasingly godless and immoral, more restrictive laws and regulations are required resulting in bigger government, more lawyers, and the use of coercive force. In addition, there is the 20th and 21st Century *loon's* attitude toward law and order whereby "situational ethics" is the legal standard, and everyone does what is right in their own sight, judges rule according to their personal ideological views and agendas, and politicians believe they are above the law and have a right to ignore the *Constitution*. Today's laws and regulations decreed and enforced by Socialists beg the question:

Figure 13: Situational ethics lacks substance because it is based on a person's state of mind and what is culturally trending for the moment.

As we learned from the 17th Century Thanksgiving crew in the previous chapter, it is easy to slip into the comfort zone, become complacent, return to old habits and take freedom, the *Constitution,* and prosperity for granted. Is the American Revolution such a distant past to us that we have forgotten what it cost to achieve freedom for everyone in our nation?

Just in case we galloped past a few important points, on the next page let's review what works and what does not work to secure and sustain a civil society.

WHAT WORKS	WHAT DOES NOT WORK
☺ Plymouth's free enterprise system, strong individual creativity, and a strong work ethic	☹ Jamestown socialism and unsustainable communal welfare and entitlement system
☺ Firm reliance on Divine Providence and God's wisdom	☹ Self-centeredness and ignoring God's guidance and wisdom
☺ Ethics, morals and laws based on unchanging principles as definitively stated in the Bible	☹ Ethics, morals and laws based on personal preferences and situation
☺ Knowledge and understanding of biblical principles, history and classical wisdom	☹ Lack of knowledge and understanding of biblical principles, history and classical wisdom
☺ Loving God and loving our neighbor	☹ Hating God and taking advantage of our neighbor
☺ Respect for and consent of the governed	☹ Disrespect for the governed and overriding their consent

Now let's venture further into the process of drafting a constitution and forming a governing structure. We have introduced a few biblical principles that supported the foundation for America's governing documents and structure. These principals were more than sufficient to facilitate liberty and justice for all. The Founders knew that:

> ✓ In the *tyrannical mindset*, individual citizens have value only as far as they benefit the government and support the political and economic agendas of the State[58]; therefore, those in power have a vested interest in controlling the thoughts and actions of the collective by *coercive restraint* of individual liberty.
>
> ✓ *Anarchists* have no consideration for individual welfare and freedom apart from "self," and they are opposed to any authority that seeks to restrain their ill-conceived behaviors that, if left unchecked, eventually devolve into chaotic savagery forcing into play another type of tyranny and hopelessness for the masses.

Therefore, they knew it was important to: (a) have a balance between the power of the people and the power of government; and (b) maintain a system of checks and balances in the governing structure by establishing such a system in America's legal governing instrument.

The Constitutional Convention convened in Philadelphia on May 25, 1787 at Independence Hall. Delegates from twelve states met, and Rhode Island delegates were absent. Their purpose for meeting was to amend the *Articles of Confederation;* however, after much debate, the delegates decided to write a new constitution on May 29. As is the nature of politics, when you rub two politicians together, invariably sparks will fly while they politely address each other as "my good friend, the Honorable Senator Jones" while secretly thinking, "My fine-feathered *loon,*" and having visions like this one:

Figure 14: What we would like to do with bobble heads and loons...

I guess folks just naturally assume that being able to say one thing and think another is a required skill for politicians and lawyers. In today's politics, we could really have a great debate over exactly which political party has the highest number of *extremist loons* and bobble heads. Sometimes the *political* process mirrors sandlot ball games.

Mom was the high school basketball star in our family, so I assumed that I had inherited her fleet-footed agility gene. I often had visions of flying through the air with the greatest of ease, winning relay races to the other end of the basketball court and scoring points on the big board. Oh quite the contraire—there was no flying, no racing, and definitely no scoring. I never quite got the hang of dribbling and running at the same time; in fact, walking and chewing gum at the same time was a real effort (mothers' remedy was ballet lessons, but sorry Mom, that dog didn't hunt either).

My first attempt at shooting hoops revealed my lack of eye-hand coordination—instead of the ball landing in the hoop, it landed on my head. In my first official game, there was the scary sight of several hundred pounds of human flesh hurling towards me; since I knew I couldn't outrun the mass of flying arms and legs, I sat on the ball in the middle of the court thinking it was more important to hold onto the ball rather than risk bodily assault. The most I could squeeze out of a basketball game was laughter coming from my teammates, the coaches, and spectators. After that, the team coach benched me, removing all the fun out of the game for everyone.

I eventually found a few sports I was good at. The first game I excelled at was single-player baseball where I was the pitcher, batter, catcher, and fetcher (no running allowed); I even managed a few homers. The other sport was Equitation and Dressage (English-style precision horseback riding) which I took up at age 24 and managed to win a few colorful ribbons before retiring from the sport at age 30. A bum knee, nearly broke neck and back, and a few crazy horses later sparked wisdom within that screamed, "Not worth the risk if you want to survive past 30." It was always the 17-hand horse, not the short ones, that dumped me, then turned around and sneered while asking that stupid question horses ask, "What are you doing down there?"

Huffy   **Ms. Flower Power**   **Wimpy**

Figures 15: Modern day politicians

As I reviewed our government's history, the political debate process reminded me of sandlot ball games where folks don't play nice like we do here in the South, and with kids (and some politicians) it becomes a survival of the fittest, king of the mountain, or perpetual tug-of-war game. Eventually, someone gets mad or hurt, the game ends with huffy or wimpy taking his ball and running home, while the "flower power" hippy trying to "redistribute" the love and negotiate for peace at all cost. Sometimes I have flashbacks of those "sandlot moments" when I watch house representatives debating in the House, or, more often, not debating, but talking without saying much of anything.

Even though politics seem petty and distasteful at times, we all must come to the same conclusion that the Founders came to: some government is necessary, and law is essential for the survival of a civil society. If we want the process to work, then we must stop inviting Huffy, Wimpy and Ms. Flower Power to political parties. In addition, we have to stop settling for second best whenever possible just because we think they can beat the incumbent (and stop favoring our relatives when there is a more qualified candidate who is willing to go toe-to-toe with the establishment and ruling elite). Vote principles and character, not popularity, great looks, or win ability. We have thrown some candidates out because we think they cannot win, and perhaps they are the very ones who could beat the odds.

My heart cries out for men and women candidates who have integrity and the courage of their convictions to stand up to America's Goliaths. Does your heart cry out too? Admittedly, finding qualified candidates today has become more challenging because of the failure to educate our youth in true American History, basic, sound principles of constitutional government, and the importance of values based on a strong faith-based worldview. Instead, the focus is on feelings about a matter and indoctrination in socialism, thus producing more radicals, entitlement groups, and *extremist loons*.

It took the Continental delegates four months to draft, debate and consent to approve, complete, and sign the new *Constitution*, whereby 39 Congressional members initially agreed on a national government with the power to tax, defend the country against foreign threats, preserve order at home, and protect property.[59] *Consent to approve meant that the Congressional delegates worked hard toward consensus rather than forcing compromise* (i.e., allowing common agreements on sound principles rather than forcing a single person's will over another regarding issues and personal interest of the representative or their state). Stated briefly: **Principles trumped self-centered interests**.

Before proceeding, let's review a few key principles and laws in the *Declaration of Independence* and *Constitution* on the next page.

41

KEY GOVERNING PRINCIPLES & CONSTITUTIONAL LAWS
✓ Equality of persons (having a common human nature and the capacity for reason and liberty, but not possessing the same abilities, initiatives, and possessions)[60]
✓ Equal God-given unalienable rights to life, liberty, and the pursuit of happiness (no one may usurp *personal will* or arbitrary control over the natural rights of others)[61]
✓ Consent of the governed by equal representation (government derives its power through the consent of the people whereby the people and the government are in a covenant relationship)[62]
✓ Accountability and separation of powers at all levels of government
✓ Freedom of speech and freedom to peacefully assemble, including the freedom to address grievances with those in authority
✓ Freedom of religion, not freedom "from" (freedom to publicly and privately express and exercise one's faith according to one's belief system; no national or state religion may be established; religion and government may coexist without usurping each other's power or authority)[63]
✓ The individual right to purchase and possess property and in free exchange of goods and property, but not the equal distribution of property or goods (different interests, abilities, and wealth determines acquisition of property and possessions)[64]
✓ The right to keep and bear arms to protect self, family, and property from harm, intrusion, coercive force, or theft
✓ Rule of law whereby everyone knows and is equally bound by the laws, and by law the government is subject to the supreme law of the land (the *Constitution*) and limited in its power based on the principles of equity and justice [65]
✓ Individual protection from arbitrary and retroactive laws, illegal search and seizure, arrest without probable cause warrants, and being tried for the same crime twice; and the right to legal counsel and a speedy trial[66]
✓ "Government exists to preserve rights that stem from the people themselves, and the powers of the national government are limited to those granted to the Federal government in the *Constitution* only. All other governmental powers are reserved to the states or to the people themselves"[67] (i.e., securing individual and state sovereignty)
✓ The *Constitution's* "Bill of Rights" (Amendments 1-10 of the *Constitution*) limits the power and authority of the Federal Government's designated powers of Article 1, Section 8 (i.e., the "welfare clause" cannot violate the individual and State rights listed in the "Bill of Rights)."

Congress sent a signed *Constitution* to each state for approval and ratification, and some states would not sign the document resulting in the addition of the first ten amendments to the *Constitution* known as the *Bill of Rights*.[68] Congress did not cram it down the states' collective throats; each state had a choice to sign or not sign. Nine states ratified the *Constitution* and *Bill of Rights*, and America's first official legal governing document went into effect in June of 1788.[69]

The Congressional delegates had achieved what no other nation has been able to achieve prior to the *Constitution*, and none has achieved since its ratification although there were some who had come close. Five major structural achievements that accomplished "coordination without consolidation"[70] (avoiding investment of major power in single body or part of the structure) included:

FIVE MAJOR STRUCTURAL ACHIEVEMENTS OF COORDINATION WITHOUT CONSOLIDATION
1) 'the balance of power within the Federal government and between the local, state, and national levels of government;
2) keeping the power base close to the people and emphasizing strong, local self-government;
3) the two legislative bodies, the House and the Senate, must agree on a law before it can become law, thus maintaining balance between the will of the states and that of the people;
4) establishing a strong Executive (Presidential) office with limited powers as bound by the law of the land (the *Constitution*);
5) the judiciary branch tasked with the guardianship of the *Constitution* and the interpretation of it according to its original intent of unchanging principles.'[71]

In short, the Founders structured the government and its governing instrument as a "***democratic republic***" that established a balanced relationship between the government and the people, and a governing structure in which both the minority and majority have a voice and are equally represented in the decision making process. This had been proven throughout history as stated in the next two paragraphs.

Pure democracy without a republic means everyone votes and the majority rule, but the minority are left out in the cold resulting in inequality and injustice. A pure democracy also would have ensured that the larger states could maintain control thus cancelling the power of the smaller states. Someone once defined pure democracy as *mob rule*. A democracy becomes unmanageable and out of control as the population grows, resulting in a large centralized government that eventually digresses into an ineffective socialistic government.[72]

The *"republic"* part of our democratic republic is based on equal representation according to districts and their population. However, it is flexible enough to expand as the population increases in each district and state, thus maintaining equal representation. Under a republic, laws are regulated and enforced according to fixed principles.[73] Representatives elected by the people in a republic are theoretically supposed to be those who are best qualified to represent their constituents and who can maintain their integrity by legislating according to principles and not party allegiance or personal stakes.

Do we truly comprehend what we are doing when we run to other countries with our military forces to help those countries set up democracies? Pure democracy does not work without the "republic" component. In fact, the Marxist and Communist state that pure democracy is the first step toward socialism, and socialism is the transitional stage towards Marxism or Communism. From what we have witnessed in the past several decades, many countries that we have helped to become democracies turn into a survival of the fittest tribe or political party. Egypt is an example where the strongest faction, the Muslim Brotherhood who has ties to terroristic groups, has gained control of the governmental seats of power. So what have we really accomplished? Democracy has no solid foundation without a republic based on unchanging principles and fixed laws.

The two previous charts encompass the body of the *Constitution* and the first ten amendments (the amendments historically known as the *Bill of Rights*). These first ten amendments were to be applied to the federal government only, and not applied as "prohibitions of state action." However, in 1925, the Supreme Court began using the "doctrine of incorporation" as a way to restrain state government liberties and authority.[74] Folks, the "doctrine of incorporation" is a Progressive code word for "consolidation of power" by the federal government designed to usurp local state authority and subvert the freedom of individuals and private businesses.

The American *Constitution's* preamble begins with, "We the People" which establishes the people as the fundamental authority. It further states that the government's areas of responsibilities are:

> ➢ "safety and security;
> ➢ rule of law, which fosters domestic prosperity;
> ➢ establishment of justice, promotion of the general welfare;
> ➢ and formation of a more perfect Union—all for the sake of securing liberty."[75]

No governing structure in any other nation has come close to what we have had in America, and no other justice system has secured and sustained life, liberty, and pursuit of happiness to the same degree as what we have enjoyed in America in the past.

However, there have been intentional efforts to undermine America's constitution, and one major blunder made by the judicial system was to allow the insidious redefinition of constitutional rights, from God-given endowed rights to "human rights," thus opening Pandora's Box of self-centeredness, immorality, and lawlessness and relieving people of personal responsibility for their behavior and actions. Other judicial bloopers include the subversive and unconstitutional redefinition of the "the general welfare," and the abuse of the commerce clause to ram rod over state sovereignty and institute government mandates that force individuals to purchase health insurance against their will, all of which push us further into the abyss of socialism.

We must reverse the curse and restore sanity to our judicial system and vote judges out or petition to impeach them if they willfully and defiantly use their own political agendas to undermine the true meaning and original intent of the American *Constitution*, or are using International Laws, or guidance from other nation's constitutions to make their judicial decisions.

In Chapter 4 we will review a few historical attempts to use social engineering to *fundamentally transform* America.

21ˢᵗ Century Truth or Consequence Question: *How many more huffies, wimpies, radicals and flower powers can we continue to put into the Senate, Congress, Judicial system, the White House, and local*

governments before the whole system collapses into tyranny, and how do I think this will impact me, my family and local community?

Dig Deeper

1. Heritage Foundation web site resources on the *Founding of America* and *Constitutional Government* at the following address: http://www.heritage.org/initiatives/first-principles/primary-sources#constitutional-government
2. Matthew Spalding, *We Still Hold these Truths* (Washington, DC: The Heritage Foundation, 2010).
3. Visit www.blackstoneinstitute.org for news information and resources on the Constitution and law.
4. David Gibbs, Jr. and David Gibbs III, *Understanding the Constitution* (Seminole, FL: Christian Law Association, 2006 by Gibbs Law Firm, P.A.).

Figures 16: Time for a Beverly Hillbilly's road trip- Hee-Hawww!

CHAPTER 4
INSANITY MULTIPLIED AD INFINITUM

"Train up a child in the way he should go, and when he is old he shall not depart from it."[76]

One of the goals of this book is to bring everyone up to speed by presenting mini-snapshots of American history in areas that affect individuals and families the most. Below are a few definitions to clarify different human control systems.

Similarity and Difference between Human Control Systems
Similarity- their goal is to concentrate power in the hands of a few. The Communists, Fascists, and Marxists start out as Socialist, and then digress into tyranny.
Difference- Socialists attain power gradually and by deceit (smoke and mirrors strategy), whereas the Marxists, Fascists, and Communists take sudden power by coercive and violent force.

As revealed below, there are more similarities than differences between progressivism, socialism, Marxism, and Communism. Lenin (USSR) used "socialism" and "communism" interchangeably; however, the term "socialism" indicated the transition phase wherein a society transforms gradually from a free enterprise system to communism by means of class warfare and social engineering.[77] The Preamble of the 1977 *Constitution of the Union of Soviet Socialist Republics* states, "Developed socialist society is a natural, logical stage on the road to communism."[78] The German National Socialists (Nazis), Italian Corporate Socialists (Fascists), and the Union of Soviet Socialist Republics (Communists) were all socialist governments.[79]

Defining Human Control Systems
Progressivism- "to enlarge...the scope of national government" (i.e., centralized government) "to respond to economic and social conditions; to move beyond the...principles of the American *Constitution* as originally intended" and God;[80] also called secular humanism, liberalism, and post modernism.
Socialism- "government ownership or control of all the means of production (farms, factories, mines, natural resources) and the means of distribution (transportation, communications, and the instruments of commerce)."[81] The "State" (national government) distributes the goods according to needs and the common good; this is in contrast to a free market enterprise system.
Marxism- is a materialistic/economic concept of history that envisions a superior communal society in which the working class forcefully ceases the means of production, material environment determines human identity and purpose, and there is no private property ownership.'[82] The goal is economic equality, but is never permanently accomplished. Lenin took it further by advocating imperialism and centralized control by a vanguard party ("State").
Communism- "a theory or system of social organization in which all property is owned by the community and each person contributes and receives according to their ability and needs."[83] Karl Marx defined it as abolition of private property ownership and free enterprise. Communism was a version of Marxism rooted in the political philosophy of socialism. The "community" was the "State."

Round Three: Piggybacked onto the first two rounds of socialistic communal experiments in America mentioned in Chapter 2 were the *Owen* and *Fourier's* movements of 1826 and 1843. Eleven *Owen* communities did not last beyond three years, and a majority of the 34 *Fourier* communities failed within two years (only one lasted for eighteen years). The estimated population of the combined communities was 8,641, all of whom died young. "The main idea of both was the enlargement of family—the extension of family union beyond the little man-and-wife circle to large corporations"[84] which was not exactly pro-family in the biblical sense.

These socialistic movements paralleled American Christian Revivals of that time (led by Nettleton and Finney of Connecticut), but differed by offering an alternate ideology of "communism of property"[85] for the unregenerate heart of European Socialists immigrants. Noyes observes that if the immigrant communal movements had embraced Christian revival in their hearts, then their communal experiments would have succeeded. At this point, I strongly disagree with Noyes because you cannot put socialism on like a glove and expect it to fit on the hand of Christianity. To put it another way, European socialism does not fit well on the hand of American liberties as defined by the *Constitution* and as originally intended by the Founders.

Noyes attempted to link the failure of *Owen* and *Fourier* socialist communities to their tendency toward procuring large land acreage and only focusing on *collective* farming[86] but later admits in his conclusion that 'general depravity and self-centeredness were the major causes of their failure.'[87] Noyes also reveals the Socialist mindset to co-op the church in their attempt to win the masses by stating:

> "If the churches cannot be put into this work, we do not see how Socialism" can "be propagated…Our hope is that church-es of all denominations will…begin to grow and change, and finally…burst forth into Communism."[88]

Guess what- Socialists have found a way to accomplish this by co-opting and infiltrating religious institutions and by adding and mixing a few code words into church and cultural lingo. Today, collective communism shows up in our churches, pulpits, Sunday Schools, and community organizations as collective salvation, social gospel, shared sacrifice, and social justice (in-depth coverage in Chapter 5).

Past Socialists and current Progressives know that changing words is not enough, so they try to undermine and alter America's *Constitution* and bury the *Declaration of Independence* knowing that socialism will never work in America as long as a constitution and declaration founded on God's unchanging principles exists. In fact, they have worked hard over the past 100 years to sterilize, glorify, gloss over, or eliminate historical events from our American history books to hide their agenda to overturn the *Constitution*.

"Progressive" is a term used by far left liberals to mask their real ideological identity which stems from secular humanism and socialism. They all have the same vision- to establish Utopia in the world or a

"New World Order"; the word "Utopia" originated with Sir Thomas More in 1516 that refers to 'an imagined place where everything is perfect.'[89] There is no honor in how they pursue their goals; it is a game pseudo-intellectuals play with people's minds and life where they trample over others to occupy high places in every sector of society and stop at nothing to maintain their control. In the limited Socialist Progressive worldview, it is a survival-of-the-fittest war with winners and losers. Guess who the losers are according to socialists.

The good news is that there are more winners than losers. This means that **non**-Socialist Americans win if we accept the challenge to say, "ENOUGH," and retake the freedom ground lost by wielding the sword of truth and defending with the shield of faith. This will require a restoration of common sense in how we conduct our personal and family lives, and how we function in governmental and free enterprise market system and society as a whole.

Now we have come to the important question of how Progressives amassed so much power in America. In the 19th Century, there was a storm brewing that would gradually turn our country into a Welfare State and rob Americans of their God-given rights and liberties (review "Key Governing Principles and Constitutional Laws" on page 42). This storm originated in the mid-19th Century through Engels and Marx.

Marxism blew into England as *economic and democratic social-ism* and was promoted by the Fabian Society (1884) founded by George Bernard Shaw and taught in the London School of Economics established in 1895 by Beatrice and Sidney Webb and George Bernard Shaw.[90] Beatrice Webb vigorously advocated welfarism, supported cradle to grave entitlement programs for the poor and elderly and coined the phrase "collective bargaining" in 1891.[91]

George Bernard Shaw also spearheaded the Malthusian and Galton eugenics[92] movement in England whereby he recommended death chambers as a solution to societal problems such as poverty, the physically and mentally challenged, social misfits, and other persons deemed not useful for the advancement and progress of the human race.[93] Eugenics is all about population control and survival of the fittest and was the inspiration for Margaret Sanger's Planned Parenthood organization; she advocated 'mandatory sterilization of the poor, the mentally and physically inadequate, and immigrants (i.e., non-Caucasians or Anglo-Saxons).'[94]

To avoid alarming leaders and scaring the willies out of the public, Socialist societies adopted a Machiavellian strategy of gradualism (or incremental change), that is "a policy of gradual reform" by unscrupulous and deceptive means "rather than sudden change or revolution"[95] by penetration and permeation. In fact, Shaw applauded Lenin and Stalin (USSR Communist leaders) for using "Fabian methods of stealth, intrigue, subversion, and the deception of never calling socialism by its right name."[96] To get the "New World Order" ball rolling the Socialists used education, churches, economic initiatives, news media, and civil service platforms to propagate socialism.

The Socialist storm continued crashing into America through an exchange program between British and American professors, writers, and scholars. Sidney Webb arrived in America in 1888, and then in 1890 published *Socialism in England*, which was widely circulated to American universities by the American Economic Association.[97] This exchange program birthed a crop of American Fabian Socialists who established the Intercollegiate Socialist Society (ISS) and by 1905 had ISS chapters in Columbia, Harvard, New York, and Princeton University and the University of Pennsylvania. The once honorable institutions that stood as the front guard and perpetuators of American liberties based on unchanging principles gradually transformed into proverbial insane asylums, experimental laboratories, and breeding grounds for the Fabian Socialist's new world order activists.

The ISS was renamed League for Industrial Democracy (LID) in 1921 and from LID sprang forth the Students for Democratic Society (SDS); the name of the game is if you get a bad reputation or become unpopular with the masses, change your name.[98] ISS and British Fabian influence produced a crop of American Socialist leaders such as 'John Dewey (education), Charles Beard (historian and political scientist), Walter Rauschenbusch (theology), Walter Lippmann (government and press), and Supreme Court Justice Felix Frankfurter.'[99]

American Socialists began chopping away at the Spirit of Liberty Tree by promoting their Socialist propaganda wherever they could secure a platform. Horace Mann, "Father of American public education," set up a government school structure in 1852 by adopting the Prussian/Spartan education system while serving on the Massachusetts State Board of Education. This educational system included a national testing system to classify students as to what occupation they were best suited for and whether they had an aptitude for college studies, teacher certification standards determined by the State, compulsory attendance, and a national school curricula shaped by the State.[100] The ultimate goal was to instill 'subordination and obedience to State authority, and national uniformity in thought, word, and deed.'[101] Compulsory education was and still is a major tool of totalitarian regimes to maintain control over their slaves.[102]

Figure 17: Student's response to compulsory psychosocial education

The intent of this system was to ensure the proper training and curriculum design to advance socialistic teachings. The Americanized Prussian school system became the epitome of social engineering of our children thus removing parental authority and transferring it to the State. Mann's strategy of implementation is a pattern consistently followed by Socialists and Progressives:

1) Identify a cause or issue of the weak or disenfranchised
2) Develop a program to meet their need
3) Implement the program at the highest level of government and work it into the government budget for taxpayer's to pay for
4) Actively lobby the Federal House (Senate and Congress) until the program is adopted at the Federal level
5) Identify a representative to champion the cause or issue or secure a seat at the Federal table to establish a department to regulate and run the program thus usurping local control

By adopting the Prussian system, Mann had established a platform that would eventually transition the American school system into an experimental laboratory for American Socialists to indoctrinate children to equip them for the New Social Order. The testing program measured the student's aptitude and was used to determine their fitness to advance to college or university and if they were "intellectually superior" enough to be useful servants of the political state or government subsidized businesses. Mann's Prussian-style system spread to other states and set the stage for future Federal control of local schools and a shift from reading, writing, and arithmetic to psychological and sociological development and social studies.

The American Fabian Socialists used "academic freedom" to counter attacks by U.S. constitutional liberty advocates. Fabian faculty gradually forced out anyone who opposed their extreme viewpoints, leaving *extremist loons* in charge of educating and mentoring university students.[103] Whenever the traditional university and college guardians resisted the American Socialists, the latter would establish new schools such as *The New School of Social Research* in Greenwich Village, New York. From the day of its founding in 1919 until today, *The New School* remains a Socialist "think tank" center and producer of progressive elites in liberal and creative arts (or at least in their own mind they think they are elite). John Dewey and Charles Beard were among the founders of this new school.

Shortly after Mann institutionalized education in Massachusetts, the socialistic vision and scientific methodology continued spreading to other secondary and post-secondary schools. The next step was to train elementary and secondary schoolteachers in the new Socialist's methodology, and write instructional materials (teacher's guides) and textbooks for the compulsory education model.

John Dewey championed "progressive" education by developing his pedagogical model of elementary and secondary education at Columbia University and later moved his socialistic venture to *The New School*. The word *pedagogue* "is Latin for a specialized slave class assigned to walk a student to the schoolmaster...the master creates instructions, the slave pounds it in."[104] In that same spirit, Dewey's educational model became a systematic and coercive reprogramming system that stripped students of their individuality that mentally forces them into a collective group so that they will serve as slaves to the will of the State. In other words, individual students were not allowed to advance beyond the collective group or have independent thoughts or interests apart from them. Under this system, children do not develop reading and writing skills at the elementary level, logical thinking skills are not developed, the moral values instilled by parents are constantly questioned and undermined, and students are manipulated psychologically and socially on a daily basis.[105]

John Dewey   **Charles Beard**

Figures 18: Loony birds of a feather flock together and swim in the same muddy pond

After Dewey, pedagogy became an institutionalized system that required a vast bureaucracy beyond the local citizen's control to enforce and maintain.[106] Ryan observed that in 1932, there were 128,000 local school districts, and today there are only 15,000 school districts, demonstrating that control had shifted from the local communities to the centralized national power base. Because of this shift from local parental control to Federal control through the NEA (National Education Association), teaching materials became more 'politicized and standardized in which one-size-fits-all, failing to recognize children's individual strengths or sufficiently address academic weaknesses.'[107]

This politically standardized education system *teaches children what to think but not how to think* and is designed to produce mindless carbon copy drones of the State. Individual diversity, interests, and talents "permit the growth of specialization and division of labor on which civilized economies depend."[108] According to George Harris, there are three basic stages of functioning human groups (listed on the next page:[109]

Three Stages of Functioning Human Groups
Savage stage- "savagery is uniformity; principal distinctions are sex, age, size, and strength. Savages think alike or not at all, and converse therefore in monosyllables."
Barbarism stage- "marked by increased variety of functions. There is some division of labor, some interchange of thought, better leadership, more intellectual and aesthetic cultivation."
Civilized stage- "shows the greatest degree of specialization; distinct functions become more numerous" whereby "mechanical, commercial, educational, scientific, political, and artistic occupations multiply."

The conclusion is that the more variety there is among human groups, the more civilized they are, and the less variety (sameness and perfect equality), the more savage and immoral they become. Socially engineering our children into groupthink mentality, to be codependent on the State for all their cradle-to-grave needs, and to expect absolute equality in every way according to the socialistic vision is to cause a decline in our civilization thus catapulting us into barbarism or savagery and eventually into totalitarianism, which impedes progress spiritually, culturally, and economically. Consider this: Only robots made from the same pattern or design can be considered equal. Lenin called his robotic adherents "useful idiots." *Does Occupy Wall Street (OWS) ring a bell?* How long will we continue to tolerate Socialist indoctrination of our children? Common sense tells us that it takes a family to raise a child and to ensure he or she receives quality education, **not** the village *loons*.

Just about the time I think I have dug up all the weeds in the Progressive education garden, more appear the next day. There is no way to include everything, so I encourage all of my readers to *dig deeper* to get the whole scoop. However, it is important to highlight major Progressive thrusts that affect our families the most so that we may focus our energies on what will turn the tide back to common sense and sanity. To solve the problem, we have to know what went wrong and find the source of the problem (i.e., the root of the problem). So hang in there while we continue on the education track because it is one of the key instruments used to undermine and destroy American families, liberties and the economy.

If your head hurts after reading this chapter, then I feel your pain. So, to lighten things up a bit, I thought we would peek at kitty's response to compulsory education and intimidation.

Figure 19: Principal to kitty: "Skippy, if you miss another class, there'll be no more catnip for you young man."

Since early attempts to establish American Socialist farm communities failed as demonstrated by the Owen and Fourier collectivist communities, education became the alternate experimental laboratory for the advancement of socialism's *New Frontier*. While at Columbia University, John Dewey's Progressive train was at full throttle as he fueled the engines with an overarching purpose to establish primary, secondary and post-secondary public education communities as the sole providers of moral and social training and to replace traditional families as the primary influence of children and future leaders. As we will see, through his efforts and those of his followers, in every part of American society insanity was multiplied ad infinitum. The Dewey Express and Progressives were not content with a small corner of America- they wanted to own America's heart and soul.

There are a few facts we need to review about John Dewey before diving knee deep in Progressive education's muddy waters:

- he advocated materialism, naturalism, Hegelian philosophy, and William James' pragmatic philosophy of relativism (truth is always changing) and denial of absolute truth
- built his philosophy on the foundation of functional psychology which is deeply rooted in Darwinian evolution
- started a Progressive education movement that was rooted in a humanistic/global social anti-God philosophy
- applauded Soviet Russia as a "new world in the making"
- wrote a glowing report in *The New Republic* of how the Bolsheviks were using social experimentation to counteract the influence of parents and the church (1928)
- co-authored and signed the *Humanist Manifesto I*, advocating a synthesizing of all religions to dismantle the influence of Christianity in American society, and promoted the social evolution theory (social Darwinism) (1933)
- served as vice president (1930) and president (1939) of the League for Industrial Democracy (LID, formally known as ISS of the American Fabian movement at Columbia University)
- he labeled expressions of individuality as insanity[110]

In route to Utopia, passengers who called themselves the *Frontier Thinkers* boarded the Dewey Express to nowhere. George Counts, a tenured professor at Columbia University and steeped in the *social gospel* teachings of his home church, jumped on board and helped transition American educational system into a collectivist-training center for the new social order. He studied Russia's educational system and socialistic philosophy extensively, and wrote *The New Russian Primer* and *The Soviet Challenge to America* in **1931** promoting socialistic strategies to re-order American society.

In **1932** Counts wrote *Dare the School Build a New Social Order* to train teachers in Socialist principles and encourage them to secure the power reigns of curricula, school policies, and administration. The monograph was a collection of three speeches by Counts including, *Education through Indoctrination* and *Freedom, Culture, Social Planning, and Leadership*. To this current day, training materials for teachers and school administrators continue to use quotations from this monograph. On the next page are a few key quotes from George Counts.

George Counts' Key Education Strategies
▪ "reconstructing society through the school
▪ promotion of *social welfare* through education
▪ teachers should deliberately reach for power...to influence the social attitudes, ideals, and behavior of the coming generation
▪ if democracy is to survive, it must seek a new economic foundation...and abandon its individualistic affiliations
▪ if property rights are to be diffused...natural resources and all important forms of capital will have to be *collectively* owned
▪ our democratic tradition must...evolve and gradually assume a...*collectivistic* pattern
▪ in a planned, coordinated, and *socialized* economy...the individual would not be permitted to...organize a business purely for the purpose of making money"[111]

In other words, the *New Frontier extremist loons* deliberately planned and executed socialistic programs to undermine individual and family freedom, strip people of the right to own property, establish America as a welfare State, use social psychology to reprogram our children into a collective new world order mindset, and to transform America into a collectivist society. So tell me America, how is that working out for our families and the economy so far? Parents who have been forced to surrender their children to the Progressive *collective* should be shouting, "Give us back our children and get your collective commie paws off of them."

I am not suggesting that every public school and university teacher and administrator is a Socialist, but there are a significant number of stealth Progressive activists within the system. If you have been one of the courageous and honorable standard-bearers of American liberties as originally intended in our *Constitution*, educating and equipping our children for success as individuals and functioning members of American society, and not turning them into collective commie robots, then I offer my sincerest appreciation and thanks for your integrity and endless hours of hard work. If not, please consider changing your mindset and modus operandi and cease trying to transform our children into citizens of a new social order, or immediately find another occupation and stop poisoning the wells of education and contaminating America's youth and social institutions.

It was not enough for Dewey to propagate socialism on American soil and grow a crop of Progressive educators in his psychosocial laboratories. He felt it was his duty to facilitate importation of Marxists *loons* from the *Frankfurt School* in Germany (during the Nazi regime-1934) and disburse them into American educational institutes, organizations and the media. The *Frankfurt School* was a radical Marxist research center focusing on social theory and modeled after Moscow's Marx-Engels Institute. Prominent figures connected with the school were G. W. F. Hegel, Karl Marx, Erich Fromm, Sigmund Freud, and Friedrich Nietzsche. The school followed the philosophy of Immanuel Kant and Hegel and developed the *critical theory*.[112] These theories became the underlying foundation of Progressive education theory and "political correctness" movement in America. [113]

By **1934,** Socialists seized significant power and occupied most teacher training institute positions, rewrote multiple textbooks, and gained control of the largest teacher's organization, the National Education Association (NEA). By 1950, "20% of all… school superintendents and 40% of all teacher college heads had received advanced degrees under Dewey at Columbia University."[114] Today, indoctrination in theories of social collectivism and brain washing techniques are prerequisites for teacher certification in the American public school system, and my heart goes out to those who really love teaching and have been unwittingly sucked into the Socialist machinery.

BTW[115]: According to Socialists, teachers do not need an in-depth working knowledge of the subjects they teach.[116] Teachers just need to know how to get in touch with students' feelings, perform social and psychological manipulation designed to provoke children to resist authority figures such as their parents and alter their morality, conduct extensive testing, be literate about multiculturalism, and knowledgeable about every religion but Christianity. Isn't that a kicker; leave out the one faith foundation that made this country strong, prosperous and great and emphasize every pagan and pantheistic religion that has come down the proverbial gutter of humanity's mind. If that isn't enough, Progressives champion the celebration of religions that want to kill all the infidels or strip people of their God-given uniqueness.

GET THAT HAND OFF THE TAR BUCKET AND FEATHERS! You know deep down that Americans have royally screwed up by focusing on self-gratification, self-interest, chasing after utopian theories and idolatrous religions, and allowing the anti-family and anti-God *extremist loons* to unseat the guardians of our faith and systematically dismantle the backbone and glue of American liberty which is faith and the family. Progressives have reached many of their goals by using weapons of mass delusion such as forced compromise cloaked as consensus building, multiculturalism, *extreme* tolerance, political correctness, pluralism, deceptive rhetoric, welfare programs, and diversity without assimilation. It is time to face the Progressive Goliaths and sling shot truth squarely between the eyes, frustrate their plans, challenge and stop objectionable and unconstitutional federal actions, unseat them from their high positions, defund their programs, and keep our children far, far away from their grasp until our children are old enough to defend themselves with truth.

After the British and American Fabian Socialists realized it would be impossible to advance their agenda by inciting class hatred because of the 'right to private property ownership' article in the *Bill of Rights*, they encouraged young Socialist faculty to deconstruct and rewrite American history and slant it in such a way as to provoke class envy and division. This type of provocation is a classic Marxist trademark. Charles Austin Beard of *The New School* and faculty member of Columbia University, started the revisionist *New History* movement rolling by writing *An Economic Interpretation of the Constitution* (1913) in which he accused the Founders of writing a constitution to advance their own personal economic gain and oppress the weak. He then churned out another revisionist high school U. S. history textbook series, highlighting economic and social injustices by portraying American Founders and business entrepreneurs as greedy politicians and capitalists while whitewashing Socialists. This revisionist strategy nurtured victim mentality that blossomed into entitlement attitudes among those who were not at the same level of social and economic status as other Americans entrepreneurs and workers.

Beard went further by insisting the Supreme Court Justices exercise control over legislation by interpreting the *Constitution* according to evolving systems of social justice. Beard and other revisionists chose

60

to re-interpret history through the lens of sociology, psychology, philosophy and economics instead of taking the direct word of primary source documents, recorded facts, and eyewitness accounts of folks who lived the history of their time.[117]   Adolph Hitler stated, "Let me control the textbooks, and I will control the State."

Would it surprise you to know that Charles Beard, who was on the board of the Frankfurt School, was an avid student of Marxist and Socialist theories of John Ruskin at Oxford University in England, utilized the pro-fascist historical methods of Benedetto Croce, and associated with radical Socialist from about 1900 until his departure from earth in 1948?[118]   Britain and Germany declared war on America's *Constitution* and sought to undermine America's moral purpose. Beard was the golden boy for the British, the Frankfurt School and the Fabian Socialist Society and tasked with carrying out their agenda by deconstructing and distorting America's history.

Beard also advocated judicial control of congressional laws by revisionary activism whereby Supreme Court justices reinterpret the law according to their biases and political agenda and not according to the original intent of our *Constitution*.[119]   To continue the assault on the Constitution, Faulkner, Kepner and Merrill in *History of the American Way* (**1951**) followed Beard's revisionist history lead by describing 'the Constitutional Convention as attended by conservative, slow to change delegates who were the property holding class, while they conveniently left out the fact that at that time 90% of Americans owned private property.'[120]

Other members of this textbook propaganda machine were George Bancroft (trained in German universities and well versed in socialism), and Harry Elmer Barnes who advocated denial of the Holocaust. To continue their tradition, F. A. Magruder promoted class struggle themes and welfarism as he put down fiscal and family responsibility and saving money in a chapter titled, "Welfare of the People from the Cradle to the Grave," in his *American Government* (**1952**) textbook.[121] Now isn't that a fine flock of *loons*?

As if manipulating the minds of our children was not enough for these *loons*, school administrators and teaching heads add insult to injury by coercive control of parents. This control is by condescension, intimidation, denigration, and accusations that parents are not smart enough to raise and teach their children and cannot hope to grasp the so-called complexities of teaching methodology and discipline. The reason school administrators and Progressives do this is because they are indoctrinated in worldviews that instill arrogance, a messianic or godhood complex, and an 'above the law' attitude.

This same scenario also plays out when citizens try to deal with government bureaucrats. Is it becoming clear that a definite pattern is revealing more of the bureaucrat's true colors as autocrats assume positions of power and stick their noses in every part of our private and public lives? Now let's look at the Socialists' track record below.

Track Record of Socialist Education in America
☹ Focusing on class struggle and welfare indoctrination of school children increased government welfare spending from 51 million in 1910 to 849.5 billion in 2010; expenditures more than doubled since 2007 from 422.3 to 849.5 billion[122]
☹ 33% of fourth graders and 26% of eighth graders scored "below basic" in reading[123]
☹ "A 2005 study from the National Center for Education Statistics found that just 31% of college graduates were able to 'read a complex book and extrapolate from it.'"[124]
☹ In 1992-93 there were 57 violent homicide/suicide deaths and 43 in 2007-08 in pre-k through 12th grade (40 and 26 of these were children in 1992 and 2007 respectively).[125] Even though there was a slight decline partly due to the fact that schools are run like prison systems (lots of security, police presence and restricted movement), in my book, this is totally unacceptable; just one child lost to a violent death is one child too many.
☹ Some public schools have to pay students to attend their schools[126]
☹ The cost of all this fine education rose from 458 million in 1910 to 918.3 billion in 2010 [127]

We have covered just a few examples from a long list of radical Socialists who occupied Ivy League schools and positions of educational influence in the past. After 100 years of shifting the focus from reading, writing, math and logical thinking to socialistic ideology and politically correct curricula, their legacy to date demonstrates how far the system has digressed into the abyss of dismal failure.

Take one wild guess as to who pays for education's failures—you are smarter than a fifth grader if you guessed the current and future American taxpayers. Can we continue underwriting socialist czar programs before America implodes and we have rioting in the streets? Oh silly me, that's right, rioting and *OWS* protest slumber parties are already happening; and how much is that costing taxpayers for law enforcement, garbage and human waste cleanup.[128]

News flash folks: Taxpayers are not an eternal spring of money; the treasury has run dry. So let's get our act together and revive individual initiative, entrepreneurship, small family businesses and a consistent work ethic, and get off the government gravy train because it has run dry, and we are living on borrowed time and borrowed money.

We have dug deep into the education trenches because it was the first Socialist foothold that quickly transitioned into the primary stronghold and dispensary of Socialist propaganda today. Every American needs to pay attention to what our children are taught in the textbooks and the classroom and confront the educrats or find alternatives for our children's education (we will discuss the last point in the chapter about a family survival pack near the end of this book). The life of our American youth, their sanity and our future depends on the course of action we choose to take from this day forward.

We have dug deep into the education trenches because it was the first Socialist foothold that quickly transitioned into the primary stronghold and dispensary of Socialist propaganda today. Every American needs to pay attention to what our children are taught in the textbooks and the classroom and confront the educrats or find alternatives for our children's education (we will discuss the last point in the chapter about a family survival pack near the end of this book). The life of our American youth, their sanity and our future depends on the course of action we choose to take from this day forward.

We will cover the second major foothold established concurrently with that of education in the next chapter.

↓

*21ˢᵗ **Century Truth or Consequence Question:** If my children cannot read, do simple math, write a coherent and complete sentence and logically reason through simple situations or problems, do I think it is in* *the best interest of my children, family and community to continue subjecting them to the inferior education of Socialists and Progressives?*

Dig Deeper

1. Steve Baldwin & Karen Holgate (2008), *From Crayons to Condoms* (Los Angeles, CA: WorldNetDaily).
2. John Taylor Gatto (2003), *The Underground History of American Education* (New York: The Oxford Village Press).
3. Movie: *IndoctriNation.*
4. Berit Kjos, *Brave New Schools* (Harvest House Publishers, 1995). Online at: http://www.crossroad.to/Books/BraveNewSchools
5. Jeff Riggenbach (2009), *Why American History is not What they Say: An Introduction to Revisionism* (Auburn, AL: Ludwig von Mises Institute).
6. John Stormer (1999), *None Dare Call It Education* (Florissant, MO: Liberty Bell Press).
7. Veritas Foundation Staff, *The Great Deceit: Pseudo-Social Sciences* (West Sayville, NY: Veritas Foundation, 1964).

STOP! At this point, if you are mentally overwhelmed, please put down this book, take a few days of R&R (rest and recuperation), and recharge your spiritual, physical and mental batteries. During that time, I recommend praying, meditating on the scriptures, loving somebody (children or grandchildren would be a good start), laughing, playing, fellowshipping, exercising, sleeping, and treating yourself to something delicious, then come back refreshed and dive in again.

"Yo, it's five in the morning, the only thing
I'm pointing at is the bed.!"

Figure 20: Man's best friend—friendship only goes so far

CHAPTER 5
HOW TO SPOT A LEOPARD

"He who troubles his own house will inherit the wind..."[129]

Now back to the serious stuff. National Socialism, progressivism, humanism, collectivism, Marxism, Communism, fascism and other destructive secular or pagan *isms* are hostile to faith, family, freedom, individual prosperity, and the *U. S. Constitution. Extremist loons* are determined to destroy the foundation, moral fabric, and building blocks of American civil society at all cost and by any deceptive means, including the perversion of language and truth.

Several decades ago, I attended one of those expensive elite schools of theology and earned a master of divinity degree the hard way—I went in a conservative and came out an in-debt conservative. There were many odd encounters when I felt that aliens from Mars were invading my mind, and I was definitely in some kind of twilight zone where common sense, truth and reality were not relevant. Also, at this time, I was experiencing sleep deprivation because I was pastoring two small churches in deep south Georgia, commuting over a hundred miles to attend seminary in north Georgia, and averaging two hours sleep a night for two and a half years.

I spent hours knee deep in the Progressive theological swamp and gave it my best shot to wrap my mind around all the nonsense. For comedy relief, other struggling students used to make up funny little sayings like, "The second commandment is - love your Niebuhr as yourself."[130] I tried to hang in there with chapel attendance, but when they introduced pantheistic worship rites as part of the worship, that was a line I was not willing to cross. I sat in classes where professors tried to convince me that a diagnosis of "sane" meant it was necessary to doubt God and question personal faith continuously. I did think it was ironic that one of my classmates was a confessing atheist studying to be a pastor in a mainline Christian church; I kept wondering how he was going to pull this one off in front of a whole congregation and God. I found out that it didn't matter if he was atheist because all his parishioners wanted was an entertaining sermon, a good social program, and someone who could bury and marry them; they definitely did not want to hear anything about Christ, the Bible or personal responsibility (these were Christians???).

Liberal professors and Progressive clerics gave it their best shot to deconstruct my worldview and coerce me over to the dark side of Progressive theology, the social gospel, secular humanism, and social justice (i.e., liberation theology), but these ideologies never found a permanent home in my heart and mind. I was rock solid in my relationship with God and too grounded in scriptural truth to succumb to alien ideas and theories that defied logic and God.

I learned more from two independent study courses I completed than I did from all the other course lectures combined. I remember one class where the professor knew his materials so well that he could lecture non-stop for three hours without any notes or books; the funny thing is, to this day, I cannot remember a single word he said. However, from my self-directed studies I learned a lot about the historical background of church governing documents and theological differences between Progressives and conservatives in the 18th and 19th century.

Independent-study courses I pursued gave me a working knowledge of Progressive terminology and about how some mainline Christian and Catholic churches transitioned from sound biblical doctrine to bizarre interpretations and outright denial of biblical truths. In the last class presentation before graduation, I stated in my introduction that, "I would like to hear one good thing about the Bible before I leave these halls." Several students discretely nodded in agreement. I have purposely been non-specific in identifying this school and the church I was connected with because it is not my intent to slander, and I hope that someday sanity will return to both and that they will once again embrace common sense biblical truth, stop propagating Socialist theories, and cease promoting the new social order of collectivism.

Within Progressive seminaries and churches, many capable and dynamic ministers are sacrificed at the altar of pluralistic ecumenicalism and political correctness because they will not compromise. In exchange for their integrity, they get the proverbial Progressive boot and are labeled "unfit for service" because they stand firm on biblical truths. For *extremist loons*, tolerance is a one-way street that applies to everyone but Socialist Progressives and atheists. I will take one minister with integrity and the courage to stand for truth over 100 Progressive ministers any day.

"Moses, you're just not dynamic enough for this job opening.
Show the next candidate in on your way out."

Figure 21: Ministers, does this sound familiar?

In late 1970, I started noticing subtle shifts in Christian churches away from sound biblical truths and toward liberalism. What was causing this shift and fueling its digression into a cataclysmic avalanche of self-destruction? Remember the quote written by Noyes in 1870, "If the churches cannot be put into this work, we do not see how Socialism" can "be propagated."[131]

Labor unrests of the 1870s and 1880s in America created a crisis, and the American Fabian Socialist jumped on this like a flea on a dog. In recent political rhetoric, we have heard the phrase in some form or another, 'you never want to waste a crisis.' Progressives and Marxists are rabid opportunists who seek out tragic situations or maneuver groups toward crisis to exploit them while incrementally working to co-opt or overthrow established systems just so they can secure a foothold and advance the new world order. The labor unrest crisis and poverty conditions in America created such an opportunity, and it was easy to suck churches into the Socialist welfare scheme.

Socialists began infiltrating the churches concurrently by taking over positions in education. Socialist philosophy was established through a newly created social science curriculum that replaced the classical education curriculum whereby Socialists melded together traditional classical courses like history with geography and changed it into socio-economic presentations that focused on the economic and social story of humanity that read like fiction rather than a factual presentation of true historical persons and landmark events. This 'social' epidemic spread until most course titles included the word "sociology" such as political sociology, historical sociology, sociology of religion, sociology of economic organization, military sociology, and educational sociology.[132] It all appears to have an intellectually respectable ring to it, doesn't it?

Therefore, the word "social" was already in vogue and it was not too much of a leap for churches to use the word in their preaching, publications and activist programs. In addition, since the word "collectivism" had worn out the welcome mat in elite socio-political circles, it was time to go stealth and employ the word "social" or "socialism" to divert attention away from the true agenda of the Fabian Marxists. The word "social" sounds innocent enough and has a nice marketable and user-friendly ring to it until you understand what it really means in the vernacular of collectivist *loons.* In simple terms, it means that individuals cannot function apart from a collective community and can only act for the good of the collective whole (or hole, as in pit - whichever you prefer), and all thoughts and beliefs are determined by the collective community's environment.

Over time, Progressives incorporated the words "social" and "sociology" and other marketable terms into religious lingo and church doctrine to bridge the language and worldview gap between socialism and Christianity. When Socialists bridged the gap, all that remained was to co-opt the church into their collectivist global scheme; a summary chart of this scheme is on the next page.

Would you venture to guess which Socialist schemes have been endorsed and implemented and:

1) which of these schemes are part of your current church or faith-based organization's statement of faith, governing documents, curricula, sermons, teachings, and budgets,

2) or does your church or organization align with or support other churches and organizations that advocate or actively participate in such schemes?

Master Plan to Nudge America into a New Social Order
1. Void absolute truth and propagate doubt and unbelief by mixing humanistic philosophy in with church doctrine
2. Deconstruct the Bible and replace sound doctrine and validity of its truth with faulty, deceptive, and entertaining interpretations
3. Do away with God as being involved in human affairs and make humanity the center of the universe
4. Excommunicate Judeo-Christian worldview and biblical principles from the public square and human consciousness
5. Convert individual salvation into collective salvation whereby salvation becomes dependent on works, and salvation of the whole community that ultimately requires a human savior
6. Formulate a class-victim theology that can be easily used to create a crisis or stir up class warfare
7. Nudge everyone towards pantheism and propagate a one-size-fits-all generic global religious system that focuses on man and not God
8. For a more manageable human population, dehumanize humanity and equate them with animals
9. Eliminate traditional family structure as the building block of civil society, devalue individuality, and promote communal living by nudging everyone into co-dependent relationships with a collective community and dependency on centralized government to meet our needs while hurling us toward a tyrannical new world order
10. Promote redistribution of wealth, advocate communal ownership of all property and assets by a centralized authority, and demonize private property ownership

Better yet, instead of guessing, let's investigate whether Socialist's schemes are in operation in your faith group. Some of the terms you may be familiar with are social gospel, liberation theology, collective salvation, ecumenical, social justice, multiculturalism, and pluralism. We will disarm the cloaking device of Christian socialism and learn how to spot these leopards in America's jungles.

Remember the Progressive takeover of America's educational institutions. In concert with this Socialist academic revolution, new faculty regimes gradually replaced orthodox Christian faculty; this scheme ushered in a flood of strange theologies further priming the pump for the ultimate American Socialist revolution. Socialistic worldviews were mixed with biblical doctrine thereby producing a watered-down, human-centered theology and for all practical purposes, giving God and his revealed truth the Machiavellian boot.[133]

By using the word 'social' in front of the gospel and justice, the true meaning of *"socialized"* theological terms remained concealed and socialism could be propagated as something noble and fit for humanity and as the answer to society's problems.[134] Even though Socialists have successfully hidden in American society up to this point, more Americans are beginning to see the insanity of their plans and pro-grams. As Socialists become more emboldened by America's compla-cency and complicity, they no longer have to hide their agenda, and they can openly reveal their plans for aggressively transitioning us to socialism while arrogantly bragging that they are 'fundamentally trans-forming America.'

First, we will survey an example of how socialism infiltrated Amer-ican religious groups and then follow this with an historical overview chart and a few definitions. As mentioned before, labor unrests and poverty conditions of the late 1800s was the crisis that sucked Christian churches and organizations into the Socialist welfare scheme. Edward and Francis Bellamy believed that humanity's destitute condition was due to character shortcomings, and a flawed social, economic and polit-ical environment thus successfully merging Marxism and Christianity. In response to the conviction and execution of five American anarchists responsible for the bloody 1886 Haymarket Square Riots in Chicago, Edward Bellamy wrote *Looking Backward* (a fiction novel advancing the idea of a Socialist utopia created by peaceful and gradual means to bring about universal economic equality and security. In Bellamy's *fictitious* utopia, everything was held in common at the public store; each individual was assigned a job according to the State's needs and issued the same credit each year to use at the communal store.[135]

In 1935, John Dewey and Charles Beard praised this *fictitious* book as the most influential one published between 1885 and 1935. In fact, it was so popular that Bellamy Clubs began popping up everywhere (later renamed the Nationalist Clubs). Nationalist Clubs pushed for public ownership of the economy by increasing government regulations to gradually eliminate private ownership of property and businesses. They also sought equal wages for everyone. This was an early stage of the Progressive Era movement.[136]

The auxiliary of the Boston Nationalist Club Number One was the Society of Christian Socialist (1889), and from this sprang Francis Bellamy's Christian Socialism, both of which had connections with the Fabian Society. Its basic philosophy was that God gave everyone an equal claim to economic rights and power, and that capitalism was based on selfish individualism and was the cause of social problems.[137] Below is a comparison chart highlighting basic differences between Christian economics and Socialist economics:

Christian Economics	Socialist Economics
Individuals and their immediate family are primary recipients of individual labor income[138]	The collective and communal storehouse is the primary recipient of individual labor income
Individual giving is direct and voluntary; individual decides what and how much to share with those who are unable to meet their own needs[139]	Giving is mandatory and taken by coercion or force, if necessary; centralized authority decides who gets what and how much; State needs are met first
Each person earns a wage according to individual skill and level of production[140]	Every person earns the same wage regardless of skill and level of production
Indolence reaps poverty[141]	Indolence is rewarded with provision for basic needs
God's storehouse never runs out and there is an abundance of provisions for those who take personal responsibility to earn their income[142]	The State storehouse is eventually depleted because welfare becomes mandatory, incentives for earning are removed, and many take advantage of free handouts

Now it is time to sprint through Christian socialism's history and highlight some of the major personalities and points along the way. See Historical Overview of Christian Socialism chart on next page.

	Historical Overview of Christian Socialism
Pre-1870s	Christian Socialist movement began in Great Britain and Germany as Christian Socialist labor parties often led by clergymen. Charles Kingsley and Frederick Maurice were the first British Christian socialists; the latter wrote *The Kingdom of Christ* (1838).[143] Robert Malthus (clergyman and economist) bridged political economic science with traditional theology to address overpopulation and was the inspiration for evolution and utilitarian social theory.[144]
1870s- 1890s	Washington Gladden was a pastor and early Progressive Era leader who called for government intervention, advanced social justice reform, and work-force unionization. Josiah Strong tags movement as *The Coming Kingdom* (1898).[145]
1900s- 1930s	Walter Rauschenbusch writes *Christianizing the Social Order* (1907) based on Christian socialism & *A Theology for the Social Gospel* (1917) to identify socialism as a valid religious movement.[146] Christian Socialism is politicized through the Federal Council of Churches (FCC is now the NCC) public policy statements and as churches incorporate Socialist ideology into their doctrine and social creeds, they demand government intervention; social creeds were a significant part of Woodrow Wilson's *Fourteen Points* and FDR's *New Deal*.[147]
1940s- 1980s	Marxist style liberation theology briefly sweeps through America then settles into Latin America. Global initiatives increase to equalize power and economic conditions for every nation and peoples. Christian Socialist go global through the World Council of Churches (1948-today), linking with UN initiatives for a "just participatory and sustainable society."[148] Liberal churches and Socialists support disarmament and encroachment of American sovereignty using the Declaration of Human Rights and International Law as defined by the UN.
1990s- Today	Christian Socialists influence government policy, using church and community groups to promote environmental protection from big bad private property owners and capitalists and to advocate for universal healthcare; they lobby for increased government regulations, laws and International treaties in conjunction with UN Agenda 21.[149] They also meld with spirituality-type churches such as the Modern Ecumenical Church that propagates "modern, agnostic and communitarian spirituality."[150] The latest church trend is the "emerging" church, which mixes in generous portions of the social gospel and social justice, focusing on collective salvation and globalism.[151]

Figure 22: Socialists appear to be deep thinkers; however, when confronted with truth, they react emotionally or become mean spirited because they lack logical answers and can't handle the truth

For individuals and families, the ultimate consequence of "Socialist economics" cloaked as good intentions is servitude to the State, and communal living instead of private property ownership. Although there were some examples of communal communities in the Bible, their existence was short lived, and this communal-type lifestyle did not become a permanent institution. The early church's communal life ended with their being scattered because of persecutions, and there was never a permanent re-establishment of such communities although there have been many unsuccessful attempts to do so. One explanation for this is that God knows our nature. We have witnessed in our own local community experiences that when certain individuals or families establish themselves as the power base behind local authorities, be it secular or religious, the system becomes corrupted, and economic benefits go to the power base and most often to those who administrate the will of that power base.

European Fabians and Marxists saw America as a rich field for their Socialist seeds, so they used German theologians to influence American theologians and gain access to America's heart and soul. While there were many just causes such as reforming child labor laws and laborer's working conditions and addressing poverty, it was not necessary to enslave an entire population on the *for the greater good of the collective* platform. We have a vivid historical example whereby Hitler rose to power with the help of Christian Socialist churches who were clueless as to his true intentions. They were deceived because they left their First Love (God), abandoned biblical truth, and were steeped in humanistic psychosocial ideologies. In addition, some were even involved in pagan spirituality (theosophy).

Some of the more prominent organized churches became easy pickings for a mad man and his house of horrors, because the church oligarchy desired restoration of their former power that they enjoyed before the Reformation at the national level. To avoid retaliation, some German churches signed an agreement that they would refrain from opposing Hitler in exchange for his protection, and Hitler knighted them as the official United Reich Church of Germany as they waved the flag showing the cross superimposed on the swastika.[152]

So, let's rattle a few Christian Socialist worldview cages and see if we can spot Socialist leopards in our own backyard jungle.[153] Why is it important to address religious worldviews in the secular context? Some folks may say, "We are not supposed to express our religious views in the public square because of that 'separation of church and state' thingy. My response is, "Good luck with that." We all function within the parameters of what we do or do not believe about God, the nature of humanity, and our morality or ethical values. Whatever worldview we consciously or unconsciously embrace influences every area of our lives, and the greatest impact is on American families and individual freedom.

Figure 23: Socialist leopard seeking whom he may devour[154]

It seems that the separation of church and state only applies to Christians. The real irony is that American Humanists frantically wave the *red* flag of "separation of church and state" at every opportunity as they seek to undermine biblical truths and morals, but when it comes to anti-biblical, socialistic agendas and other religious pagan worldviews, there is complicity to advance these causes by our government and legal system. This is hypocritical on the part of Humanists (Socialists).

If there is to be an absolute separation of church and state, then human-ism should get out of government, education and the public square since the IRS recognizes it as a tax-exempt religious organization and based on the humanists' own admission.[155]

News flash: Human-centered ideologies have consequences; it is detrimental to individual freedom and family wellbeing to continue fol-lowing Progressive pied pipers. If you really care about your family and neighbors, stop following them, no matter how popular, good look-ing, or trendy they may seem. Progressives rarely consider the long-term consequences of their so called "smart" plans that are sold as *for the common good*, and when things go south, they cling to lame brain explanations such as *unintended consequences*, or worse yet, *accepta-ble losses* as citizens continue losing their freedom, property, heritage and dignity, and all just for a bowl of Socialist stew.

Breaking Christian socialism's word code is like using a machete to cut through a jungle. Let's take a few swipes and define some terms to gain insight into how Christian socialism is religiously packaged and how it manifests in social creeds, statements of faith, and governing documents (see Appendix A for further explanations).

- *Collective salvation*- salvation obtained by helping to save everyone else first
- *Ecumenism*- one world religious organization that accepts all religions as equally valid and true
- *Humanism*- no need for God or moral absolutes because man is good and can reach self-godhood
- *Liberal theology*- each person constructs his or her own truth and all beliefs are relative and equal
- *Liberation theology*- equalizing human conditions for every-one by any means necessary
- *Pluralism*- all religions are valid paths to salvation and God
- *Social gospel*- man building an earthly kingdom of God (uto-pia)
- *Social justice*- equalizing justice and economic opportunity for everyone based on human needs or demands
- *Unitarianism*- a religious group that formed the basis for lib-eral theology

Entrapping churches in socialism required a gradual and systematic dismantling of sound biblical doctrine by reinterpreting it through a social and cultural lens, thus making man the center of the universe and pushing God to the side or completely out of the picture.

Liberal Theologian's Methods of Bible Interpretation or Criticism
Hermeneutic of doubt or suspicion- a type of interpretation that questions the inerrancy of the Bible (being without error); the meaning of scriptures and its authority depends on whatever the community or individual decides it is; they also believe that humans wrote the Bible; therefore, they deny that the Bible is God's revealed truth.[156]
Deconstructionism- a type of hermeneutic that deconstructs a text and separates it from its true meaning to create novel interpretations with no regard for valid truth and logic.[157]
Historical-critical method- (higher criticism is old term) a hermeneutic of doubt that assumes biblical history is unreliable and uses a scientific method of interpretation. Spinoza developed this theory because he believed that theology was "the source of all political problems"; further developed by F. D. E. Schleiermacher (father of classical liberalism).[158]
Socio-critical method- a type of interpretation rooted in pragmatism, utilitarianism and postmodernism whereby a community's culture determines the meaning of scriptures; it applies the hermeneutic of suspicion to biblical interpretation, "asserts that truth is what is good for the community," and it originates from the philosophies of Hegel, Marx (Neo-Marxist social theory), Freud, and Nietzsche. Liberation and feminist theology are examples of this type of biblical interpretation. [159]

Figure 24: When it comes to theological stuff, I empathize with you.

I guess all those "smart" theologians forgot about 2 Timothy 3:16-17: *"All scripture is given by inspiration of God, and is profitable for doctrine, for reproof, for correction, for instruction in righteousness, that the man of God may be thoroughly equipped for every good work."* Simple biblical truth is much more effective and practical for the real world than highfalutin socialistic interpretations of scriptures; the good news is that the Holy Spirit is more than sufficient to guide us into knowing and understanding.[160]

The most disturbing and destructive characteristics of Christian socialism are:

1) Casually discarding God's supremacy over humanity and perverting His truth as revealed in the scriptures
2) Intentional perversion of God's moral compass for humanity that He established in His Word
3) The arrogance that people think they can save society through human effort without God
4) Destroying our freedom and cloaking it as *for the common good* thereby forcing shared misery on everyone
5) Thinking it is okay to steal from hard workers by draining their family resources to feed co-dependent people who refuse to work
6) Cherry picking scripture verses to support socialism's ideological viewpoints and not acknowledging truth stated in the surrounding context of those verses and other bible passages

Walter Rauschenbusch clearly stated his intention to create a theology based on psychosocial sciences when he wrote in *A Theology for Christian Socialism*, that "...for the first time...Christianity has a... chance to form a working partnership with real social and psychological science."[161] Therefore, in the next chapter we will examine the root system of Christian Socialism to gain further insight and understanding of how detrimental it is to American families and individual freedom.

A few thoughts before moving to the next chapter- there are many Christians and numerous churches in the body of Christ that champion God's truth and remain faithful witnesses of His redeeming feature, and to these churches, I say, "THANK YOU, and God bless you for your faithfulness and courage." However, some church members are unaware of what is happening. This is not the time to turn a blind eye. Ultimately, it is each individual person's responsibility to examine his or her own worldview and make adjustments to realign with God's truth and then be alert as to what is taking place, stand strong, and graciously speak out in love if truth has been replaced with a lie.

"We assumed 'Comparative Religions' would
restrict itself to the more respectable religions."

Figure 25: What are they really teaching in those Ivy League schools?

21ˢᵗ Century Truth or Consequence Question: *Is compromising and yielding to Christian Socialists just for a few temporary indulgences worth sacrificing my children's future?*

Dig Deeper

1. The Bible
2. Documentary: Ken Connolly (host), *The Indestructible Book* (DVD, 2004).
3. David Noebel (2006, 2ⁿᵈ Edition), *Understanding the Times* (Manitou Spring, CO: Summit Ministries: Summit Press).
4. Fritz Ridenour (2001), *So What's the Difference* (Ventura, CA: Regal Books). (A brief overview of various religions).
5. Documentary: Vision Video (2005), *Hanged on a Twisted Cross* (DVD/VHF presentation about the life of Dietrich Bonhoeffer). Not appropriate for young children.
6. Edgar C. Bundy, *Collectivism in the Church* (Church League of America, 1965).

CHAPTER 6
POISONOUS FRUIT

"Beware lest anyone cheat you through philosophy and empty deceit, according to the tradition of men, according to the basic principles of the world, and not according to Christ."[162]

As we learned in the previous chapter, there are deliberate efforts to undermine the simple gospel of Christ and God's role as central to matters of the human heart and soul by distorting biblical truth through deconstruction and reinterpretation. If socialistic political ambitions and utopianism were to be successful, it would be necessary to ensnare churches in the cause of socialism.

Early socialistic philosophies and utopianism ran concurrently with one another throughout humanity's journey on terra firma. Biblical truth remains in the cross hairs of both movements because it is diametrically opposed to the enslavement of humanity, destruction of families, establishment of an earthly human kingdom or utopia, and worship of anyone or anything other than the one true God and His incarnate Son, Jesus Christ who clearly stated that, "My kingdom is not of this world."[163] How many earthly human kingdoms have come to a catastrophic end, and how many more will collapse before we get the message that *absolute power* in the hands of any person or ruling elite group *corrupts absolutely* because it is the nature of the power of the beast for the worst in humanity to rise to the top.[164]

Mitchell's (2007) *Charts of Philosophy and Philosophers* helps with navigating the maze of major philosophies and philosophical movements with the added component of "theology" that shows a gradual wedding of human philosophy with biblical faith and their eventual divorce from universal truth established by God. Navigating this maze starts with understanding foundational philosophies that keep

79

feeding American socialism's Goliath, philosophies devised by empty vessels who have a rotten root system that produces poisonous fruit as illustrated in the *Spirit of Bondage Tree* below:

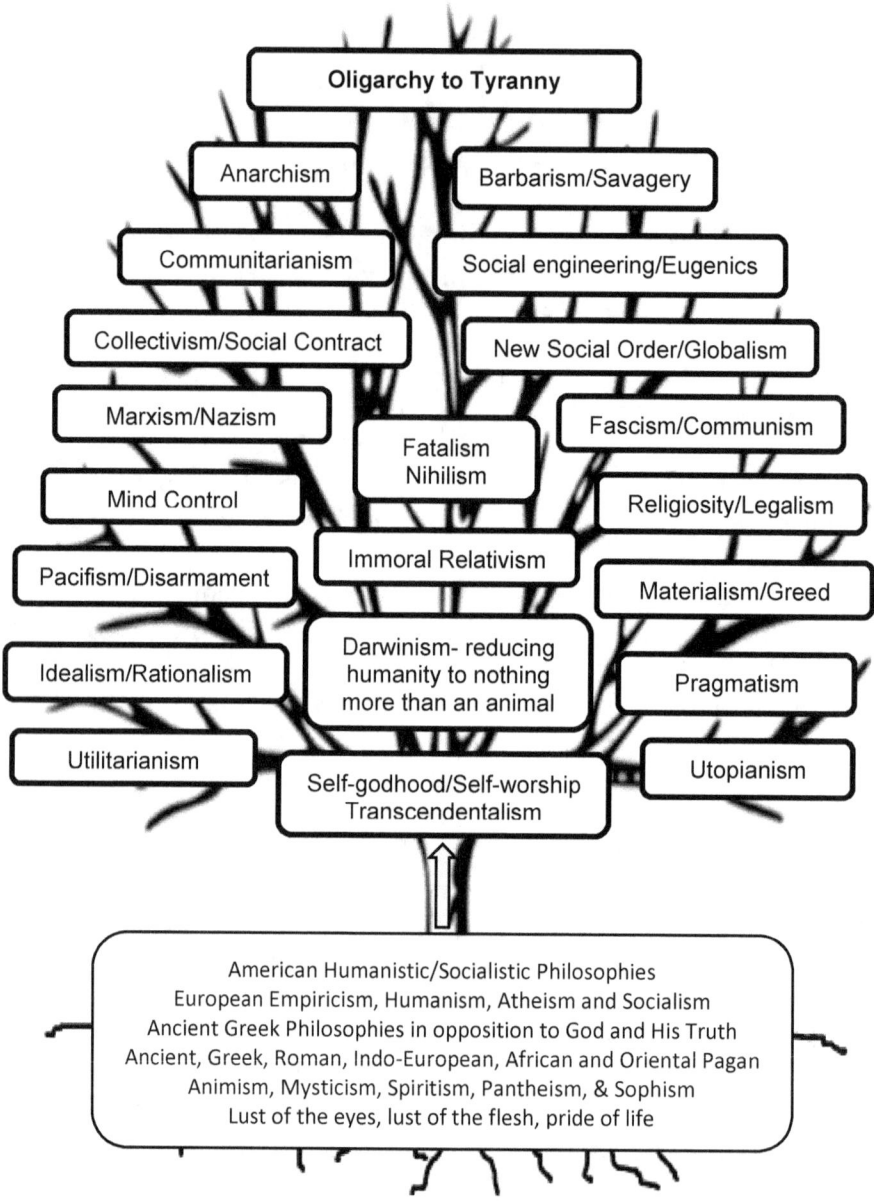

Figures 26: Spirit of Bondage Tree[165]

For anyone wanting a deeper understanding of the historical development and digression from fixed truth based on God's character and nature, Appendix B provides a brief overview of three major philosophical eras and some prominent trends that relate to faith, freedom and the family. In addition, some of the fruit-*isms* of the bondage tree are explained in this appendix thereby revealing a constant struggle between God-centered vs. human-centered philosophy and theology. In sum, the following illustrates devastating results of human-centered philosophies and theologies.

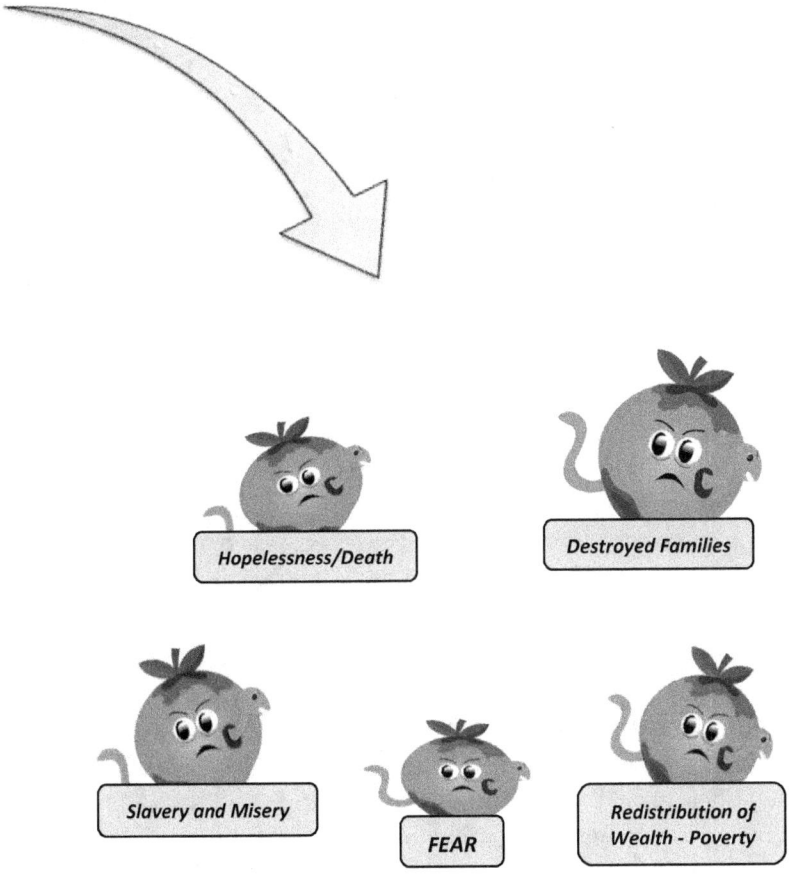

Figure 27: Fruit falling from the Spirit of bondage Tree (devastating consequences for faith, family and freedom)

After reviewing philosophy's history and trends in Appendix B, it was easy to track the shifting sands of philosophy and theology as they drifted further away from God-centeredness and biblical truth. The consequential shift was toward elevating humanity as the center of the universe with little or no room for God.

I loved hanging out with Dad in his workshop building bookcases. One of the basic principles I learned about design, manufacturing and building was that all copies must be cut from the master template to maintain the closest facsimile to the original template's size and shape, ensure a perfect fit, and guarantee structural integrity and functionality. If this basic principle is not applied when building a bookcase, the finished product will be crooked, have gaps at critical points of support, will be unstable, tend to mimic the Leaning Tower of Pisa, and will not stand the test of time and use. I still have one of those bookcases that Dad and I built, and its structural integrity and functionality are intact after fifty-two years of being dragged all over several southeastern states.

After Dad died, I worked through the loss by rebuilding a crooked separator wall using his old hand drill, hammer, leveler, wire cutters, screwdrivers, and circular saw. Just me and Dad's tools in action helped in the healing process and also brought back memories of some valuable lessons Dad taught by example. Memories are the most valuable and enduring part of us that we leave behind, and they can be either healing or painful memories- the choice is up to each person, which is why we need to be mindful of memories we are making every day for our children and grandchildren. It is a tradition to eulogize the departed; unfortunately, for some family members I have known over the years, it took a little Jack Daniel's courage to muster up something good to say about the deceased. What will your legacy be?

Philosophy can be a tool of construction or destruction. In the mind of skilled thinkers who have a solid foundation in God's truth as a starting point, and humility to stabilize their course, life's challenges are worked through with the application of sound reasoning and unchanging moral principles. However, in the hands of other philosophers who doubt or deny absolute truth, create their own fantasy world of ideas, elevate humanity into self-godhood and dismiss God, philosophy becomes distorted, confusing, deceiving, destructive, and downright illogical for anyone who has a shred of sanity and common sense. The reason the latter is so illogical is that human-centered philosophies are built on previous philosophies, and the new versions either argue against or add to an original philosophy, spinning off in a direction unintended by the original philosopher or Supreme Ruler of the Universe.

That last dog won't hunt because when someone makes a copy of a copy, it never fits, especially when dealing with reality, thus sending humanity in an uncontrollable tailspin of self-destruction or self-fulfilling prophecy. In other words, the further one moves away from truth to create an alternate reality like a new social order or utopia, *versions* of the truth are corrupted and reality becomes distorted and unmanageable.

So, "How do human-centered philosophies and theologies play out in real life; do they enhance faith and freedom for individuals and families, and do they secure peace and tranquility for a civil society?" To answer these questions, we will begin by skipping a rock across Darwin's shallow pond. Darwin had the opportunity to construct a healthy pond with some real depth and maybe even a little happiness.

"Croak something romantic, will ya?"

Figure 28: Happiness in a deep pond...

Instead of acknowledging God as Creator and honoring his fixed Laws of Nature, Darwin deliberately shoved God out of the picture to build a shallow pond of purposelessness, hate, and destruction. There is significant evidence proving that during most of his life, Darwin was one oar short of a good boat ride. He had agoraphobia (fear of crowds) complicated by a tormenting psychoneurosis which was probably "provoked and exaggerated by his evolutionary ideas," and the disapproval of his theories by his wife toward whom he was codependent.[166]

83

Darwin wrote in his diary, "describing fits of depersonalization, hallucinations, suicidal thoughts, bizarre behavior, and sadism (...inordinate love for killing animals)."[167] He also classified women as inferior to men. This is the man some still insist on celebrating every year on Darwin Day and religiously following his theories despite all the scientific evidence disproving evolution. Birds of a feather really do flock together and swim in the same muddy pond; we can say one thing about *extremist loons*- they are consistent in their loyalty.

When I dredged Darwin's shallow pond, I discovered that he did not originate the theory of evolution, but copied other theories and dark philosophies (dark *isms*) such as:

1) The natural selection and evolutionary or transmutation theories of Erasmus Darwin (his atheist grandfather), Robert Chambers, Jean Baptiste Lamarck, Robert Grant, Carl Vogt, Edward Blythe, and Patrick Matthew

2) Struggle for existence from Thomas Robert Malthus' principle of population (a promoter of population control through eugenics and infanticide)[168]

3) The racism of his cousin, Francis Dalton, and faked data of Ernest Haeckel who believed that the human embryo was at the lower stage of evolutionary development and devoid of conscience

4) George Cuvier's theory of the earth claiming that multiple catastrophes produced progressive creationism

5) Charles Lyell's dismissal of Genesis as history, and advocating uniformitarianism (took millions of years for earth to form)

6) Other materialistic philosophies of the Birmingham Lunar Society, an industrial think tank seeking to improve humanity through psychosocial engineering and without God's help or wisdom (does Looney society ring a bell)

On pages 86-87, is *Darwin's Fatal Fruit Tree* illustrating some of the poisonous fruit produced as a result of his loyalists feeding from his polluted pond and applying evolutionary theory's struggle for survival and racism as a means to psychosocially engineer humanity.[169]

We have already discussed in a previous chapter the connection of Margaret Sanger, founder of Planned Parenthood, to the European eugenics movement. In her own words, "More children from the fit, less from the unfit -- that is the chief aim of birth control." *Birth Control*

Review, May 1919, p. 12.[170] During the early 1900's, American Socialists were supportive of the European eugenics movement and racial purification projects.

As we will discover over the next several pages, millions who have waded in Darwin's pond, have come to a tragic end; Darwin's ultimate goal in developing and establishing his theory as far as he was concerned was like committing murder.[171] What slithered out of his pond was not pretty, so brace yourself.

It is not within the scope of this book to debate the pros and cons of Darwinism; however, there are excellent resources that more than adequately address the errors and invalidity of the theory of evolution (see "Dig Deeper" section of this chapter).

I have adapted a chart by Dr. Kelly Ross on moralistic relativism showing the political application of *pseudo-scientific socialism* and secular humanism by tyrannical leaders revealing its end game as digressing into immorality and insidious relativity (italicized words in chart are mine based in further research).[172] Remember the definition of moralistic relativism (Appendix B)- there is no absolute standard for morality and each person decides what is right or wrong in each situation (i.e., situational ethics), which changes according to human will and circumstances, and cannot always be expressed rationally.[173]

Moralistic Relativism		
	Moralism	**Moral Aestheticism**
Nazism	• totalitarianism • no privacy • no free speech • no free association • collectivism • race enemies	• beyond good and evil • *justified* mass murder[174] • beyond bourgeois morality[175] • survival of the fittest • evolution
Communism	• totalitarianism • no privacy • no free speech • no free association • collectivism • class enemies	• beyond good and evil • *justified* mass murder • beyond bourgeois morality • scientific socialism • dialectical *materialism*

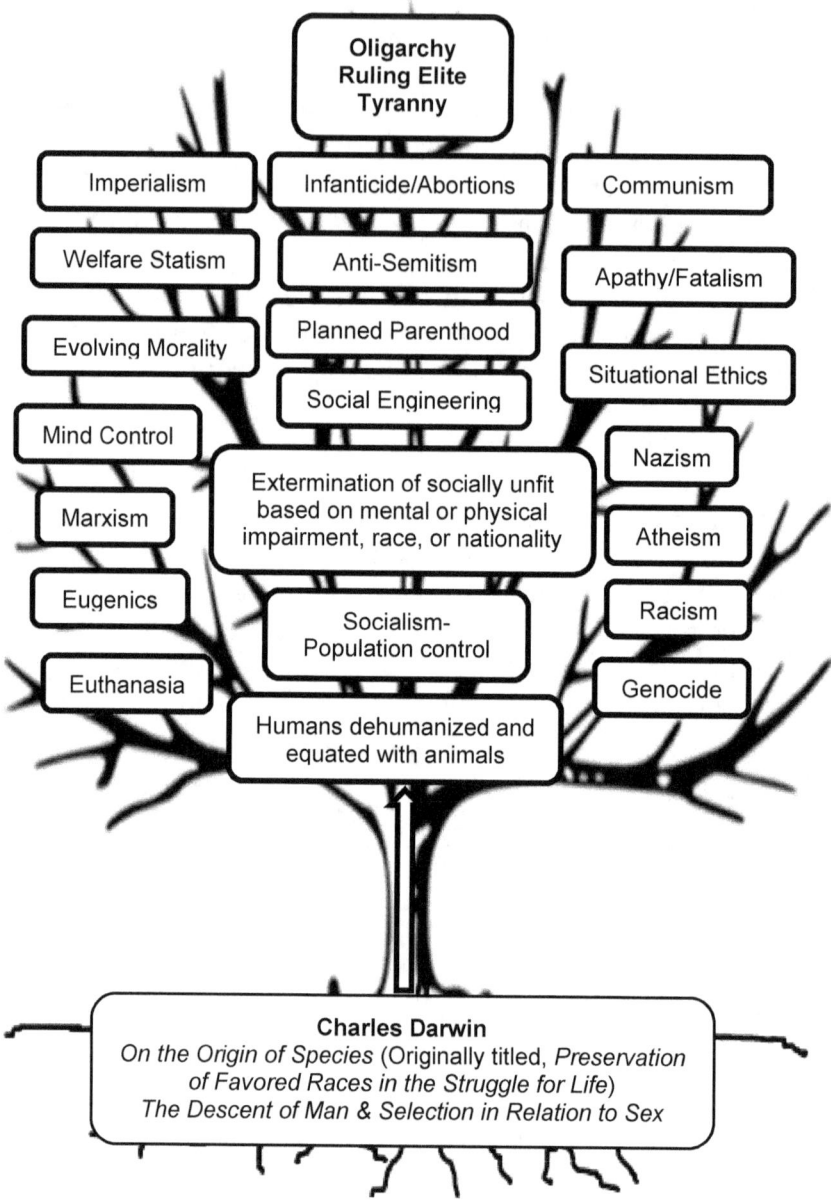

Figure 29: Darwin's Fatal Fruit Tree

As demonstrated in Nietzsche's "beyond good and evil" philosophy was applied, and both political systems purposely avoided using God's standard of morals and values. There was one more kick in the gut for individuals and families, and that was the justification of racism and mass murder by the Nazis based on Darwinian evolution, Marxist advocacy to eliminate reactionary races, and Himmler's occultism. Hitler used evolution theory, Houston Chamberlain's German race supremacy ideology and Himmler's theosophical occultism, the last of which was rooted in Greek anti-God philosophies, paganism and the belief in the racial superiority of the Germanic/Teutonic race (Aryan). Building on

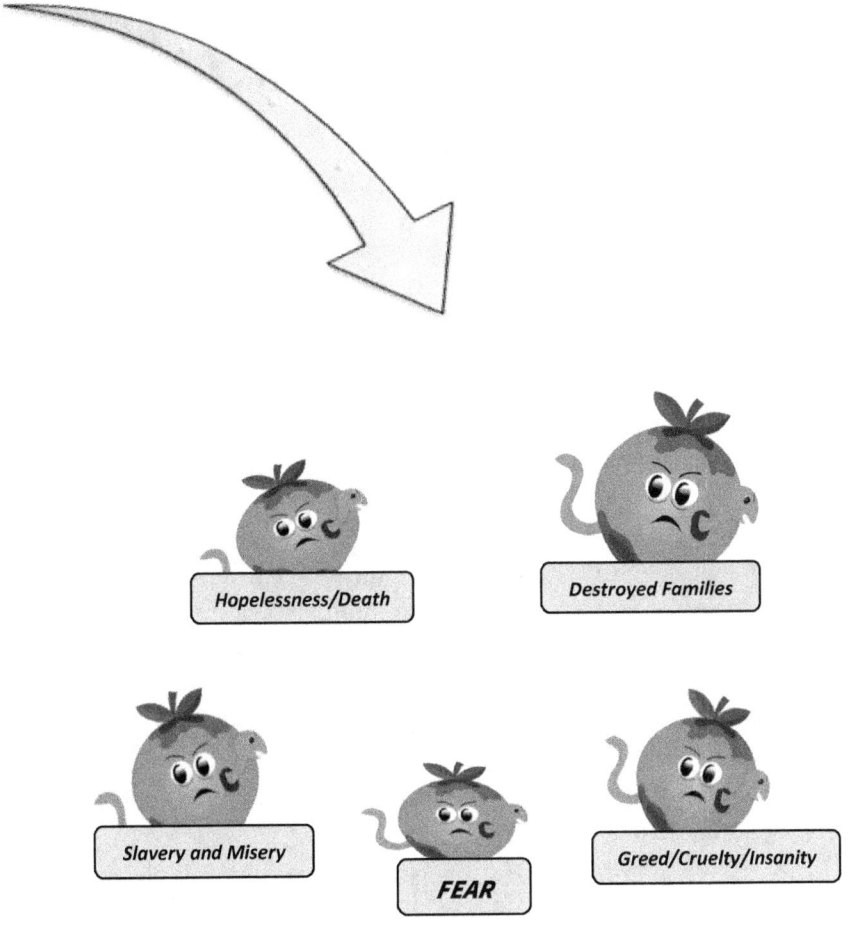

Figure 30: Fruit falling from Darwin's Fatal Fruit Tree (devastating consequences for faith, family and freedom)

insanity, Nazi thugs felt they were "morally obligated" to use eugenics (sterilization, abortions, infanticide) and genocide to cleanse and purify their Germanic race; among those deemed unfit for the new Reich society were the psychologically and physically impaired, Jews and other persons of non-German descent, gypsies, homosexuals, and religious and political dissenters.[176]

Over the past two millenniums, humanity has reaped the consequences of the philosophies of those who thought they knew better than God did. Below are statistical results of Communism and Nazism from just the past century:

Tyrannical Socialism's 20th Century Murder Rate:[177]

Soviet Union (Communist) (1917-87)	61,911,000
Chinese Communists/Nationalists (1949-87)	48,914,000
Nazi Genocide[178] (1933-1945)	20,946,000

Combined total murder rate in the 20th century by Marxists, Communists, Fascists and other oppressive regimes and governments was approximately 169,202,000 men, *women* and *children*.[179] Ethnic cleansing is another word for genocide, and genocide includes sterilization, birth control and/or abortions imposed upon a targeted group (based on ethnicity, race, or religion), although the latter three types of genocide were not included in the above statistics even though they were implemented.

I thought about including a few pictures of Hitler's legacy of horrors, however, they were too horrific to subject gentle souls to. Should you need empirical evidence, feel free to visit the Holocaust museum or any web site that contains photographic documentation of Hitler's death camps and chambers. We should never forget the high cost in human lives of atheistic and socialistic ideologies, especially the lives of children who suffered and died horrendous deaths at the hands of sadistic egomaniacs.

Based on the oppressive political practices and statistics, there is not one shred of evidence indicating freedom for individuals and families; both political systems demonstrated a perverted political moralism in play that was hazardous to one's health and welfare. Any way you slice *pseudo-scientific socialism's* pie means a generous serving of death, destruction and misery for anyone caught dining in socialism's cafeteria.

When a nation shoves God out of its picture and succumbs to socialism and its band of related *isms*, that nation goes dark as depicted in the satellite photography in Figure 31 below. Nazism, Communism, and Fascism are all grounded in atheism, evolution, and socialism, which are all part of Postmodernity.[180] We are deceiving ourselves to think that socialism, secular humanism, progressivism and any other human-centered *ism* will ever result in heaven on earth and safety for families and America; it is obvious that under these philosophies, it isn't Zion we are marching to.

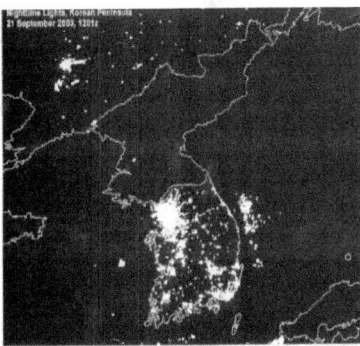

Figure 31: Night-lights of South Korea (moderately free) and North Korea (not a glimmer of freedom shining except for the ruling elite)[181]

You may be thinking that America is not equal in character to those of totalitarian regimes of Hitler, Stalin, Lenin, Mao Tse-tung, Khadafi or Kim Jong-Il, or at the least, well on the path to equality with tyrannical regimes. Let's take a peek at what teachers in North Carolina are required to teach their students regarding values:

- ✓ "There is no right or wrong, only conditioned responses
- ✓ The collective good is more important than the individual
- ✓ Consensus is more important than principle
- ✓ Flexibility is more important than accomplishment
- ✓ Nothing is permanent, except change
- ✓ All ethics are situational; there are no moral absolutes
- ✓ There are no perpetrators, only victims"[182]

Using Appendix B as a guide, can you spot the different philosophies that show up in the above list? After reading the previous list of values required to be taught to children, what kind of society do you think we will have when these children become adults? How long do you think the elderly will survive when these children take government leadership positions in relation to the recent 2010 healthcare bill passed? I will repeat what I have said before: *Secular humanism is a form of socialism, which is a stepping-stone to some form of tyranny.* Moreover, so goes a nation who gives God and His moral compass the Machiavellian boot from the public square and from human consciousness, and makes man the measure of all things and center of the universe. It will cost us our freedom if we continue marching to the dark side of philosophy's *isms*, especially those packaged as secular humanism, liberalism, progressivism, or socialism (or whatever name is culturally trending).

Before moving to the next chapter, let's review Historical Eras and Philosophical Trends (Appendix B) and note several things that stick out in this chart:

1) On the heels of the *Reformation* (1517 to about 1648) came an explosion of dark philosophical *isms* (dark *isms* are those philosophies that deny God and His light of truth and elevates humanity to self-godhood and the determiner of truth).

2) As humanity moves toward being the measure of all things and the center of the universe, logic moves from being a vital part of thinking until it gradually digresses into irrelevancy (see point 1 of the Pre-modern Era, point 2 of Modernity Era, and point 2 of Post-modernity Era of Appendix B). The real irony is that when logic began to wane in the Modern Era, this era was knighted as the *Enlightenment* or *Age of Reason* (1650-1700) (example: what is good is called bad, and what is bad is called good). Based on the fruit produced by the dark side of philosophy's *isms*, the Modern Era period should be called, the *Age of Insanity.*

3) When God and logic became irrelevant in the mind and heart of humanity, new levels of understanding diminished, and most of the dark *isms* became a regurgitation of previous *isms* (i.e., copies of a copy). Note the decrease of original philosophical ideas in the Postmodernity Era and that most of the dark *isms* of this era are copies of previous dark *isms*.

In Chapter 7, we will return to America's historical path and see how much we have digressed toward courting total chaos and how this impedes individual and family freedom.

21ˢᵗ Century Truth or Consequence Question: Review the chart and stats in this chapter- Are we going to remain caught up in our own little world and allow America to become the next notch in the tyrannical Socialist belt? Or, are we going to put the brakes on American Socialist leaders, vote out politicians who refuse to follow the constitution, rescue our children from Socialist educators and teach them biblical truth, constitutional principles and the difference between right and wrong according to God's moral compass for humanity?

Dig Deeper

1. Documentary: Kevin Miller, Ben Stein (actor), *Expelled: No Intelligence Allowed* (Premier Media Corporation, Inc.).
2. Jerry Bergman (2011), *The Dark Side of Darwin* (Green Forest, AZ: Master Books).
3. Tom DeRosa, *Evolution's Fatal Fruit* (Fort Lauderdale, FL: Coral Ridge Ministries, Inc., 2006).
4. Jonathan Sarfati (2004), *Refuting Compromise* (Green Forest, AR: Master Books, Inc.). His books titled, *Refuting Evolution* and *Refuting Evolution 2* are also recommended.
5. Maddoux, *Public Education Against America* (New Kensington, Penn.: Whitaker House, 2006),
6. Tammy Bruce, *The Death of Right and Wrong* (Roseville, Calif.: Prima Publishing 2003).
7. Jeremy Noakes and Geoffery Pridham (eds.), *Nazism: A History in Documents and Eyewitness Accounts*, 1919–1945, Vol. 1 (New York: Schocken, 1983).
8. Movie: Nora Lamb, *China Cry.*
9. Movie: Corrie Ten Boom, *The Hiding Place.*

CHAPTER 7
COURTING TOTAL CHAOS

"And this occurred because of false brethren...who came in by stealth to spy out our liberty which we have in Christ Jesus that they might bring us into bondage."[183]

Chapter 6 revealed that the further humanity drifted from God, the more insane and illogical their thought processes became. There was a serious knee-jerk reaction to the *Reformation,* and it was as if intellectuals lost touch with reality, entered a no-fly mental zone and landed their thoughts in a parking lot full of unintelligent life forms. I say this because of the inordinate number of pseudo-philosophies produced during philosophy's modernity and postmodernity eras, and the mortality rate of people subjected to them.

To connect philosophy to history, David Bebbington identified five philosophical schools of history (see Appendix D). To simplify the basics of these five schools of history, I have synthesized them into three models of history: (1) Linear History, (2) Cyclical History, and (3) Chaotic History. I have combined Bebbington's last three schools into the Chaotic History model, because they have interchangeable parts, and the last school of historical materialism is a copy of a copy of several different philosophies. On the next page is a simple graphic depiction of each historical school.

It doesn't take much to figure out which schools spell *futility* and *hopelessness* and which one offers hope. The first one demonstrates purpose and destiny; the second is a series of never ending cyclical journeys; and the third has no meaningful purpose or direction. Granted, the linear pattern has its ups and downs because life rarely travels in a straight line. However, even with all its challenges, the human spirit is free to accept God's way and purpose that leads to life here and in the hereafter, not to speak of His eternal love that conquers fear and sustains us in the good and not so good times.[184]

Linear History   Cyclical History   Chaotic History

Figure 32: Three Models of History

Bebbington listed cyclical history before linear history in his ordering of these schools, probably basing it on revisionist history in which the pagan worldview (such as those of the ancient Orientals, Indian and Graeco-Romans) was seen as predating Old Testament history. Cyclical history model was based on Darwinism and *pseudo-scientific* dating to accommodate the theory of evolution. However, I believe linear history comes first based on the fact there had to be a First Cause and an Intelligent Designer who was the first principle driving force of Creation (as "In the beginning God...").[185]

Chaotic history appears to be the current trend regarding American Socialists who are involved in social experimentation and who maintain a materialistic focus that translates into chasing money and power with no discernible direction or pattern. Both chaotic and cyclical models of history are rooted in fatalistic cycles of constant struggles and perpetual changes that seek immediate pleasure or temporary relief with little regard for long-term consequences.

The next question is, "How does socialism play out economically?" We have had several "rounds" illustrating attempts to establish collective communities or utopia in America's history and an overview of socialism's rise in America (review Chapters 2-4). This brings us to the European Industrial Revolution that crossed the Atlantic and landed on American shores. Concurrent with this revolution were the Gilded Age's (1873-1901) social and economic challenges that opened Pandora's Box of unions and government regulations. The green-eyed monster (i.e., *the love of money and power*), consumed politicians, the upper middle class union leaders, and industrialists and businessmen who had embraced materialistic philosophies void of truth and a stable moral compass. As a result, this generated a series of crises for American families, laborers and the economy. This was when America drifted further away from freedom and *Constitutional* self-governance and hurled toward dependence on the federal government to "save" them and meet their needs.

Unions are the major vehicle Marxists used to gain control and maintain power over the working middle class. Therefore, in line with this Marxists strategy, American Socialists via the Socialistic Labor Party (unions) used the Gilded Age's crises to force government to pass laws favoring centralized planning and control thereby severely restricting private ownership of property and businesses. To gain further insight into this labor party's platform and its demands in 1887, go to the first web site listed below, and then compare it with the Socialist Party USA 2012-13 platform detailed in the second web site. Both of these platforms are based on Marxism and Communism, and reveals what today's Occupy Wall Street protests are about, which is to nudge us further toward anarchy or tyranny.

1) 1887 Platform: http://www.slp.org/pdf/platforms/plat1887.pdf
2) 2012-13 Platform: http://socialistparty-usa.org/platform/

Both platforms demand compulsory education run by the federal government. Below is a 2011 photographic example of the quality of education these demands have produced over the past 124 years.

Figure 33: Example of socialism's compulsory education effectiveness

There were courageous Christian clergymen who boldly spoke out against American socialism; Charles Spurgeon was one of those brave souls. In his sermon that exposed the dangers of socialism, he summarized the main point of his message in one statement: "I would not have you exchange the gold of individual Christianity for the base metal of Christian socialism."[186]

Now let's fast forward to the early 1900's and review a few government programs designed to nudge America toward collectivism of a *new social order* through non-violent social revolution. A majority of these programs were brought to us by administrators leaning so far left that we have nearly fallen off the cliff several times, which brings us to the socialist programs of *big government* presidents beginning with the administrations of Teddy, Woody and Franky who worked to advance progressivism's socialistic agenda.

Theodore Roosevelt (1901-1909), Woodrow Wilson (1913-1921) and Franklin Roosevelt (1933-1945) held fast to the social Darwinist view of government and the *Constitution* as being living organisms that were in a state of constant change and needed complex, expandable administrative mechanisms to control and regulate it.[187] Wilson said, "All that Progressives ask or desire is…to interpret the *Constitution* according to the Darwinian principle."[188] This is in direct opposition to American traditions that held to fixed principles, a moral compass based on truth, and the ingenuity and creative abilities of Americans, local authorities and businesses to manage their own affairs.

One example of this expandable administrative mechanism was the creation of The Department of Interior (DOI) in 1849 that escalated into a government land-grab initiative over time whereby the DOI and various other federal departments have seized or laid claim to 30% of America's total land mass. In 2008, the federal government owned 84.5% of Nevada, 69.1% of Alaska, and 57.4% of Utah.[189] I would be the first to speak out for wildlife preservation, and I understand government's need for workspace, but this is beyond ridiculous, especially considering the fact that the government is running a 19+ trillion dollar debt and cannot even balance its own budget.[190]

How does this affect you and your family; this means that (1) each American taxpayer living today would have to pay approximately $160,000+ to bail out the government and its welfare dependents, and

(2) does imminent domain ring a bell? I just had a flashback of a video I saw where Hugo Chavez was touring one of his cities and pointing to buildings and homes he was seizing from private owners for his government's use. Have you figured out what each mortgage crisis in America is really about? Try "redistribution of property" to the federal bureaucracy's chosen ones; this is called *socializing property* (i.e., theft).[191]

Teddy, Woody and Franky were among the first to start an *avalanche of presidential power grabs* and establish centralized bureaucratic control systems designed to wrestle freedom and control from the hands of individuals, families, businesses and local authorities. Each successive presidency since Woody meant an exponential increase of federal bureaucracies under the President's direct control. Beginning with Teddy's *New Nationalism* and *Square Deal*, presidents began to think BIG, as in BIG GOVERNMENT. The growth of government bureaucracies mushroomed during Woody's *New Freedom* programs and Franky's *New Deal* and continues to grow at an insane rate today. Guess who the brainpower was behind these initial plans; try Dewey's Ivy League *loons* who served as advisors and members of the president's think tank or brains trust, most of whom were Columbia University's Fabian Socialists (i.e., Progressives).[192]

To wrestle control away from Congress and the Senate, and effectively bypass the checks and balance system of the *Constitution*, Wilson devised an elaborate administrative structure to expand the president's power beyond those intended by the *Constitution*.[193] As of today, the President has executive control over 21 Presidential Cabinet Departments, as well as hundreds of Independent Agencies, Government Corporations, Independent Regulatory Agencies, Commissions and Committees (each having multiple sub-agencies). For a full picture of the size of our government, go to the A-Z Index of Government Departments and Agencies at the following link:

https://www.usa.gov/federal-agencies/a

Guess who is tagged to pay for these *deals* of a lifetime? Thanks to Woody's *16th Amendment* income tax bill passed in 1913, hardworking American taxpayer's are footing the bill. Some of these government

97

deals were designed to aid the poor and weak; however, gradually they developed into entitlement co-dependencies and out-of-control raw deals for average Americans, their children and their grandchildren, and potentially for many generations to come.

Whenever the government jumps in to help, there is always a consequence- whatever goes up must come down according to the law of gravity. Sound wisdom says, ***"Get off the Federal and State gravy train before they derail."***

Figure 34: Redistribution in action- there is always a down side to dependency on government to supply all our needs and demands

What is bizarre is that anything deemed detrimental or in opposition to the progress of American socialism has been gradually outlawed by legislative action, government regulations, judicial activism, or executive orders. It is no stretch of the imagination to include free speech and privacy rights as freedoms that have been outlawed by national security, hate crime laws, and Homeland Security's broad definition of domestic extremists in their lexicon (*Constitutionalists, Christian patriots* and *opposition to abortion* are just few examples).[194] Visit the following to see if you qualify as an extremist:

http://www.fas.org/irp/eprint/lexicon.pdf.

On March 16, 2012, the President signed an executive order, which is a revised version of EO 8248 and 12919's *National Defense Resources Preparedness* in which the words "under both emergency and **non-emergency** conditions" added to Section 201(b). This means that in non-emergency situations, the government can confiscate all material, service and facility resources, including food, water, energy, transportation and healthcare resources, all of which will be reallocated or *redistributed* by the federal government, giving them the power to tell you and your family where to live, what to eat.[195]

Most Homeland Security guidelines and related executive orders were passed into law under the cloak of securing our safety. This explanation does not pass the logic test. Even if the government takes away every means we have to defend ourselves, this will never make us totally safe because those who seek to do us harm will always find a way to get what they need to do what they want. Did we not learn anything from Hitler's legacy of horrors? One of the laws passed by Hitler's regime was that a gun license could not be granted to anyone who was a Jew; Hitler then had all the defenseless Jews moved into fenced ghettos while reassuring them that it was for their safety. The next stop, after the less than livable ghetto situation, was death camps, again under the "for your safety" explanation. As Jews were loaded into boxcars, the Nazis played songs like the *Viennese Waltz*.

The key strategy used by genocidal maniacs and *extremist loons* is fear; another name for this is *psychological terrorism*. The game plan is to scare people until they are willing to give up their personal freedoms to "be safe." Under Darwinian socialism, laws of the jungle apply, and to win in this jungle, fear must be invoked at every turn to render victims powerless, weak, or unable to move.

Figure 35: Too scared to think or move; for extremist loons and psychosocial terrorists, every day is Halloween

Wafa Sultan, a *former* Muslim, gives us a detailed picture of how *psychological terrorism* works. She pointed out that *fear of lack* is the first wave, then *fear of the unknown*, and from there it quickly escalates into *fear of death*. When one or all of these fears become a mindset or habit, the next step is for the fearful to respond with either a plea for a human *savior* or violence. She also stated that the strong would devour the weak "in a society that is not governed by the rule of law, but by the law of the jungle…and both justify the status quo as an inevitable divine decree."[196] The God of love gives us a simple cure for fear by giving us His love and a sound mind, but we have to choose to accept His gift of love.[197]

The main purpose of terrorist attacks on 9/11 was to invoke fear in Americans. Guess what, it worked. Does this look familiar?

Figure 36: Non-porn x-ray view- what they actually see is more sexually explicit, and folks, this is just downright obscene and creepy.

How many different ways are we paying for TSA agents to gawk at or touch our stuff—how about taxes, surcharges and increased air fares just to name a few. I staged my own private sit out and refused to purchase another airline ticket just for the indignation of being gawked at or groped. Have we even bothered to consider what impact this has on children who are subjected to this lunacy?

With the recent passage of the 2010 health law, there seems to be no end in sight of the avalanche of government bureaucracies and debt increases. The main reason for this is that government economic policies are based on Keynesian economics that is entrenched in Fabian socialism; Keynesian economics is a government interventionist welfare system (based on Hegemonic principles).[198] In short: Spend other people's money like a drunken sailor, increase taxes on everything (including the dead), maintain large deficits, regulate small businesses to death, get as many people dependent on government aid as possible, never balance the federal budget, bankrupt the nation, lie about the economy, and ridicule, marginalize or vilify anyone who disagrees with these insane Socialist plans. Sound familiar?

Below is Robert Murphy's mini snapshot of Rothbard's "Consequences of Free Market Enterprise versus Welfare Economics:"

Consequences of Two Diverse Economic Systems[199]	
Free Market Enterprise	**Welfare Economics**
Individual freedom	Coercion
General mutual benefit (maximized social utility)	Exploitation of one group at the expense of another
Power of man over nature	Power of man over man
Harmony/peace	Conflict/war
Efficient satisfaction of wants	Disruption of consumer wants
Economic calculation	Chaotic calculation
Incentive for production and advancement in living standards	Destruction of incentives and regression of living standards

Franklin Roosevelt was one of the key figures in establishing welfare entitlement schemes. To get his economic machinery rolling, he created rights based on manufactured needs. Some of these needs were generated naturally by crises, but Socialist politicians and special interest groups took advantage by manufacturing more needs in backroom deals. Since the original meaning of *unalienable rights* given by God in the *Constitution* had no political force, FDR had to substitute a different humanistic standard for determining rights whereby the State "defined, created, and expanded rights and gave them to individuals in order to bring about social change."[200] FDR bypassed the *consent of the governed* to address social problems of the collective, thus creating an *unconstitutional* second Bill of Rights.

The intent of the Founding Fathers in the original Bill of Rights was equality of persons (i.e., having a common human nature and the capacity for reason and liberty, *but not possessing the same abilities, ini-*

tiatives, and possessions).[201] By arbitrarily creating an Economic Bill of Rights to establish social and economic equality for everyone, FDR had steamrolled over the *Constitution.* This meant that individuals were relieved of responsibility to provide for their own needs and could depend on American taxpayers to bail them out. Over time, these rights were extended to illegal, non-US citizens.

Roosevelt's administration arbitrarily established guaranteed rights. This included the right of every family to have a decent home, the right to adequate medical care, the right of provision by government during old age, sickness, disability due to accidents, and unemployment, the right to earn enough to obtain adequate food, clothing, and shelter, and the right to a good education.[202] Today, the cost per person for welfare programs (if everyone paid taxes) has risen from $1,808 (1910) to $27,519 (2010) per year just for entitlement programs.[203] Under current government deficits, there is no way to separate welfare programs from redistribution of wealth initiatives, so we can anticipate more of our hard earned dollars being taken by the government without our consent through mandates, laws, regulations, and executive orders as welfare spending continues to increase.

According to the *Index of Economic Freedom,* America dropped from 6th place (2009) as a free nation to a new low of 11th place (2016) as *mostly* free in her ranking among economically free countries; size of government was a major cause for the decline.[204]

The main problem we have had for several generations is that socialists strive to be masters of the universe and are hell-bent on playing god in people's lives while stealing other people's money, and as Margaret Thatcher once said, "The problem with socialism is that you eventually run out of other people's money." Hence, I predict that American socialism will fall because of the inevitable self-implosion of our current social welfare system. What can we do? Take personal responsibility and make a deliberate effort to get off the government gravy train, return to our roots of individual ingenuity and entrepreneurship, and get out of debt; *"...if any would not work, neither should they eat."*[205] If we continue to be a part of the problem and allow leaders to lead us to socialism's slaughterhouse, then, please forgive me, we are stuck on stupid and courting total chaos. If we don't act now, we can kiss liberty goodbye.

In summary, there were specific events in our history whereby the political establishment implemented programs to undermine our *Constitution* and subvert individual freedom. These "progressive" programs were designed to displace American liberty for individuals and families, destroy the free enterprise system, and establish a Progressive version of utopia in America. The good news: we can refuse to participate.

↓

21ˢᵗ Century Truth or Consequence Question: Read the following "Ten Measures of the Communist Revolution" *from Karl Marx's* "Communist Manifesto" *and check off which ones are in effect by law, regulation or policy mandates in America today.*

- ☐ "Abolition of property in land and application of all rents of land to public purposes
- ☐ A heavy progressive or graduated income tax
- ☐ Abolition of all rights of inheritance
- ☐ Confiscation of the property of all emigrants and rebels
- ☐ Centralization of credit in the hands of the state, by means of national bank with State capital and an exclusive monopoly
- ☐ Centralization of the means of communication and transport in the hands of the State
- ☐ Extension of factories and instruments of production owned by the State; the bringing into cultivation of wastelands, and the improvement of the soil generally in accordance with a common plan
- ☐ Equal liability of all to work. Establishment of industrial armies, especially for agriculture
- ☐ Combination of agriculture with manufacturing industries; gradual abolition of all the distinction between town and country by a more equable distribution of the populace over the country
- ☐ Free education for all children in public schools. Abolition of children's factory labour in its present form. Combination of education with industrial production"[206]

Dig Deeper

1. Zygmundo Dobbs (1969), *Keynes at Harvard: Economic Deception as a Political Credo* (Austin, TX: A Veritas Study, Perry Press, 2009). Online version at: http://keynesatharvard.org
2. Star Parker (2003), *Uncle Sam's Plantation* (Nashville, TN: WND Books).
3. Ronald Pestritto and William Atto, *American Progressivism* (Lanham, MD: Lexington Books, a division of Rowman & Littlefield Publishers, Inc., 2008).
4. Ambassador Terry Miller & Kim Holmes, *2012 Index of Economic Freedom* (The Heritage Foundation and Dow Jones & Company, Inc., 2012).

CHAPTER 8
LOONYVILLE

"Do not love sleep, lest you come to poverty; Open your eyes, and you will be satisfied with bread."[207]

As stated before, Woody and Franky started an avalanche of socialistic programs. They established fourteen (14) government agencies staffed by over 2.5 thousand people, which grew to over sixty-nine (69) agencies staffed by 2.11 million people by 2012 (not including the USPS).[208] The federal government has increased its workforce by 14% since 2008, while private sector jobs have decreased by 5% (i.e., five million private sector workers became unemployed).[209]

What is the current State of the Union that politicians and mainstream news media are not stating? How about a few of the consequences of FDR's redefinition of rights, *The Great Society's* "War on Poverty" program, 20th and early 21st century political redefinition of poverty, and expansion of categories classified as part of socialism's welfare entitlement programs (see Appendix E), stated below:

- Welfare program expansions discouraged work and marriage; unwed birth rate rose from 5.3% (1960) to 41% (2009) thus increasing number of welfare recipients.[210]
- Welfare spending increased 44% from 1964 to 1996 and skyrocketed to $714 billion a year in 2008. Projected welfare, entitlement and subsidy programs will increase $1 trillion dollars a year at taxpayer's expense.[211]
- Total federal spending going to government dependence programs rose from 28.3% (1962) to 70.5% (2010).[212]
- Welfare recipients receive assistance from six or seven programs, averaging welfare income of $32,748 (2010), up from $7,314 (1962).[213]

- 49.5% of Americans pay no income tax.[214]
- In 2010, 91.2 million Americans are dependent on government aid (up from 33.6 million in 1962; the 2010 Healthcare bill will add another 25 million people to government welfare rolls and increase taxes.[215]

With 29.5 % of the U.S. population dependent on government support (including government employees and benefits) in 2012 and only 50.5% of Americans paying income taxes, current size of government (average government employee salary is $76,586/year), and $212 trillion in unfunded liabilities, government welfare and entitlement spending is **unsustainable**.[216] On what planet does anyone think taxpayers could foot the bill for the 2010 Healthcare bill and not pay the price in reduced medical services and threat to wellbeing?

Just in case you missed this point earlier or forgot it, I did state and still strongly believe that *government is necessary to maintain a civil society*. The issue we are grappling with is how much government is absolutely necessary.[217] Thomas Jefferson said, "A government big enough to give you everything you want, is strong enough to take everything you have."

In FDR's 1941 State of the Union address, he listed *"freedom from want...for everyone in the world"* as one of the freedoms he desired for everyone in the world (i.e., extreme equality). The big question is, "If he truly believed in freedom from want for everyone in the world and was so concerned about hungry folks, then why did he enact the *Agricultural Adjustment Act* (AAA) in 1933?" This *New Deal* law paid farmers at American taxpayers' expense to kill livestock and not plant crops in order to raise prices on food and meat during the Great Depression when unemployment was at thirteen (13) million and families were going hungry. FDR's hidden agenda was for government to have full control of farmers and farmland by giving the Secretary of Agriculture broad discretionary powers. Rexford Tugwell, a hardcore Fabian Socialist professor of Columbia University and member of FDR's Brains Trust, was ecstatic over having a hand in creating a *planned society* as undersecretary of agriculture.[218]

FDR's federal machinery hired over 100,500 men from America's farming communities to enforce AAA laws, thus increasing the size of government; Woody and Franky redefined job creation as starting new federal programs at taxpayer's expense, centrally controlled by the feds with multiple offices throughout the United States. The AAA program resulted in an underproduction of crops and livestock, thus forcing a drastic increase in food imports and food prices and eviction of tenant farmers who were *resettled* by the government into American cities at taxpayer's expense. Uprooting and coercing people into living in cities are Marxist strategies based on the belief that cities are the hub of social change and transformation. In other words, it is easier to control a large population of people if they are located in a small dense area rather than spread over miles of rural areas.

Do you think for one minute that government freebies did not influence how AAA employees and resettled tenant farmers voted; how do you think FDR managed to be elected as president for three more terms? Re-election is the primary driving force behind government dependence programs such as welfare, entitlements, and subsidies. It is to politicians' advantage to keep welfare programs going and increasing the number of dependents on government aid.

While there are legitimate disability and extreme hardship cases, there is no reason for those who are able to work to remain on government aid. To perpetually remain as a nanny-state dependent when able to provide for one's self is equivalent to stealing from taxpayers and becoming the government's useful idiot. BTW: Do you think midwestern tenant farmer families were happy with their new digs in the city after a few years (see below)?

Figure 37: 1930's Downtown Los Angeles Slum[219]

After two decades of Woody and Franky's government power grab and psychosocial engineering of America, we had officially entered

107

Loonyville's twilight zone. *Loonyville* is my pet name for the kissing cousin of all fantasy utopias concocted by socialists and other pseudo-intellectual *loons*. In review, the one element that the three philosophical eras in Appendix B have in common is the idea of *utopia* that envisions a perfect earthly society. Ironically, in classical Greek, *utopia* translates into English as *not a place*, which, in our lingo today, means *nowhere*.[220]

Utopia is a mentally contrived fantasyland that never existed or ever will exist in this lifetime. Therefore, *Loonyville* represents no particular place on earth and is simply a fantasy. Below are some key characteristics of utopias as revealed in Mark Levin's *Ameritopia*:[221]

1) is parasitical and dehumanizing by nature
2) is irrational because no one can plan for human complexities and shifts of needs, wants and attitudes, and not everyone is absolutely equal
3) requires a surrender of personal liberty and assets for the common good
4) human, natural and material resources are held in common and managed by a central administrative body controlled by the ruler
5) needs and wants are met in exchange for total loyalty and servitude, thus devolving into a two-class system of ruler(s) and servants
6) needs of the State or common good supersede the family
7) the independent and industrious are viewed as threats to the collective
8) digresses into anarchy if needs and wants are not met by rulers
9) ends in tyranny to restore order due to chaos generated by anarchy

In summary, all of these characteristics translate into a futile cycle of insanity with wealth and wellbeing reserved for top dogs (i.e., ruling elite) while everyone else is conscripted to servitude. Arguments for equality made by *Loonyville loons* go something like this:

(1) "We are all equals.
(2) Equals ought to be treated equally.
(3) We are treated equally by redistributing wealth.
(4) (Therefore) we ought to have our wealth redistributed."[222]

Premise (3) is false- when you forcibly take from one person to give to another, that is an unequal and unjust treatment of the one from whom the resources are taken and strips them of their freedom of choice and right to benefit from their own labors (not to mention the theft of resources and inheritance from family). Therefore, this argument cannot be taken seriously as a logical argument that can withstand the test of truth. Mark Levin gave a great explanation of equality and inequality when he stated:

> "Equality, as understood by the American Founders, is the natural right of every individual to live freely under self-government, to acquire and retain the property he creates through his own labor, and to be treated impartially before a just law. Moreover, equality should not be confused with perfection, for man is also imperfect, making his application of equality, even in the most just society, imperfect. Otherwise, inequality is the natural state of man in the sense that each individual is born unique in all his human characteristics. Therefore, equality and inequality, *properly comprehended*, are both engines of liberty."[223]

As illustrated above, there is a major disconnect from truth, facts, logic, and reality by Socialist *loons* when they redefine *equality*. During their reconstruction of *equality*, they eliminated all personal responsibility and accountability for decisions and actions of individuals and the collective hive. Not much logical thinking going on here is there, especially in light of long-term *consequences*. By the way, while attending a seminar on stress management, I was politically corrected when I used the word "consequences"; apparently, this word causes some people to stress out. *Extremist loons* consider it a judgmental word, especially when they are trying to dodge accountability to God's moral and ethical principles and natural laws.

Now that we have taken a couple of laps around the mulberry bush, let's get back to our original topic. It was not enough for American Socialists such as FDR to increase the size of government and the number of those dependent on government for support; FDR and his wife, Eleanor, had global aspirations. Based on presidential power grabs and the demands of American Socialists, the endgame was to expedite social and economic justice globally at the expense of taxpayers and business entrepreneurs. Remember, FDR was very clear in his intentions when he included the phrase "everyone in the world" in his 1941 speech, which meant extending *social justice* beyond our borders. Some of the same ideas of redefined *rights* and *equality* advocated by FDR were included in the UN's *Universal Declaration of Human Rights* (ratified December 10, 1948); Eleanor, as one of the authors, considered this one of her greatest achievements.

Thanks to American Socialists, US taxpayers were on the hook to fund the UN at $3.978 billion for 2011 with an estimated increase to 5,326.2 billion in 2017.[224] This does not include the $8+ billion dollars the US spends on foreign aid each year apart from the UN budget requests, which is projected to climb to $25 billion a year by 2015 thanks to political *loons* making insane promises and signing away America's future at a breakneck pace.[225] Please do not misinterpret what I am saying; I believe in promoting and facilitating peace among nations and giving temporary assistance and a hand up until folks can get on their feet and provide for themselves. However, I am not in favor of coercively taking from hard workers to provide a perpetual flow of handouts for those who refuse to take personal responsibility for their own provisions and defense.

How effective are handouts? In Memphis, Tennessee, ninety-two of 229 or 40% of the homes provided for recipients through Habitat for Humanity and government Housing Trust Fund went into foreclosure or bankruptcy within the first year of occupancy.[226] The biggest American Socialist flop has been Fannie Mae (1938) and Freddie Mac's mortgage backed securities whereby 93-100% mortgage loans were doled out like candy to borrowers who made little or no equity investment and did not have to demonstrate an ability to pay back the loan over an extended period. Due to foreclosures, bankruptcies, and major defaults on home loans, the housing market bubble burst, causing prices to plummet by 30-50%. Responsible homeowners have lost thousands in home equity value, making it impossible for them to sell their home or refinance at lower interest rates because appraised values are less than what they originally paid for their home and less than what they owe on their mortgage. For example, a home bought for $150,000 in 2008 dropped to $86,000 in 2012 and had an outstanding loan of $119,000; this means the owner loses $31,000 in equity and will have to cough up a minimum of $33,000 plus closing costs in order to sell or refinance the home.

The other government housing scheme was low-rent HUD housing that started out as decent housing but eventually turned into slum housing over time. The pictures below are vivid examples of government attempts to be a landlord and provide affordable housing for everyone.

Figure 38: Government's affordable housing

Perpetual wells of free handouts do not work. Not everyone is equal in regards to taking personal responsibility because not everyone will invest the same personal sweat equity if one can get free stuff, because the convenience of freebies is preferred over **self-reliance**. Once folks are hooked on free handouts, they develop a brain freeze and mantra, "I *demand* free stuff." For example, OWS protestors cannot seem to coalesce around a common cause or issue except, "I demand free stuff" as demonstrated in a *Party for Socialism* protestor's sign that read, "Money for child care, not bank bailouts."[227] OWS expects the government to give out free money for childcare at taxpayer's expense instead of working for it themselves. Of course, as we have discovered, bank bailouts did not work so well either.

American Socialists (Progressives) bemoan the fact that the *US Constitution* is a major roadblock to their accomplishing their agenda. So, they figure if they can't come all the way through the front door, then they will come in the side door through the UN by *using children, the poor, the economy, the environment, climate change, and social*

111

justice to do it. To guarantee the need for radically changing America, a crises-generating mechanism had to be created. The following is one example of a "Progressive" strategy. In 1966 Richard Cloward and Frances Fox Piven, two American Socialist professors at Columbia University School of Social Work, formulated the Cloward-Piven Strategy and published their scheme in *The Nation*, a Humanist and Socialist magazine. The Cloward-Piven Strategy was designed to create chaotic social and political crises by increasing welfare dependency on government and forcing an economic collapse in order to replace the federal welfare system with a national guaranteed annual income to end poverty.[228] Anybody with common sense would recognize this as economic terrorism with the sole purpose of keeping people in a constant state of fear to enslave him or her to a central planning bureaucracy.

A "guaranteed annual income" sounds like a great idea doesn't it. What they failed to mention is that everyone but the centralized bureaucracy is conscripted to servitude and limited as to how much is redistributed from the common storehouse and federal bank to each person or family just so everyone could live in *shared misery* except the ruling elite. This spells Communism or some other form of radical tyranny and slavery.

America, you are being played like a fiddle if you think for one minute that the plans of Democrats and Progressives for solving poverty or other economic problems are noble plans. Do you think that the federal government run by American Socialists can effectively manage such a large-scale scheme when they can't even balance their own budget? Politicians make a big deal out of how much they are cutting the budget while in actuality they are increasing spending at the same time; most of the time spending increases outpace budget cuts.

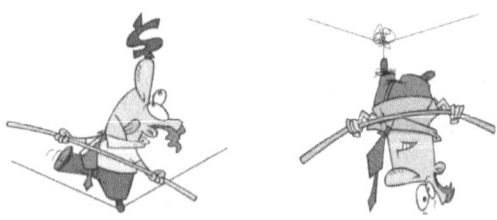

Figure 39: When Progressives and moderates fake balancing the budget, with no safety net, the American economy is left hanging by a thread.

112

Under FDR's *New Deal*, ecological programs exploded in growth thus establishing a foothold situation that enabled American Progressives to chip away at private property rights. It started as an anti-pollution program that had some merit in the beginning, but quickly mushroomed into a giant ecological octopus called the Environmental Protection Agency (EPA) established in 1970. This was Richard Nixon's power grab over everything to do with the environment, increasing the size of government by adding "three federal Departments, three Bureaus, three Administrations, two Councils, one Commission, one Service, and many diverse offices."[229] EPA tentacles eventually extended as a massive government control of America's natural resources and anything else labeled as "environmental."

Let's throw this train in reverse for a moment. Remember the first *redistribution of wealth schemes* in Chapter 2 and 4 (i.e., Round One, Two and Three of Socialist experiments) and the fact these experiments were failures? As if FDR's *New Deal* and other social justice schemes of American socialism were not enough, let's really go crazy and go global. Apparently, there is no end to stupidity. Is mutually assured economic destruction really what they envisioned just so every person in the world could be economically equal and have his or her needs met by someone else? We will dive deeper into globalization and the greening of American socialism in Chapter 9.

*21ˢᵗ **Century Truth or Consequence Question:*** *Do I expect my children and grandchildren to pay for my universal healthcare, and if not, what are my plans to provide this for myself and/or my family?*

Dig Deeper

1. William Beach & Patrick Tyrrell, *The 2012 Index of Dependence on Government* (Washington, DC: The Heritage Foundation, SR104).
2. Mark Levin (2009 & 2012), *Liberty and Tyranny* **and** *Ameritopia* (New York: NY: Threshold Editions).
3. Ryan Messmore, "A Moral Case Against Big Government: How Government Shapes the Character, Vision, and Virtue of Citizens"

No. 9 of the First Principles Series (Washington, DC: The Heritage
Foundation, February, 2007). Can be obtained online at:
http://www.heritage.org/research/reports/2007/02/a-moral-case-
against-big-government-how-government-shapes-the-character-
vision-and-virtue-of-citizens

CHAPTER 9
THE OTHER SHOE

"There is a way that seems right to a man, but its end is the way of death."[230]

To guarantee success in undermining American citizen's freedom to own land and keep most of their paycheck, and to strip local communities and local governments of their right to self-govern, the socialist environmental octopus morphed into a United Nations (UN) green Trojan horse of global environmental programs. Global environmental regulations and laws are designed to supersede local, state and national sovereignty and override personal property and asset rights. This green Trojan horse rolls under the power of UN treaties, international law, and global taxation schemes. This Trojan horse was named the *Green New Deal* because it borrowed three planks from FDR's *New Deal*:

- ↓ strict regulation of the cause of the problem
- ↓ funding of *New Deal* infrastructure by increasing taxes on the rich and big business
- ↓ investing billions of taxpayer's money in government infrastructure projects such as bridges, highways, and dams[231]

This green Trojan horse is Keynesian economics and the *New Deal* on steroids. We now have a flock of green agenda socialist *loons* who are in a frenzy to force global taxation laws on Americans (such as the cap and trade bill introduced in Congress a few years back). It's ironic that in the mind of *extremist loons*, cuts will not work, but green spending will, claiming that global taxation will reduce public debt, create jobs, and cut carbon, when the opposite is true as we learned in the Solyndra debacle. Take one wild guess who chose the winners and losers in these redistribution of wealth scheme?

115

Back to the three planks borrowed from the *New Deal, h*as anyone bothered to ask green agenda *loons* what building bridges, highways and dams have to do with saving the environment? Think with me for a moment-, do any of the following infrastructure projects benefit or help the environment, wildlife or improve air or noise quality?

- laying down more concrete or tar-based roads
- building bridges to nowhere
- cutting down trees and wiping out natural greenery to make way for concrete and steel structures or wider roads

Did we all of a sudden forget that trees absorb CO_2 and produce oxygen or that they clean the air, reduce heat, keep soil from eroding, and absorb dangerous pollutants? Trees also act as windbreakers; have you ever noticed what a desert looks like and how easy the wind can kick up the dust? Then why do politicians go straight for nature's jugular and promote projects that destroy wildlife's natural habitat? Politicians will claim as a defense that it is to stimulate the economy and create jobs. Has anyone noticed how many infrastructure spending bills Congress passed since the early 1900s, how many more government employees are added to federal payrolls at taxpayer's expense and how many "emergency transportation spending" bills are passed? How many road projects start just shortly before general elections, and which politicians make a habit of pushing infrastructure projects? So tell me America, how's that working out for taxpayers.

How many folks are aware that anytime local governments accept money from the feds, be it through grants or loans, they rescind their self-governing rights to the federal bureaucracy that only cares about maintaining power over citizens and local authorities? Here are some things to consider: (1) the federal government can recall loans at any time and as they deem necessary; (2) government grants have a ton of attached requirements and regulations that impede the local economy; and (3) many times local governments have to cough up matching funds for grants and agree to certain restrictions. If local authorities do not dance to the tune of federal requirements and restrictions, the feds can bankrupt local governments by recalling loans or by withholding the remaining grant funds. In addition, the federal government will sometimes bend over backwards to grant funds to states and cities, but then will accept foreign bids to do US construction jobs. For example, the following construction jobs were awarded to China:

> "Construction Engineering Group (CSCEC)"...has constructed bridge segments for a 2,050 bridge in California and transferred Chinese workers to do the installation. They "already built seven schools in the US, apartment blocks in Washington DC and New York and are in the middle of building a 4,000-room casino in Atlantic City. In New York, it has won contracts to renovate the subway system, build a new metro platform near Yankee stadium, and refurbish the Alexander Hamilton Bridge over the Harlem River."[232]

Whenever politicians and environmental activists chirp about raising taxes to protect the environment and create "green" jobs, be very suspicious. Develop the habit of doing your own research and follow the money (i.e., who is benefiting financially and politically and does the money go where it is supposed to go in the budget). If we discover that government projects do not benefit American laborers, the environment and our local community, then we should expose and challenge projects that do not reap a return for American workers, taxpayers and our local community. Gather facts, document with hardcopies and notify the media by writing an editorial or holding a press conference, and then write or call your representatives to protest with respect and civility. We will cover more about strategy and solutions in the next four chapters.

Now back to the *Green New Deal*. We cannot begin to unravel the entire Progressive Socialists' game plan unless we take a serious look at what role the UN plays in their plan and how entrenched America has become with the UN's agenda. While the UN has contributed to peacekeeping efforts and has been somewhat effective in the past, regarding the treatment of wounded, prisoners of war and civilians through the Geneva Convention, and feeding the impoverished, their effectiveness has diminished due to expanding beyond their primary duty to maintain world peace and curb the abuses of tyrannical leaders. Today, on a scale of one to ten, how effective is the UN at maintaining world peace and curbing abuses of tyranny?

According to the original UN Charter, the role of the UN was to be restricted to the following: (1) "maintain international peace and security; (2) develop friendly relations among nations; and (3) achieve international co-operation in solving international problems."[233] Howev-er, concurrent with the last 70 years of presidential power grabs and the world domination aspirations of various national leaders, the UN octo-pus has exploded in size and power at a phenomenal rate. The immoral part is use of the poor, children, women, economy, the environment, and related crises as so-called just causes to increase the UN's power base and fill the coffers of nations who hate America and Israel. By creating a massive global bureaucratic control system, UN tentacles can now reach into every area of life thereby establishing a UN foothold situation in every nation with the full intent to override national sover-eignty and individual liberty. One of their key goals is to crush the American free enterprise system and recreational activities by defining and controlling *unsustainable activities* (see Appendix H).

The chart below represents the other shoe that has been "progres-sively" falling on America's head since the establishment of the UN in 1945; that is the UN's plan for "Global Governance", historically known as the *new world order* or *new social order* fashioned by Fabian Socialists and other Loonyville *loons*. American politicians and the ruling elite view America's interconnectedness with the UN's central bureaucracy as a good thing. However, below we will uncover the UN's version of utopia and how it has gradually increased its power and accumulated mandated monetary commitments from wealthy na-tions while American taxpayers foot a high percentage of the bill (22%+ of UN budget as of 2011 projected to increase yearly).

UN's Plan for Implementing a Global Utopia
☑ *Reconstruct word meanings*- initiate a comprehensive propaganda mechanism to manipulate people into consensus with UN goals.
→ FDR started this ball rolling by redefining "human rights" and stretching the scope of "equality" beyond reasonable and logical limits (review page 115).
→ Reconstruct the meaning of *prosperity*. For example, Tim Jack-son's *Prosperity without Growth* describes prosperity as follows: "Prosperity consists in our ability to flourish as human beings— within the ecological limits of a finite planet."[234] This translates in-to environmental initiates and regulations designed to impede the growth of free enterprise and reduce private property ownership. Prosperity is limited in that nobody prospers unless everybody

prospers which is called *shared prosperity* but ultimately results in *shared misery* for those who are not part of the ruling federation.

→ *Equality* means to equalize everyone in every respect (except for the central administrators who get the largest piece of the pie first).

☑ ***Develop code words to cloak true agenda-*** use code words and propaganda slogans to deceive people and hide true intent and purposes of programs and projects.

→ See Appendix F for list of UN education buzzwords used in global education and administration plans and student teacher curriculum implemented through the National Education Association (NEA) to local school districts (i.e., buzzwords are what parents are told so that the true meaning and intent of the words are masked). This is important information for parents to know when meeting with the PTA, school board, or local school administrators and teachers and when reviewing school curriculum. Appendix F chart was written by an educator.

→ Examples of code words in relation to environment, economy, and human equality- shared prosperity, sustainable development, smart growth, co-housing, sustainable lifestyles, sustainable consumption, carbon footprint, redistribution, common good, animal rights, environmental regulations, world class, human rights, Earth rights, universal rights, and unsustainable activities.

☑ ***Devise a comprehensive platform that assures cooperation of all nations and social groups-*** by interconnecting and melding together economics, the environment and human equality, mutually assured economic destruction is guaranteed for non-compliance by any nation.

☑ ***Devise plans for getting prosperous countries to pay for redistribution of resources projects-*** the UN periodically writes program proposals for UN member nations to vote on that propose global taxation schemes. Under such global taxation schemes, nations would have to surrender their sovereignty in order for citizens to be taxed by the UN, and taxpayers of rich nations would foot most of the tax bill.[235] Another planned strategy is for UN to set prices on "environmental externalities" which would be added to the price of products, thus increasing cost to consumers.[236]

☑ ***Indoctrinate younger generation to accept UN values and agenda-*** For the UN, equality means thinking and acting the same as reflected in the global curriculum developed by UNESCO to indoctrinate children in UN ideology, an Earth-centered focus, and a *global citizenship* mindset to prepare youth to serve the UN's international workforce.

This is accomplished through such programs as the *UNCyberschool-bus.org* targeting primary through high school age children.[237] The postsecondary version of UNESCO's curriculum is the *UN Academic Impact* initiative designed to instill UN values and principles in college curriculum, teaching, and student indoctrination.[238] For more in-depth information, read *Brave New Schools* by Berit Kjos.

☑ ***Write policy statements and guidelines for achieving goals*-** one example is the *United National Millennium Development Goals (MDG)* which includes the following along with the UN's real agenda stated in the parentheses-enclosed text:[239]

→ eradicate poverty and hunger for everyone (use other people's money and resources to achieve equality for everyone regardless of personal efforts of welfare recipients to provide for themselves)

→ achieve universal primary education (using UN, socialistic and earth-worshipping curriculum [pantheism])

→ empower women (release them from family-oriented desires and responsibilities and break down the family unit to advance communitarianism)

→ ensure environmental sustainability (nature trumps humanity)

→ develop global partnerships for development using consensus (override local authority and national sovereignty)

☑ ***Establish various centralized bureaucratic systems to control the world economy and resources*-** The UN is comprised of five principal organizations with 88 associated departments, agencies, groups, commissions, bodies, programs, institutions and sub-organizations.[240] The following are directly or indirectly controlled by the UN (reminiscent of FDR's expansion of the President's cabinet and executive offices):

→ *International Law Commission (ILC)* - along with multiple other UN committees, commissions, agencies and the *International Criminal Court (ICC)* are tasked with codification and Progressive development of International Law.[241] Should the US decide to become a member of *ICC*, US troops could be put on trial before foreign judges and tried without *US Constitution* protections for doing their duty and following orders which *ICC* could deem as "war crimes." In addition, the UN and its political supporters in the US Congress and Senate have attempted to put the US under an international climate treaty controlled by the UN, thus opening US citizens and businesses to prosecution and conviction by the ICC if they violate UN climate change regulations.[242] It is critical that American citizens let their representatives know that any treaty enforceable by the UN that overrides American sovereignty is totally unacceptable.

→ *Various UN Treaties*- treaties written by the UN are enforceable by UN military forces and legal arms such as NATO and the *ICC*. For a treaty to become law in each nation, it has to be ratified by the governing body or congressional representatives of the people. Once ratified, the treaty becomes law, and the UN military force and *ICC* have full authority to enforce treaty laws. A few examples include the following:

  ▪ *Arms Trade Treaty (ATT)* - creates an international gun registry that is the preemptive measure for a full-scale gun confiscation, which, if enforced, would supersede the *US Constitution's* Second Amendment right to keep and bear arms for Americans.[243] This is an NGO led movement.

  ▪ *Law of the Sea Treaty (LOST or UNCLOS)* - grants legal jurisdiction over all of the world's seas, oceans and continental shelves to the UN. If a nation ratifies the treaty, such as the US, then it would be open to a barrage of climate change lawsuits, global taxation, and regulations restricting US benefiting from royalties on mineral resources of the American continental shelf mined by other nations.[244]

  ▪ *Various other disarmament and environmental treaties*- intended to weaken nations and override national sovereignty, thus making it easier for UN to occupy and control.

→ *International Monetary Fund (IMF)* - centralized international or world bank. The World Bank seeks to push nations into accepting a regional bank scheme, such as the European Union, which would ultimately be controlled by the UN World Bank.[245]

→ *UN Educational, Scientific and Cultural Organization (UNESCO)*- develops global programs and curriculum that teaches UN values, philosophies, and religious perspectives aimed at indoctrinating students to accept global solidarity and Social Democracy (i.e., utopian socialism), and to compliantly serve the "State" with little interest in valuing and honoring national sovereignty and individual freedom.[246]

→ *Non-Governmental Organizations (NGOs)*- NGOs are non-governmental organizations that "maintain official relations with UNESCO"[247] and are committed to the UN's Agenda 21 plan whereby they act as lobbyists for the UN's *sustainability* programs such as sustainable consumption, sustainable development, and sustainable lifestyles (mostly made up of environmental groupies). They work at the local and regional level through public-private partnerships (PPP) to apply pressure from the bottom up, and at the international level to apply pressure from the top down to promote and coerce compliance with sustainability guidelines of the UN. At the end of this chart is an illustration of what is promised vs. what is delivered when there is a public/private partnership, followed by terms NGO planners like to throw around when pitching a UN plan. UN suggestions for forcing sustainability guideline compliance includes: "greening the market through regulation," increasing cost of products to account for environmental impact to control consumer consumption of products, co-housing (eliminate private residences), car sharing (to eliminate single driver commuting), and bank loans going only to companies who add value to the environment or society (as determined by the UN).[248]

☑ *Adopt a common religious worldview that is Earth-centered and as an alternative to traditional values and Christianity*- in the 1996 UN Conference on Human Settlements (Habitat II) in Turkey and the 2006 UN World Urban Forum, the UN presented models of planned communities and city zoning law recommendations respectively. Each UN model community made no provision for Christian churches or Jewish synagogues but instead advocated the establishment of interfaith worship locations.[249] Because Christianity and Judaism are considered incompatible with UN socialist philosophy, the UN aggressively pushes for a melded conglomeration of religions that are Earth-centered (such as New Age and other Eastern religions) and have similar ritual practices such as: "trances, dreams and visions, divination, Spiritism, magic and sorcery, charms and amulets, Solstice rites, serpent worship, and sacred sex."[250]

☑ *Create and promote a common enemy to secure global and social solidarity*- sort out those who oppose UN plans for global governance and social solidarity and paint a big target on their backs. The UN's chosen enemies are Jews, Christians, middle class Americans and free marketers (capitalists). For more insight into the UN working against the interest of Israel visit the following web sites:

http://www.meforum.org/3299/war-against-jews;
http://www.humanrightsvoices.org/victims/ngos/

☑ *Promote sustainable development of densely populated urban cities and discourage population of rural and suburban areas (urban sprawl)*- promotes a strategy to move people from rural and suburban areas into densely populated cities consisting of concrete and steel, multi-story apartments, and sparse foliage. Sustainable development or smart growth schemes put control of natural resources such as natural habitats, water, food and energy into the hands of a global government such as a UN world federation. See Appendix G for a glimpse of the UN's plan for your living situation; sounds like a good plan, but read text highlighted in grey for true UN meaning and purpose. The name of the UN sustainable development program is Agenda 21: "**Agenda 21** is a comprehensive plan of action to be taken globally, nationally and locally by organizations of the United Nations system, governments, and major groups in every area in which humans impact the environment" (i.e., NGOs and PPPs).[251] One UN NGO that works within many local communities to advance Agenda 21 goals and guidelines is the *International Council for Local Environmental Initiative (ICLEI)*, which works for the common good of the UN and not for the good of your local community.[252] **Important:** See UN's list of unsustainable activities in Appendix H.

"…Pruitt-Igoe had several "features" that housing planners thought would improve the lives of the tenants. Elevators stopped only at the first, fourth, seventh, and tenth floors, forcing tenants to use the stairs to reduce "congestion." Communal corridors on the third floor of every building housed a communal room, laundry, and a garbage room; these corridors quickly became covered in graffiti and littered with garbage and human waste. Pruitt-Igoe was completed in 1955; by 1968, HUD was encouraging people to move out, and in 1972 the buildings were demolished…it turns out that Pruitt-Igoe cost 60% more than the… national average for public housing."[253]

*Figure 40: What was promised: 1950 Architectural plans for the Pruitt-Igoe housing complex proposed to St. Louis, Missouri **VS.** What was delivered because of public-private partnership of the federal and state governments and private construction firms*

The chart on the next page lists a few words planners like to throw around when pitching their sustainable development schemes:[254]

★ Environment	★ Best Management Practices
★ New Economy	★ Outcome Based Education
★ Equity	★ Endangered species[255]
★ Consensus	★ Invasive Species
★ Affordable housing	★ Restoration
★ Friends of ...	★ Public/Private Partnerships
★ Action	★ Common good
★ Protect	★ Regional
★ Preserve	★ Collaborative
★ Quality of life	★ Inter-disciplinary
★ Benefit of all	★ Stakeholder
★ Sanctuary	★ International Baccalaureate
★ Social Justice	★ School to Work
★ Watershed	★ Historic Preservation
★ Facilitator	★ Vision
★ Traffic Calming	★ Sustainable Medicine
★ Triple Bottom Line	★ Livable Communities

We can summarize the UN's agenda for global governance with their slogan that is showing up on bumper stickers: Think Globally – Act Locally. Even though the US funds 22% of the UN's general budget, it only has one vote and no veto power. 128 nations out of 178 nations have a majority vote (mob rule) even though they only contribute 1.3% toward the entire UN budget.[256] In other words, this type of social democracy is equivalent to majority or mob rule purposely intended to cancel out the voice of the minority even though that minority (American taxpayer) is footing a large percentage of the UN bill.

The bottom line is, in the land of *Loonyville*, everyone is manipulated into believing in absolute equality for everyone, including animals and plant life; and *extremist loons* will not be content until they own your children, your property, your family, your money, your soul and anything else that is not nailed down—let's face it, they even want the nails. By the way, the UN is as adept at balancing their budget as the federal government is, and is relentless in its self-expansion as evidenced in its 114% budget increase over a two years period.[257]

Can we afford the UN and its intrusive policies on our national sovereignty and should American taxpayers continue underwriting 22% of their bloated budget? To answer these questions, we must examine what is at risk for American families and freedom and assess whether the UN's basic worldview is in harmony or in conflict with our *Constitution* and its foundational principles.

In addition to your application for a building permit being denied,
we intend to confiscate your property for the sake of the common good!

Figure 41: UN plans for businesses and private property in America[258]

It is way past time to pull back the curtain and take a straightforward look at what is behind the UN and whether or not American taxpayers can continue to be a major supporter of UN agendas and proposed programs. Very few of our leaders seem to be willing to acknowledge the gorilla in the room and ask, "**What is at risk?**" Based on what we have learned so far, we can conclude that the following is at risk in America:

- Children and families
- National sovereignty and security
- *Constitutional* protection from unjust and arbitrary international regulations and laws
- Security of natural and material resources including food, water and energy
- Private property ownership
- The means to protect one's family and self
- Freedom of choice for housing, education and transportation
- Military personnel
- America's natural resources (including food and water)
- National economic interests
- Local communities and states to self-govern without interference
- The *US Constitution*
- Christians and Jews

Don't believe me? Then let's look at the following example and read what was stated in the UN Conference on Human Settlements (Habitat I) in which they advocated implementation of their *New International Economic Order* (underlining added to emphasize main point):

"Land… cannot be treated as an ordinary asset, controlled by individuals and subject to the pressures and inefficiencies of the market. <u>Private land ownership is also a principal instrument of accumulation and concentration of wealth and therefore contributes to social injustice; if unchecked, it may become a major obstacle in the planning and implementation of development schemes.</u> The provision of decent dwellings and healthy conditions for the people can only be achieved if land is used in the interest of society as a whole."[259]

The UN NGOs and PPPs will stop at nothing to subvert the US *Constitution* and American liberties. One of the UN-driven efforts to achieve equality for everyone in the world was an attempt to pass Senate bill S.510 that would have turned American food sovereignty over to the UN within ten years. Fortunately, the bill did not pass. However, as with all UN initiated plans, walking-dead House bills advocated by the UN will periodically do the Zombie shuffle and hit the floors of the Senate and Congress until victory is achieved for global *extremist loons*.[260] The Open Society Institute/Foundation, an ultra-left socialist group, is a big donor to the UN's sustainable development planners (*ICLEI* to be specific).[261] Watchmen, remain vigilant.

2012   **2016**   **2018**   **2020**

Figure 42: New World Order transportation plan for Americans according to American Socialists, EPA and the UN.

In 2020 A.D., transportation mode will be work boots because everyone but the global elite will be working in the international workforce or labor camps—that is, unless we take back our country NOW).

UN *extremist loons* and their public-private partners never seem to run out of ways to repackage and re-justify their plans for global control. When "sustainable development" wore out the welcome mat in America, "smart growth, comprehensive planning, and growth management" took its place. To demonstrate the absurdity of UN justification and desperation for its plans to solve food inequality and the so-called global warming problem, it recommended we eat less meat to curb "global warming" stating that human consumption of meat and raising cows and other livestock for meat consumption causes huge greenhouse gas emissions. The UN official making the recommendation happened to be a vegetarian from India where cows are considered sacred.[262] Makes you wonder if they expect carnivorous animals to go on a vegetarian diet. How do you think Mr. Leopard would like that idea?

The basic philosophical foundation of the UN goals and administrative policies include secular humanism, Darwinism, eugenics, egalitarianism, utilitarianism, social justice, and socialism.[263] Much of the original UN Charter was fashioned after the USSR's constitutional principles of social solidarity and collectivism. So how does the UN model line up with the principles of the US constitution model as originally intended? Berit Kjos compared the models (the UN paradigm is in sync with postmodernity dark *isms*) in the chart below.

Original US Constitutional Model vs. UN's Model of 21st Century World[264]		
	Constitutional Paradigm	UN Paradigm
Beliefs	Based on Bible	Blend Earth-centered religions (i.e., pantheism and New Age)
Culture	*Individual/Family Unity*	Global solidarity
Values	Based on the Bible *(absolute, unchangeable truth)*	Based on human idealism *(easy to manipulate)*
Morals	Moral boundaries	Sensual freedom
Rights	Personal freedom	Social controls
Economy	Free enterprise	Socialist collectivism
Government	By the people	By the few who control the masses

Are you aware that the UN socialists have been dictating American primary, secondary, college and student teacher textbook content through the National Education Association (NEA) and publishing companies like Houghton Mifflin, Allyn and Bacon, and McGraw Hill, and that the Robert Muller School's curriculum design and content was adopted as the primary curriculum? Several US presidential administrations have fully cooperated with and helped promote the UN's World Conference on Education for All (WCEA) goals in American education whereby educational partnerships (PPPs) were facilitated to advance educational equity for everyone in the world by the year 2000 which progressively gives the UN global control of classroom and textbook curriculum, including America.[265]

We have already witnessed the UN's double standard of demanding tolerance for everyone but Christians and Jews in their listing these as *unsustainable attitudes* in their global biodiversity assessment (review Appendix H). Then the UN arrogantly turns around and demands inclusion and application of multiculturalism in classroom curriculum and teaching, but diminishes or excludes references to Christianity or Judaism. Instead, they demand observance of multicultural mythology, pagan worship (such as the worship of Gaia, the Earth goddess), pluralism, 'multicultural *storytelling*, fantasy, changeable values and attitudes, subjectivity, experiential feelings and imagination (key to occult thinking), group consensus, politicized and speculative pseudo-science (i.e., climate change based on Darwin's evolution and other faked science), and collective responsibilities.'[266]

Of course, to dupe a whole nation into accepting the UN model of global governance and social engineering, the *Green New Deal* groupies will have to repackage their deal. And guess what? They already have it covered; their green Trojan horse will soon gallop in under the steam of *sustainable history* and *Transhumanism* philosophy (*H+* or *TH*). Not to worry, however, you will already be aware of what these really mean because *sustainable history* is a mix of *Cyclical* and *Chaotic History* discussed in Chapter 7, and *Transhumanism* was devised by a neurologist and is a regurgitation of all those philosophical dark *isms* of the *Modernity* and *Postmodernity* eras.

H+ doubles down on the application of Darwinian evolution and eugenics, and combined with mind-control drugs or implantations, and human genetic and anatomical reconstruction using Nano technology and other techno apparatuses.[267] To make this repackaged deal palatable and justifiable, a dash of mind-numbing transcendentalism and cosmic humanism is thrown into the mix.

Why should this matter to American families? Do you really want to give up your individual and family freedom and surrender your

American citizenship to be a Global Citizen? Still not convinced this is a real possibility. Think again. Robert Muller was invited to present his New Age *World Core Curriculum* at the Global Citizenship 2000 Youth Congress in April 1997. During the UN meeting, Muller presented his Global Passport program originally devised by Gary Davis of the World Service Authority (WSA, www.worldservice.org), whereby Global Passports were being issued and are now currently accepted by several nations. To obtain a WSA passport, one must agree with the World Citizen Credo and accept "an affirmation of global citizenship and allegiance to world government." A key part of this affirmation to which one must agree is:

'As a World Citizen, I affirm my planetary civic commitment to WORLD GOVERNMENT, founded on three universal principles of One Absolute Value, One World, and One Humanity which constitutes the basis of World Law. As a World Citizen I acknowledge the WORLD GOVERNMENT as having the right and duty to represent me in all that concerns the General Good of humankind and the Good of All.' (All capitals are in original)."[268]

Living with the Psychic

Figure 43: Cosmic humanism in action

BEWARE: Leaders who promise collective salvation and equality through government intervention and advocate universal solidarity are dangerous. When Progressives and UN green *loons* finish destroying America's constitution, stripping us of our liberty and forcing us to abide by International Law, whom do you think will be left to rule the roost? Communist, socialists, and Islamic extremists groups have been weaseling their way into the UN from the beginning of its establishment, and these *extremist loons* are all about money and power.

How do you think Sharia Law would work out for your family, especially for women and children? Go to www.religionofpeace.com to see what they have in store for you and your family if this ever comes to full fruition. As you will discover, there is nothing user-friendly about Islamic <u>Extremists'</u> law and religion or any other oppressive tyrannical legal code or occult practice devised by mad men.

Michael Carl, an experienced political consultant, reported on Islam's release of a 23-page booklet, *The Global Islamic Civilization: The Power of a Nation Revived,* outlining plans for Muslim world domination, which promises that "Islam will conquer the hearts of all Christendom," and "those nations who resist will be placed under a police state." In addition, Sheik Al-Mohammedi states that, "Christianity should be destroyed and wiped from the face of the earth," and that "non-Muslims have no place in his vision for the world." Pamela Geller, an Islam analyst, points out that *The Global Islamic Civilization* booklet is "a call to warfare against and subjugation of non-Muslims under the Sharia" which is in line the Muslim Brotherhood' goals.[269]

Now that you are up to date as to what modern day socialists have planned for American families, NOW is the time to grab the collective bull by the horns and give American socialism a proper burial. In Chapter 10, we will outline key strategies to accomplish this task.

21ˢᵗ Century Truth or Consequence Question: Is the following example of Dharavi's urban planning advocated by British and American Socialists what I envision for my children and grandchildren?

Figure 44: Socialist idea of a sustainable community benefiting from its "locally sourced materials" (i.e., garbage refuse) according to utopian Progressives[270]

If not, then America:

Get off the...

and DO SOMETHING!

It's time to

on the Progressive donkey, and send American Socialism, Darwinism, and the *Green New Deal* packing.

Figure 45: For the sake of our children, stand up and take action

Dig Deeper

1. www.freedomadvocates.org
2. Ron Taylor (2011), *Agenda 21: An Expose of the United Nations' Sustainable Development Initiative and the Forfeiture of American Sovereignty and Liberties* (Kindle Edition: available for .99 cents).

3. Free pamphlet online on Sustainable Development/Agenda 21: http://www.freedomadvocates.org/images/pdf/SD%20A21%20pamphlet-2010.pdf
4. Tim Jackson (March 2009), *Prosperity without Growth: A Transition to a Sustainable Economy* (London, UK: Sustainable Development Commission).
5. Article by Wendell Cox, Ronald Utt and Brett Schaefer online at: http://www.heritage.org/research/2011/12/focus-on-agenda-21-should-not-divert-attention-from-homegrown-anti-growth-policies
6. Article by Brett Schaefer: http://www.heritage.org/research/reports/2012/01/us-must-ensure-that-un-accounting-gimmicks-result-in-real-cuts-to-bloated-un-budget
4. http://www.eagleforum.org/un/2011/11-05-16.html- UN seeks to lower living standards for Americans
5. Heritage Report about the UN on Family and Marriage (2001): "UN Committees Take Aim At Family Structure and Morality, Analyst Says" (article available online).
6. Article by Ana I Eiras online at: http://www.heritage.org/research/reports/2003/09/imf-and-world-bank-intervention-a-problem-not-a-solution
7. http://www.crossroad.to/Excerpts/chronologies/un.htm

CHAPTER 10
RESTORING SANITY WITHIN

"Behold, You desire truth in the inward parts, and in the hidden part You will make me to know wisdom."[271]

Remember the *Spirit of Liberty Tree* on page 18 and its fruit on the next page, i.e., courageous faith, strong families, and responsible freedom. Responsible freedom, strong families and courageous faith are keys to preserving well-balanced American liberties. We will begin with responsible freedom that involves being a good American citizen through responsible stewardship of freedom.

There is no magic wand anyone can wave to make everything instantly okay. We did not arrive at our current state of affairs overnight; it took over a hundred years for us to digress toward insanity. We can give it our best shot to shorten the time it will take to restore sanity in America, but in the end it will still take time, effort, and determination.

What has become clear from the beginning is that each individual American citizen is responsible for the success or failure of America as a free country and relying on politicians' empty promises has been counterproductive. Either we can embrace these inconvenient truths, or we can continue blaming politicians, mainline media, public educators, college professors, the Supreme Court justices, district judges, and the UN. Granted, we have plenty of reason to be frustrated, apathetic and even angry, but to remain so is to risk becoming a full-fledged totalitarian police state. There is a way out of the current ruling caste system's insane asylum. Either we can remain frozen by fear and apathy, or we can roll up our sleeves and do the hard work of re-securing our liberties and preserving them for the next generation.

Therefore, *restoring sanity begins with each individual.* Within my own heart and mind is where my journey began toward being a better citizen by taking personal responsibility to become an active and engaged part of the solution instead of part of the problem. Self-examination is good for the soul and produces amazing results if we are honest and courageous enough to make the necessary changes in our attitude, decision-making process, and behavior as individuals and families in relation to responsible citizenship. Below are a few questions that would be good to ask ourselves periodically.

- ☐ Do I know the difference between the truth and a lie?
- ☐ Do I have the necessary logical thinking skills to distinguish between logical arguments vs. illogical ones **or** facts vs. personal opinion?
- ☐ When I hear or see information in the media or on the internet, do I automatically believe it, or do I verify whether the information is based on facts and backed by reliable sources?
- ☐ Can I spot anti-American or socialist lingo when I see or hear it?
- ☐ Do I know when others manipulate me, and if so, do I know how to avoid or counter manipulation, especially when it is group manipulation?

Being the sharp tack that you are, you have noticed that this checklist highlights required skills to be a responsible steward of freedom. So, let's ferret out a few jewels of wisdom.

Responsible stewards of freedom seek the truth and have the integrity and courage to base decisions and actions on the truth. Marx recognized eternal truths (i.e., God's eternal truths) as the power that undergirded a free enterprising society which he called the bourgeoisie class (affluent middle class), when he stated, "Communism abolishes eternal truths, it abolishes all religion, and all morality, instead of constituting them on a new basis; it therefore acts in contradiction to all past historical experience."[272] Translated, Marx recognized that if Communism was to be successful in enslaving a free enterprising society, anything founded in biblical truth and its unchanging principles would have to be subverted, dismantled, reconstructed or destroyed. Socialism and all its related dark *isms* require the destruction of society's eternal truths and moral compass that secure and sustain liberty.

According to Progressives, truth is "what works for each person or group, what we can experience or observe, what can be proved by reason, harmony among a set of ideas, or what we feel."[273] Even though

134

'truth is consistent with logical reasoning and experience, these theories of truth are not grounded in objective reality because truth always corresponds with reality.'[274] Think for a moment- Does truth based on the shifting sands of culture, political expediency or moral ambivalence enhance or diminish a civil society, and would liberty survive in such a society where there are no stable unchanging principles or eternal truths to ensure the safety, security and *general* welfare of everyone.

Andy Andrews presents an argument for "why the truth matters more than you think." In a short essay (listed in Endnote 274), he gallops through some historical moments and answers the question, "How do you kill 11 million people?" The simple answer was, *"Repeatedly Lie to them."*[275] Andrews succinctly recounted how tyrannical politicians and group manipulators led passive unarmed citizens to the slaughterhouse step-by-step; he challenged Americans not to follow pseudo-saviors and wannabe kings like a nation of dumb sheep.

Americans have been bombarded with lies and propaganda for over a hundred years, so it is critical that we understand the true meaning and nature of truth if we want to survive as the land of the free. Truth is an important ingredient of logical thinking and a vital part of responsible stewardship of freedom; sound logic and wisdom can only work within the parameters of truth that holds up under the pressures of validity testing. Truth means *"conformity to fact or reality; exact accordance with that which is, or has been, or shall be."*[276] For something to be true, it must always be in sync with eternal truths, facts and/or reality (on the earthly and/or in the spiritual realm).

Lawyers, judges and politicians have gotten away with murder while auctioning off our freedoms to the highest bidder by convincing the rest of us that only *grey area* half-truths matter. Perverting truth, facts and statistics is a key socialist strategy to maintain a constant state of chaos and fear. Socialists go to great lengths to ridicule or demonize anyone who dares to stand on the firm foundation of truth as defined by our Creator. However, in the absence of courage to walk in integrity and unchanging principles, there exists only a person who lacks substance and spouts an endless fountain of empty promises and lies.

Agendas, programs and plans of *extremist loons* can only be successful as long as chaos, fear and/or passivity exist. When humanity perceives itself as the measure of all things and evolving into godhood, then order is disrupted and chaotic fear thrives. The way out of this chaotic, arrogant and self-centered state is to accept that in truth and reality, God is the measure of all things, and humanity is imperfect. If there is any shred of doubt about humanity's imperfection, just watch the news for ten minutes—case closed. God is perfect and desires that we live in His truth, love and peace which are the elements of life that sustain society's natural order when given half a chance. *"Love rejoices in the truth,"*[277] and so should we.

Socialism and its constant companions, chaos and fear, cannot thrive where God is accepted as the measure of all things and where there is a consistent state of truth. Michael Novak once stated that "the most critical threat to our freedom is a failure to appreciate the power of truth." For those who have had the misfortune of going through institutions of mass instruction designed to lock people into a socialist mindset, the following resources will help undo the damage and establish a firm foundation in truth and unchanging principles that best support and preserve American liberties.

- ✶ The Bible- especially the following books: Proverbs, The Gospel According to John, Ephesians, Galatians, 1 John, Nehemiah, Exodus, Romans, Philippians
- ✶ Matthew Spalding, *We Still Hold these Truths* (Washington, DC: The Heritage Foundation, 2010).

Responsible stewards of freedom develop and consistently exercise their logical thinking skills. Hitler stated "to his inner circle, 'How fortunate for leaders that men do not think. Make the lie big, make it simple, keep saying it, and eventually they will believe it.'"[278] Lessons from history will serve us well if we refuse to repeat past mistakes.

"The most enduring lesson of Nazi Germany is that ordinary people, <u>simply concerned about living their own lives,</u> can be motivated to become a part of an evil movement through the power of compelling propaganda, intimidation, and mass euphoria...

As Richard Terrell wrote, 'Create a critical mass of people who cannot discern meaning and truth from nonsense, and you will have a society ready to fall for the first charismatic leader to come along.'"[279]

Dismiss truth, and logic becomes irrelevant, and sound thinking goes out the window. The key element in logical thinking is the ability

136

to determine whether a statement is true or false. Put another way, "Logic is the systematic study and practice of discerning and telling the truth."[280] The purpose of logic is to arrive at the truth of things. According to God's standard of truth and unchanging principles, there is a very simple objective order that requires a "yes" or "no" in the process of determining the truthfulness of statements. The objective order requiring a "yes" or "no" answer as to the truth of every statement is illustrated in the binary code of computer programming:

"At its most fundamental level, a computer chip…interprets a series of 'one' and 'zero'—a digital version of 'yes' and 'no,' 'positive' and 'negative.' This binary (only allowing two answers) language…can code and process everything you see happening on your computer screen. In this system there is no 'maybe,' 'possibly,' 'probably,' or the like…Everything from games and graphics to the most complex mathematics and engineering boils down to a series of 'yes' and 'no.' (And one improper answer can lock up the entire system!)."[281]

The American society is in a locked-up state because we have been wandering around in the desert of ifs, maybes, possibly and probably, and doing so as if there were no standard of truth and moral compass. Greek Sophists utilized *rhetoric* as a tool to twist truth and deceive for manipulating people into accepting their arguments and schemes. We see this type of manipulation frequently used in politics and our justice system. The socialist version of logical thinking (i.e., "critical thinking") weaves together a complex system of arguments that lean heavily on "possibly true" and "probably true" to determine the validity and soundness of an argument that consists of two or more premises (statements) and a conclusion drawn from the premises. In devising such a convoluted argument system void of "yes" or "no" answers, absolute truth becomes almost impossible to be determined, and, therefore, truth is purposely rendered irrelevant.

A key tool of deception is the use of fallacies. Socialists talk about fallacies in their critical thinking courses, but rarely follow their own guidelines for avoiding the use of fallacies by cleverly slipping fallacious statements into their arguments on a regular basis. By using fallacies, anything can *appear* to be true or *appear* to be false.

Some of the more favored fallacies are hasty generalization, oversimplification, slippery slope, appeal to progress, double standard, straw man, red herring, appeal to fear, poisoning the well, and false dilemma. The use of such fallacies introduces subjectivity into the thought process and bases truth on feelings or whatever is culturally trending. This creates a constant state of fuzzy thinking, confusion, or dwelling in the *grey area* where truth cannot be established as fact.

Granted, because we do not have knowledge about everything, and truth cannot always be established, grey areas do exist; however, it is illogical thinking to project our personal subjective *grey area* uncertainties on the world at large as objective truth. For example, because someone cannot physically see or touch God personally does not mean that God does not exist. To project onto the world at large a personal subjective statement about God as "not being" would be promoting a false statement because there is sufficient evidence to prove otherwise. Take one look at nature in all its intricate order and majestic wonder and the starry night display of perfect design and synchronization; then consider the fact that it is a mathematical impossibility for all of it to have happened by chance.[282] The laws of nature and order of the universe require a Master Designer of superior intelligence and power.

To determine whether a statement is true or false involves careful consideration of the facts. There are two types of facts:

- *Objective facts* are based on actual things or events which can be verified by direct observation or by visiting the thing, or verifying an event through primary sources such as original documents, photographs, Congressional records, memoirs, or diaries that record the facts of an event (as in historical facts).
- *Subjective facts* are subjective feelings or subjective experiences in the absence of tangible evidence; the truthfulness of a subjective fact is dependent on the trustworthiness of the person making the statement or claim.

In short, objective facts are things and events that can be verified, and a subjective fact is confined to the subject experiencing it and may not always be verifiable. To determine the truth, we must get the facts straight; in the absence of all the facts or concrete evidence, it is human nature to fill in the gaps with thoughts that may or may not be in accord with reality, which is how family feuds and wars get started. To separate fact from fiction and determine truth, we must establish a corresponding reality external to our mind's ideas, opinions or biases.

138

Logical thinking also involves making a distinction between relevant and irrelevant information and claims, distinguishing between emotional vs. logical thinking and objective bias vs. subjective bias (the latter is based in emotion and makes outrageous claims, or purposely misleads readers or viewers as in propaganda). To review or further develop logical thinking skills, fine-tune our ability to detect fallacies, and develop argument analysis skills, the following resources below will help.

✳ Nathaniel and Hans Bluedorn (2005, 2003), *The Thinking Toolbox* and *The Fallacy Detective* (Muscatine, Iowa: Christian Logic). Both books are appropriate for ages 13 to adult and contain practice exercises.
✳ Joel McDurmon (2009), *Biblical Logic in Theory and Practice* (Powder Springs, GA: American Vision Press).

Responsible stewards of freedom use credible sources to check for accuracies and truthfulness of statements and information. We need to stop being gullible gussies by accepting everything the mainline media, public educators, professors, politicians, lawyers, and Progressives peddle as truth and start doing our own fact checking using reliable and credible sources. Instant gratification, grasping to meet immediate needs, or a don't care attitude will tempt us to overlook the facts and not consider all the consequences of decisions or actions, but this has proven to be self-defeating and detrimental to our American liberties.

The basic rules of checking statements or information for accuracy and truthfulness are listed below (see Appendix K for more in-depth coverage of these rules):

✓ Always use credible primary sources to fact check and distinguish between primary vs. secondary sources
✓ Determine credibility and trustworthiness of author or organization presenting information
✓ Use two or more credible sources to verify information
✓ Consider background and ideological leanings of authors and organizations to determine possible distortions of information
✓ When fact checking, do not hesitate to use the *Freedom of Information Act* (FOIA) when encountering resistance by government agencies to provide requested information

139

✓ Politically charged issues require a higher level of vigilance to confirm accuracy and truthfulness of statements and information

The information age and internet have royally upset the Progressive apple cart, because their true agenda is exposed for the whole world to see. This explains why Socialists have launched an all-out assault on freedom of speech by passing laws or attempting to pass laws to diminish and silence opposition to American socialism such as the hate crime law and fairness doctrine with embedded hate speech language as defined by socialists. Granted, there are scores of cuckoo-bird web sites; however, legitimate web site information written by reputable and credible authors will cite or acknowledge their sources if it is not their original work and will back his or her information with facts.

Responsible stewards of freedom are able to spot socialist/Marxist lingo and counteract with the truth. Why is this important? So you will know when you are being lied to, manipulated or socially engineered. Most of the time when dealing with American Socialists and Progressives, it is like shadow boxing with *loons* because one never can make contact with true word meanings and the end game or agenda when dealing with Socialists. In *Loonyville*, word meanings are always evolving and shifting as determined by the environmentalist, culture or situation, or a person's imagination.

I always chuckle inside when I hear people say that there is no such thing as absolute truth; some folks seem oblivious to the fact that they have just contradicted themselves and made an "absolute" statement. Those who have bought into *relativism* and other similar loony *isms* live in a fantasy world; in the real world, loony statements like the one above fail the logic test. Granted, English can be tricky, illusive, and confusing, especially when a word can mean different things in different contexts and yet be spelled and pronounced the same way.

Time for a mental break: This reminds me of the first time I heard one of my former south Georgia church members pronounce *pecans*, while asking me if I wanted a few. The way I heard it was *pee cans*, so I wasn't exactly sure how to answer or if I should answer (was he joking or was he really asking me if I wanted a few *pee cans*). If he was serious, for the life of me I could not figure out what in the world I would use them for since there were adequate facilities in the church

140

and the parsonage. You see, in northeast Georgia I had become accustomed to hearing *pecans* pronounced *pekahns*, and that must be right because that is how Uncle Neal pronounced it; after all, he had a pecan grove in his backyard that he tended and harvested, so he must have known how to pronounce the word.

After a brief pause, I politely said, "Yes sir, I am sure they will come in handy." Well, that gave me away, and he gave me a country shire grin; I never was able to live down that faux pas. So goes life in the American language fast lane.

A word or phrase can represent two different concepts or pictures. For example, a word can be a bird or a fruit:

OR

Figures 46: Is it a Kiwi or a kiwi?

For Progressives or Socialists, a word is worth a thousand pictures, and when a word has exhausted its manipulative usefulness, it is replaced with another word or phrase to revive commitment and enthusiasm by the masses for whatever cause *loons* are into at the moment. *Extremist loons* call this tactic, *reframing the debate* by using morally slanted terminology.[283] Appendix J lists a few favorite words used by Socialists.

During the Nazi regime, Hitler and his cronies used "sanitized" terms to lure his victims into extermination camps and death chambers. For example, "When Hitler starved children, he called it putting them on a 'low-calorie diet,' and the extermination of Jews was called 'cleansing the land.' Euthanasia was referred to as 'the best of modern therapy.' Children were put to death in 'Children's Specialty Centers.'"[284] So half a century later we are still playing the socialist/Marxist word game of "catch me if you can" as word manipulation games whittle away our freedom and rob us of an occasional McDonald's treat.

There is a double standard rule in the socialist word game. For instance, *tolerance* is proudly paraded around like a prized bull appearing to promote fairness and respect for everyone. The moral duty standard is applied to guilt people into exercising tolerance indiscriminately and without much logical thinking. *Extremist loons* also seek to establish legal requirements to force the practice of tolerance that borders on violation of individual conscience and unalienable rights and serves to widen the gulf between different groups. Even though, in the minds of socialist *loons,* intolerance is considered a global threat, moral duty standards regarding tolerance applies to everyone but conservative Christians. The double standard rule kicks in, and the prized tolerance bull turns into a raging bull whereby tolerance along with its companions, fairness and respect, all of a sudden vanish. But that's all right, socialist *loons*, because conservative Christians are tough, and we have become experts at dodging verbal bullets and raging bulls.

Like a kaleidoscope, words and phrases constantly change with every twist and turn of circumstance and cultural diversity in Loonyville. With every turn of the kaleidoscope and shift in word usage, compromise becomes a constant demand in favor of what defies eternal truths and unchanging principles. However, a people who are willing to tolerate an ounce of compromise that violates eternal truths and favors evil are headed for a ton of heartache and devastation. You see, there are things about which we can compromise, but we as a nation cannot continue caving in to the demands of Progressives and Socialists who are arrogantly determined to destroy what sustains and preserves us as a free nation.

We can no longer afford to waiver on unchanging principles and eternal truths and allow our moral and ethical compass to be crushed under the heel of Satan. The extremes of multiculturalism, diversity and tolerance will be the undoing of this nation. As long as we agree to play in the polluted pond of American socialism and blindly go along to get along, we will remain trapped in the chaotic and illogical socialist maze that lacks consideration of long-term consequences.

Responsible stewards of freedom know when they are manipulated or indoctrinated and know how to counteract deception, fear tactics, and manipulation. *Change agents* or *facilitators* are professional psychosocial manipulators who are highly trained in group infiltration

142

and manipulation techniques called the *Delphi technique* devised by Hegel and perfected by Karl Marx and Lenin and is still used by current day Marxists, Communists, Socialists, Progressives, and Liberals. Because I have participated in meetings where group manipulation by change agents or facilitators was in full operation, I can confirm that group manipulation or the *Delphi Technique* (which I call being *delphied*)[285] includes the following tactical strategies. The order of these tactical strategies is not set in stone and may be adjusted to fit different groups.

First Strategy: infiltrate target group. Change agents secretly representing a non-governmental organization (NGO) committed to socialists central planning agenda, hob knob with local leadership to gain credibility within a group, or stealthily blend in and during a group meeting, these infiltrators can wait for the right moment to spring into action. If a person looks out of place or is not part of your local community, then more than likely they are an NGO, central planner, or stakeholder infiltrator.

Stakeholders who are committed to a pre-determined plan or agenda are also "invited" to attend group meetings even though they may not be a part of the group's community. Regional commission members are notorious for posing as stakeholders so that they can influence groups and steer them in a direction that best benefits the agenda of the regional planners who rarely agree with what local citizens want. Regional commission agendas usually involve money that translates into linking local cities into a regional plan that involves generating tax revenue from local taxpayers for the coffers of the regional commission's budget (railway systems and bus transportation are favorite carrots dangled in front of locals).

Second Strategy: present two opposing proposals and at an opportune moment when the group has exhausted all of its options, roll out a third plan that appears to be a viable compromise. The problem with the third plan is that it is a preferred and pre-determined option of leadership that advocates an agenda to advance socialists planning schemes. The "proposed" plan represents the desired direction and plan of the change agent, facilitator, central planner, leadership, or power players behind the leadership and sets the agenda in a group meeting. Drafters of pre-determined plans assume by their actions that a group is too stupid to come up with good recommendations, and central planners blatantly seek to crush the suggestions of individuals who think outside the political box. There are times when planning is necessary such as budget proposals, but even in proposed budgets the devil is in the details. The purpose of this stage is to manipulate groups into rejecting the first two opposing proposals so they will agree to and adopt a third pre-determined option (this is known as the Hegelian dialectic process used by Marxists).[286]

During a citizen's budget committee meeting several years ago, I recall submitting a recommended plan for a budget adjustment that would have saved money for local taxpayers. In a meeting the week before the final citizen's budget committee meeting when we were to vote on the different recommended budget plan adjustments, my recommendation mysteriously disappeared from the list of citizen recommendations. When I asked the meeting facilitator why my recommendation was not on the list, he stated that it "was not supported." This was a strange response since the group had not voted for or against each recommended plan proposed by the members of the citizen's budget committee, so it begged the question of who was not supporting the recommended plan. This was a perfect example where a recommended plan did not fit a *pre-determined* agenda and was tabled before anyone had a chance to voice his or her preference or vote. What an ultimate show of disrespect for taxpaying citizens. It was also evident that there were power players and stakeholders outside the group pulling the facilitator and budget strings despite what citizens wanted.

Third Strategy: divide and conquer. This stage may or may not be implemented depending on the size of the group and the number of anticipated resistors. This stage involves two steps: (1) Split group up into smaller subgroups and plant pre-chosen facilitators or change agents in each group; then (2) pass out pre-fabricated questionnaires to guide group discussion and solicit input from subgroup members with little or no intention of taking input seriously.

At this stage, individual input and ideas of group members answer questions regarding their needs, desires, wants or recommendations. Pre-chosen subgroup facilitators use their manipulation skills to steer the group toward the pre-set agenda. Subgroup recorders note individual ideas or write individual suggestions on a large marker board tablet to give individuals a false sense of being valued participants in the planning and decision-making process. Group facilitators and/or their assistants collect the subgroup lists and sift out suggestions that conflict with the pre-determined agenda or plan, and then the finalized list is put before the group for final approval.

Fourth Strategy: identify anyone who may object or resist the pre-determined agenda or plan. Psychosocial manipulators are highly skilled stock herders (stock as in cows, sheep, or horses, take your pick) who prefer group meetings to individual meetings because groups are easier to control and manipulate than individuals are.

Group and subgroup members are herded into a collective mentality of "we are all in this together" to get everyone moving in the pre-planned direction of the agenda. Psychosocial manipulators rely on people's unwillingness to lose face in a group to control resistors. To keep from losing face and remain an accepted member of the group, one must give up convictions and principles.[287] Most adults from the 1950s and forward have been pre-programmed by educational and government institutions to play "nice" and reject individualism and authoritarianism—a socialist strategy to turn American citizens into a collective groupthink society. Emotionally charged issue buttons are pushed by the manipulator to identify resistors and individuals who show signs of having independent thought or logical thinking skills.

The final step in this stage is to create a psychologically controlled environment whereby manipulators can transition groups into a mob mentality. As long as a mob mentality is in play, facilitators can use them to 'isolate, ostracize, ridicule, and overwhelm individual resistors.'[288] The purpose of this strategy is to humiliate or intimidate resistors into submission and/or to silence them.

Fifth Strategy: force group consensus. After silencing the voice of resistors, and evaluating group input to spot and sift out opposing viewpoints and recommendations, the facilitator maneuvers the group into a consensus or collective opinion where collective good trumps individual good. The pre-determined plan that includes a few minor tweaks is presented to the group, and if there is any residual resistance by the group, then fear tactics is used to intimate the group into submission and acceptance of the proposed plan.

145

To illustrate the above strategy, in a citizen's budget committee meeting, for example, if group participants disagree with the facilitator's proposed plan to increase property taxes to raise revenue to support budgetary spending increases, then the facilitator simply threatens to cut the budget for police, fire and emergency services. Such a threat provokes fear in citizens who agree that these vital services cannot be cut, so they cave in and agree to property tax increases. It rarely dawns on citizens that they have been *delphied* into accepting a pre-determined agenda and budget so that local governments can continue with business as usual.

The ultimate goal of forcing group consensus is so psychosocial facilitators and change agents can present their plans as having the support of the community or citizens. This is disingenuous and deceptive because there is a vast difference between consensus and majority acceptance by individual citizens. Consensus is a "collective opinion" and is intended to neutralize the right vs. wrong of issues and to eliminate consideration of the pros and cons.[289] The *Delphi Technique* is purposely structured to benefit vested interest groups and central planners to advance their agenda, bills, budgets and programs in spite of disapproval and rejection by the majority of citizens.

All of a sudden it may have dawned on you that you have encountered the *Delphi Technique* and experiencing an urge to explode; if not, then check your pulse to see if you are still alive. No one of sound mind likes being manipulated, deceived, and treated as if he or she is stupid. It helps to remember that the main purposes of the *Delphi Technique* are to shut down opposition and to get everyone on board with a pre-determined agenda. Now that we are informed about key strategies and purposes of psychosocial manipulators, we can preemptively counteract being herded into a collective and *delphied* by using the following strategies adapted from Eakman's book:

Before the meeting:
☑ Do your research and outline points you want to address
☑ Put on your psychological and spiritual armor[290]
☑ Try to identify a few like-minded citizens in the group or, if possible invite your like-minded citizen friends to join you in the meeting

During the meeting:

☑ Avoid getting sucked into agreement with the facilitator and their pre-determined proposals; be aware of the use of slogans and cloudy manipulative socialist lingo

☑ When speaking, remain calm, and avoid raising your voice (be psychologically prepared to be casual and professional in body language, attitude and tone), and use "we" instead of "I" so that the facilitator has less opportunity for singling you out as a target at which he or she can create and direct group hostility

☑ Before the facilitator has an opportunity to maneuver the group into a false sense of unity or mob mentality, reframe the debate to align with the important points and problems that need to be addressed and resolved

☑ If necessary solicit the help of your like-minded friends and tag team the facilitator to help focus the group on what is important and relevant to your community if you sense that the group is being *delphied* (this will unseat the facilitator from his or her dominant position thereby freeing the group to think for themselves and create constructive, common sense solutions)

☑ If the facilitator is open minded, work together to create constructive recommendations and then hold the facilitator accountable to include recommendations in the final list to be considered by the group

☑ Calmly with a disinterested but respectful demeanor stage a walk out and invite others to join you if the facilitator is pig headed and determined to shove a pre-determined proposal down your throats

After the meeting:

☑ Call a press conference with local papers and news media or write an op-ed to report the results of the meeting. This will inform and empower other citizens to get involved and be aware of what is going on

☑ Follow-up to make sure citizen input was given due consideration and recommendations were implemented if practically possible.

☑ If recommendations were ignored, hold another press conference or write an op-ed and shout it from the roof tops

The above strategies are just a starting point. If you are serious about counteracting manipulation, the following resource is critical to have in your mental arsenal:

✳ B. K. Eakman (2011), *How to Counter Group Manipulation Tactics* (Raleigh, NC: Midnight Whistler Publishers).

In the end, truth matters, and it is each American citizen's responsibility to secure and maintain his or her God-ordained constitutional liberties. If elected by the people, those officials need reminding that they work for "we the people," and not the other way around. Next, we will cover restoration of sanity at home.

↓

21st Century Truth or Consequence Question: *Is compromising on unchanging principles and eternal truths worth the loss of freedom for my family and me? If not, what will I do to fortify my courage to stand firm against compromise and consensus tactics?*

Dig Deeper

1. J. Budziszewski (1997), *Written on the Heart: The Case for Natural Law* (Downers Grove, IL: InterVarsity Press).
2. B. K. Eakman (2011), *How to Counter Group Manipulation Tactics* (Raleigh, NC: Midnight Whistler Publishers).

CHAPTER 11
RESTORING SANITY AT HOME

"The righteous man walks in his integrity; His children are blessed after him."[291]

Family is the primary structure and first institution of civilized society established by God. It is the basic building block of God's natural order for humanity designed to *reflect* the harmonious and diverse individuality, relationship (oneness), and *unconditional love* of God's being and personhood.[292]

> "The human race was created in the image of God, who is...one in being and three in person. Both oneness and threeness are equally real, equally ultimate, equally basic and integral to God's nature....The balance of unity and diversity in the Trinity" (Father, Son and Holy Spirit) "gives a model for human social life, because it implies that both individuality and relationship exist within the Godhead itself."[293]

The Trinity model for family reflects a "reciprocal love and communication" that overrides the social extremes of collectivism and radical individualism.[294] It is by God's design and natural order that we be in relationship with one another as a family and civil society.

According to God's original design and purpose, each family begins with the covenant union of one man with one woman whereby 'a man leaves his father and mother and joins to his wife to live as one flesh.'[295] The purpose of that union is for companionship, spiritual intimacy, pro-creation, and to establish a balanced, peaceful and wholesome order within human society.[296] "One flesh" means that each part (person) completely unites with another to make a domestic family unit, and for each part to unify completely and function as a whole they must naturally fit together. The union of two people who, according to

149

the laws of nature, do not fit together naturally and spiritually risks the health, welfare and survival of families and a civil society.

The following is a brief survey of three basic family types, key characteristics, and key factors, including some major points drawn from Zimmerman and Kurth's book on *Family and Civilization*.

FAMILY TYPES AND KEY CHARACTERISTICS[297]

Domestic Family

Structure and type of relationship- a single-family unit comprised of husband and wife and children bound together by a covenant relationship[298] of mutual love, affection, cooperation, friendship and respect. The binding commitment to be faithful and loyal is secured through God's continuing authority over marriage and presence in the family, and the domestic family relationship is maintained through God's natural order and unconditional love.[299] To be a strong, successful, normal family unit, and to reach its fullest potential, the husband and the wife must *leave* their respective parents and *cleave* to each other.

Purpose of marriage and family- marriage and family nurture the whole person and provides an environment that encourages physical, mental, spiritual, and social growth of each family member when functioning as our Creator intended. Domestic families have children whom they protect, educate, socialize, and guide, thereby enabling society to survive and thrive; a decline in birth rates and families fulfilling their familial responsibilities results in a loss of society's system of values that preserve it.[300]

Stability and longevity- originally designed for longevity[301] and stability barring any catastrophic event or extreme circumstance such as life-threatening abuse or domestic violence. Because the domestic family unit is the most basic level of a civil society, stable and enduring families facilitate and preserve stable and enduring nations. Active family solidarity, fidelity, loyalty, moral values and faith preserve the domestic family. Domestic families cannot find humane conditions and peaceful existence within the trustee family structure because the clan or tribe uses them as warring squadrons.[302] 'As long as the domestic family is given the freedom to provide for themselves and is free from bondage, it will not digress into a trustee or atomistic family type.'[303]

Social function in society- provides basic organization, structure and security for society at the lowest level and influences societal order and welfare at the highest level. Parents are responsible for passing on their faith and cultural traditions that serve to strengthen and unite a civil society. Strong domestic families preserve the basic social structure of a nation whereby society can "depend upon it as an aid in government and as a source of extreme power" for efficient functioning of government at all levels.[304] This family type also "sets the pattern of social behavior" and preserves the basic value systems of society.[305] When human nature confronts the reality of changing circumstances, time and age, the domestic family is best equipped to adapt and make the necessary adjustments.

Internal regulation of family type- the domestic family is self-governing whereby behavior and interaction are worked out within each family unit. This process is fluid based on maturity and the changing nature of personalities that requires adjustments at different stages of development. A healthy domestic family unit maintains a natural order whereby the husband is the head of the family, and the husband and wife honor and respect each other as equal partners in the relationship. The unconditional love demonstrated through the parents toward each other and their children enables the respect and obedience of children toward parental and external authority outside the home. When the family is functioning to its maximum potential, older children are expected to be more responsible, and this added responsibility facilitates character formation.[306] Unconditional love is the norm within a domestic family and serves as a stabilizing force; each member knows he or she has the support of his or her family when faced with failures and difficult situations.

External regulation of family type- predominantly regulated by the sacred documents of a faith group or religious body (i.e., church or synagogue), and ideally safeguarded by legal regulation. In a society guided by unchanging principles and specific moral guidelines, parents assume leadership in making good citizens of the next generation without undue interference from outside forces such as the government, public education, or dictatorial religious extremists.[307]

Power distribution within society- balance of power distributed between family units and other social and governmental institutions.

Nature and level of individual freedom- children remain under parental authority until they are self-supportive or set up a family of their own, and individual members are free to choose their mate. Husband and wife retain their individual personality when married but function as one. When functioning as God designed, each family member is treated with dignity, decency, and respect, and is allowed individual freedom as long as that freedom does not override the freedom of another or jeopardize family unity, safety and welfare.

Dominant worldviews- Orthodox Judaism and Christianity

Level of civility- when functioning as originally designed, this family type is the most civil of all family types.

Predominant type of government- this family type thrives in a democratic republic that is rooted in God's order and moral values.

Legal implications- the domestic family type provides a more stable foundation for society so that extreme, oppressive laws become unnecessary because citizens are trained by domestic family members and faith groups to recognize the difference between right and wrong, and to understand the boundaries of freedom and the consequences of violating those boundaries.

Economic impact- as the domestic family thrives under a free enterprise and free trade system, the economy grows. The domestic family naturally "leads to trade, commerce, migration, and modern society."[308]

Strengths and/or weaknesses- covenantal family structures maintain strong bonds that can withstand *most* storms of life; therefore, it is less susceptible to enslavement. Civil societies thrive when the domestic family is the predominant family structure in society.

Trustee Family

Structure and type of relationship- a collective clan, tribe, aristocracy or commune of multiple single-family units linked together by blood relationships or land estates (feudal landlords and their servants), and is the most primitive family structure. Marriage is a uniting of personalities or two families that meld together to form common traits or conform to traits of the dominant clan or tribe membership.

Purpose of marriage and family- is to perpetuate the lineage, strengthen the clan, preserve the clan estate and property, or to keep the throne of a ruling clan or tribe secure.

Stability and longevity- blood vengeance, feuds, incessant warfare, over regulation, clan or tribe banishment, and automatic targeting of ruling or dominant clan severely hinders stability of trustee family and longevity of clans, tribes, or feudal lords. The trustee family type is unsettled, has high birth rates, and lives in miserable primitive conditions.

Social function in society- solidifies cultural practices in society and tightens solidarity of clan relationships enabling it to withstand invasion or intrusion from outside forces of other countries.

Internal regulation of family type- because the single-family unit is considered a part of the collective trustee family, it has a somewhat limited scope of individual sway and power within the single-family unit (i.e., the balance of power in regulating the affairs of individuals and single-family units is tipped heavily in the direction of the clan or tribal leadership).

Figure 47: Trustee family types do not regard women as persons of individual worth, and they are not recognized as equal partners in a marriage

External regulation of family type- law of the land predominantly determined and regulated by the dominant clan or tribe ruling the State. "The total social processes of the society of trustee families comes under extended family jurisdiction" and function under a barbaric code.[309]

Power distribution within society- power base concentrated in dominant clan or tribe who has widest control in society. Power is "granted to head of a clan or tribe" as a "trustee responsible for carrying out public or social responsibilities delegated to the dominant trustee family at that time.[310] Trustee families attempt to control local politics to curry favor to its own family members that manifests as nepotism.

Nature and level of individual freedom- individual freedom extremely restricted in choice of marriage partners, occupation, creativity, entrepreneurship, and advancement to better one's self or single-family unit. The trustee family type does not allow for much independence for individuals of single-family units.[311]

Dominant worldviews- pagan, polytheistic, Islam, earth-centered religions; characterized by religious or legalistic extremism.

Level of civility- unless restrained by a higher authority outside the dominating clan or remuneration negotiations are in full operation in lieu of blood feuds, the trustee family becomes barbaric. It is generally intolerant of outsiders, oppressive and uncivil by nature.

Predominant type of government- dictatorship, oligarchy, totalitarian, tyranny, monarchy

Legal implications- the dominant trustee family arbitrarily determines the laws that tend to favor the ruling family and are unbalanced and unjust toward other trustee families. The trustee family is not fitted or equipped for judicial responsibilities of the State because justice is based on revenge. Property is held in common by clan, tribe, or feudal lord's estate (no private ownership of property except by a feudal lord). System of justice is inequitable in that when one member of a clan or tribe commits a crime, all the members of that same clan or tribe are held accountable and punished, and women and children are treated unjustly and cruelly because they are considered property. A trustee family settling within the boundaries of a larger nation maintain their own code apart from the laws of a nation (Tribal nations of the American Indian and clans of the Appalachians are two examples).

Economic impact- economic growth is stifled due to hindrances to individual or single-family unit entrepreneurship, trade and commerce development. The feuding nature of trustee families hinders the economic growth of a country dominated by this type family.

Strengths and/or weaknesses- prone to disintegration due to internal incompatibilities, blood feuds, violence, and the constant struggle to be the dominant ruling clan, tribe, or feudal lord. The trustee family type is not compatible with the peaceful and secure nature of the domestic family.

Atomistic Family

Structure and type of relationship- loose family units comprised of individuals who are cohabitating for mutual pleasure or benefit and bound by a fluid contract or verbal agreement. The "Chicago School of Sociology defines family as 'group of interacting personalities' and therefore an 'atomistic mass of people freed from the restraint of custom and religious ideas,' which promotes the ideas of family as a private contract."[312]

Purpose of marriage and family- if partners choose to marry as opposed to co-habitating, the marriage relationship is more of a conjugal coexistence focusing on personal pleasures and mutual financial benefits with minimal interest in child bearing and rearing. This makes the atomistic family more open to outside relationships, acceptance of sexual perversion, and disloyalty toward family members.

Stability and longevity- the atomistic family is the most unstable and short-lived family type because it is based on a fluid and private contractual partnership. The individual is more important than family and is more inclined toward mutual consent separation or divorce. It is the least supportive of children and individual family members and less likely to embrace meaning, value, and unconditional love because love is diluted down to the lowest common denominator of sensual pleasure.

Social function in society- the atomistic family is more responsible and responsive to work and government because it is less bound to family obligations because of its fluid nature and each member's focus on *self*. However, because of individual's sense of unrestrained freedom and self-interest and the lack of a stable moral compass, the meaning of freedom changes from opportunity to license and a demand for *personal rights*. Because of the void of 'internal or external guides to discipline the self, the individual transfers his misery onto others and helps to build up government institutions to remedy his or her misery, which leads to individuals following a charismatic "prophet" or political figure who promises to rescue them and cure the disease of a codependent social system.'[313] Moral and religious support systems are dismantled and eradicated in society and the public square to ease the conscience of atomistic family members (extremism regarding separation of church and state), thus erasing society's knowledge base regarding the distinction between right and wrong, which thrust the family toward chaos and extinction.[314]

Internal regulation of family type- because of the constantly changing desires of individual family members, shifting sand and confusion would best describe the character of internal regulation.

External regulation of family type- is regulated predominantly by the "State" or bureaucratic government agencies, psychosocial forces, or whatever is culturally trending whereby laws regarding family tend to be ambiguous, arbitrary, and unjust. Not by choice, hardworking taxpayers pay for the high cost of social ills brought on by the atomistic family type and its *expressive individualism*.

Power distribution within society- because this family type is a loose structure of individuals and it lacks a stable value system, it has the least power of control and action in society.

Nature and level of individual freedom- People praise the atomistic family because of its unrestrained freedom, not being tied down to any particular value system, and its high mobility potential. However, these characteristics make it

154

the weakest family type because of its lack of a stable moral code that best supports liberty and justice for all, and is more likely to be enslaved by a tyrannical or totalitarian state thereby causing society to decline into chaos and barbarism.

Dominant worldviews- agnosticism, atheism, paganism, pantheism, Humanism, Socialism, Marxism, evolutionary theories of familial nihilism

Level of civility- atomistic families eventually turn violent because of individual self-interest and antisocial nature.[315]   21st protests and violent demonstrations were comprised of youth from atomistic families who have an *entitlement* mindset that believes government (i.e., other people's money) should provide for all their needs. Chaos, violence, and police state mentality prevail in every country that has digressed toward big government, increased *entitlement* or welfarism and socialism.

Predominant type of government- is democratic government that eventually digresses into anarchism, tyranny, fascism or totalitarianism because of the *imbalanced* focus on individualism.

Legal implications- when the atomistic family type is dominant in society, "the law moves away from finding a fundamental workable truth to a function of commanding, forbidding, allowing, or punishing," which means more legislation, regulation, and repressiveness (i.e., less grace and mercy, more legalism).[316]

Economic impact- with its unrestrained freedom, this family type is void of an internal accountability and moral value system and quickly digresses toward decreased productivity that severely impedes economic growth and progress. Because of the high percentage of separations, divorces, and single heads of households, this family type has more of a negative impact on a nation's economy.

Strengths and/or weaknesses- under the contractual family structure, the ties are loose and incapable of weathering the storms of life making it more vulnerable to destructive societal forces. Because of the emphasis on individual freedom void of a stable moral compass, the atomistic family lacks internal solidarity and is more inclined toward external social solidarity, especially control by society's culture, big government, or tyrannical forces. Individuals without the stable support of a unified family structure are more inclined to distribute their misery, pushing society towards anarchy, bloodthirsty dictatorships, class warfare, orgies, increased murder rates, domestic violence, and child abuse (review the fall of ancient Roman and Greek empires). Other side effects of this family type's final stage of development include:

- ↓ Increased causeless divorce
- ↓ Population decrease because of childlessness
- ↓ Increased public disrespect for parents and children
- ↓ Demeaning of early historical heroes and great leaders
- ↓ Degradation of the sacredness of marriage vows
- ↓ Trendy redefinition of marriage and family void of decency, natural order, and moral values
- ↓ Adults and children of traditional domestic families slipping away from their family and civic obligations

155

> ↓ Rapid spread of anti-family sentiments by pseudo-intellectuals
> ↓ Increase in laws undermining the domestic family type
> ↓ Acceptance of adultery and sexual perversion as the norm
> ↓ Youth rebellion toward parents and other authority figures
> ↓ Rapid increase of juvenile delinquency
> ↓ Increased intrusion of government into family affairs and over stepping parental authority in an attempt to "fix" problems[317]

Based on the points highlighted in the previous chart on family types, the domestic family type is best equipped to perpetuate and preserve the American Dream of freedom, opportunity, prosperity, and peace. The domestic family structure is the sustaining force of America. However, since the 1950s, we have *progressively* digressed toward atomistic family type dominance where extreme *expressive individualism* such as feminism, moral ambivalence, and irresponsibility rule the day. Let's have a reality-check moment and review a few facts that demonstrate the prevalence of atomistic families.

↓ Percentage of married women dropped from 66% in 1950 to 52% in 2010, and percentage of married men dropped from 68% in 1950 to 55% in 2010[318]

↓ In 2009 there was a 50% divorce rate (i.e., of 6.8 marriages per 1,000 of total population compared to 3.4 divorces per 1,000)[319]

↓ Percentage of cohabiting adults rose from 1.1% in 1960 to 11.6% in 2010[320]

↓ 6.7% of children are living with cohabiting parent(s) and 26.6% are living with only one parent in 2010[321]

↓ In 2002, 15% males of cohabiting couples were unemployed[322]

↓ Births to unmarried mothers rose from 4% in 1950 to 40.8% in 2010[323]

The self-centered nature of an atomistic family type often morphs into extreme individualism that sometimes manifests as self-worship and poses a danger to the weaker members within a family. Left unchecked, it can quickly escalate into domestic violence, child abuse, or sexual perversion. Restoring sanity in the home and in our nation begins by acknowledging the fact that reinforcing the domestic family structure is critical to American liberty and our children's safety and future. Consider the following questions:

☐ Do I fully comprehend what undermines families and their freedoms?

☐ Is my home *in order* and functioning normally?

☐ Do I maintain a consistent balance between family, work, and
external activities?

☐ Do I stay informed and engaged with what my children or
grandchildren are taught in public, charter and private schools,
and am I fulfilling my responsibility to be the primary educator
of my children?

☐ Do I actively educate my family and the next generation to be responsible stewards of American freedom?

☐ Is my family self-reliant and living without government welfare
aid, and although hoping for the best, is my family prepared for
the worst-case scenario?

**Responsible stewards of freedom fully comprehend what under-
mines the domestic family and its freedom.** "No great civilization has
endured for any length of time without paying considerable attention to
the organization, promulgation, and protection of the domestic family."[324] Because domestic families serve as a solid foundation for civilized societies and a safeguard against tyranny, there have been forces
at work throughout history to destroy traditional and biblical domestic
families. These forces are arrogantly open about their plans as demonstrated in Vladimir Lenin's statement, *"Destroy the family, you destroy
the country,"* and it is the nature of social progressivism to separate
and divide families and hurl whole nations into oppressive servitude to
the State. In review, below are key strategies used to undermine domestic families and minimize their effectiveness in sustaining and preserving a free and civil society.

Strategy #1- Destroy moral value systems and excommunicate expressions and influence of God-centered worldviews from the Public
Square, and outlaw open and public expressions of faith.

Strategy #2- Devise a propaganda machinery to re-educate society
toward acceptance of socialist ideology and earth- or human-centered
worldviews (as opposed to God-centered worldview).

Strategy #3- Usurp the spiritual authority of Christian churches and
organizations by creating laws and bureaucratic institutions that fly in
the face of common decency and respect for the sanctity of human life
(regardless of age or stage of development).

Strategy #4- Redefine marriage and diminish commitment to the sacredness of marriage as God intended (marriage between a man and a woman), facilitate the rapid growth of social deviance by advocating contract marriages, easy divorce, and cohabitation in lieu of traditional covenant marriages and commitment to marriage vows and family, and push society toward atomistic or trustee family dominance.

Strategy #5- Usurp local and parental authority by creating a centralized public education system to re-educate children to accept socialism and loyalty to the State and to disrespect parents and traditional moral values.

Strategy #6- Reduce the availability of farmable land and livable land space for families and their heirs by declaring land and property sites to be national monuments, and institute other measures to deprive families of property ownership such as oppressive inheritance and property taxes, and declaration of lands or property as environmentally protected.

Strategy #7- Create and rapidly increase the size of government-run social institutions to be the sole provider of life-sustaining resources (food, water, healthcare), housing, and jobs, thereby depriving families and individuals of the opportunity to provide for themselves and thereby making them the government's dependents.

Strategy #8- Subvert and rewrite the American Constitution to strip families and individuals of protection from tyranny and to ban ownership of all weapons.

Strategy #9- Confiscate and redistribute family wealth and assets and restrict free enterprise ventures through heavy taxation, regulation, and monetary/market manipulation by the centralized banking system such as the Federal Reserve or an international entity such as the UN-run World Bank and International Monetary Fund.

Understanding the above strategies is the first step toward resisting and undoing the damage already wreaked by Progressive *loons*. As revealed in previous chapters, Socialists and anti-American forces have been working for over 100 years to destroy family and faith influences that preserve liberty and sustain a civil society. John Dewey's Train to Nowhere, utopian visionaries, the media, Hollywood, the United Nations, ACLU, NEA, feminists, Planned Parenthood, socialist demonstrators (OWS), Marxist professors, secular Progressive politicians, and other socialist spokespersons having eagerly championed the cause of anti-God and anti-American initiatives. Now it is our turn to upset their apple cart and restore sanity.

Redefinition of marriage and pushing families toward a more atomistic family type is necessary to accomplish the goals of tyranny and totalitarianism. Therefore, it is important that we reinforce the traditional domestic family structure and resist socialist schemes to redefine marriage and undermine families. Carefully consider the following facts:

- ♦ "Compared to married couples, cohabiting couples tend to report poorer relationship quality and less psychological and financial wellbeing. Cohabiting relationships and even subsequent marriage tend to be less enduring."[325]
- ♦ "Children born to unmarried mothers are at greater risk...for poverty, teen childbearing, poor school achievement, and marital disruption in adulthood" than children with two parents present.[326]
- ♠ Men in a committed covenantal marriage are less likely to engage in self-centered, criminal and/or violent activity, and are more affectionate and attentive to their wives and children than men in cohabitating arrangements[327]
- ♠ "Children from intact families are more likely to have positive attitudes...and higher expectations for their own marriages. In adulthood, they are less likely to form a high-risk marriage, to undergo divorce, or to cohabit, and they tend to enjoy a higher quality of marriage."[328]

Responsible stewards of freedom maintain order in the home. Government intrusion, Planned Parenthood, and the feminist movement have done much to destroy family stability but not without the complicit cooperation of everyone who has exercised unrestrained freedom, extreme expressive individualism, and indecency. God originally intended for each person to live in liberty, but not at the expense of family and other people. It is, therefore, time to declare, *"ORDER IN THE HOME,"* and put forth committed effort and individual sacrifice to restore the traditional covenantal domestic family. The survival of American civilization and our children's future depend on each one of us advocating, supporting, and preserving this honorable institution that has the power to transcend culture and thwart tyranny's intrusion.

Order in the home is restored by reviving unconditional love and respect towards one another, beginning with forgiveness, reconciliation with God and each other, prayer, and having faith that with God all things are possible. It is the father and husband's responsibility as head of the home to lead with unconditional love and respect for his wife and children that is then reciprocated by love and respect of the wife toward her husband and the mother toward her children. As dad and mom model unconditional love and respect for one another, the children will likely emulate the same response pattern.

There are a number of hindrances to mutual respect and loving family relationships. The ones that cause the most problems are stated below with some recommended solutions:

- *Failure of fathers to faithfully and lovingly fulfill their role as provider, protector, and head of the home-* solved by fathers and husbands assuming their position as head of the home and continuing to grow in the knowledge and practical application of father and husband responsibilities and skills, avoiding the use of coercion, excessive force, cruelty, and demeaning verbal tactics, and learning to play with their wives and children

Figures 48: Spending quality time together strengthens the family

- *Usurping self-interest over the welfare of other family members-* solved by submitting to one another in love
- *The temptations of adultery or sexual deviance-* solved by being committed and faithful to one's marriage mate, being a spiritual leader in the home, and avoiding compromising situations and exposure to pornography, R-rated movies or any media that glorifies infidelity and sexual perversion
- *Interfering parents who refuse to let go of their son or daughter after he or she marries-* solved by the son or daughter practicing the "leave and cleave" principle whereby the husband and wife form their own family solidarity without parental intrusiveness or parental attempts to shelter new families from learning and growing together as an independent family unit
- *Rebellious attitude towards one another (i.e., wife toward husband or children toward parents)-* solved by practicing respect for one another, maintaining parental unity, and parents applying consistent patience and sometimes tough love measures with children
- *Struggle for dominance over others in a family sometimes brought on by self-centered ego, religious or ideological extremism, or mental distress and fear-* solved by perfecting unconditional love and respect skills sometimes requiring mentorship by more experienced persons who have demonstrated success in their own family relationships, and allowing others the freedom to reach their full potential both within and outside the family
- *Mental and verbal abuse, domestic violence, child abuse, and drug addictions or alcoholism-* solved by the restoration of unconditional love and for extreme cases, immediate consultation with competent, just, and Godly counselors (in cases where life is threatened, protective and/or legal intervention may be required)
- *Outside intrusive interference that results in dividing the family-* solved by standing firm in family loyalty and resisting outside interference which may occasionally require the services of professionals who are expert at holding at bay intrusive agents using excessive power and unwanted, counterproductive and sometimes destructive influence

A few resources that will help with understanding and fortifying family relationships are listed below:

 ✵ David L. Fleet (2012), *F.A.M.I.L.Y.: The Fight to be an Unconditional Man* (CreateSpace of Amazon.com).

✳ Andreas Kostenberger with David Jones (2010, second edition), *God, Marriage, and Family* (Wheaton, IL: Crossway).

Responsible stewards of freedom maintain a balance between family, work, and external activities. Today, more often than not, mates and children experience loneliness or abandonment because one mate or both parents are too absorbed with work and external activities, and children are outsourced to the care of outside persons, agencies, or institutions. The domestic family is a nation's primary incubator of good, upright and happy citizens, and for each family member to grow and function with a high level of normalcy, quality time spent together is required. To abandon this quality time together is to sacrifice the well-being of each family member. Support for this is found in the following briefs:

✳ The Heritage Foundation, "Marriage and Family as Deterrents from Delinquency, Violence and Crime"- Brief #26 (Washington, DC: familyfacts.org). Retrieved from:
http://www.familyfacts.org/briefs/26/marriage-and-family-as-deterrents-from-delinquency-violence-and-crime
✳ The Heritage Foundation, "Family and Adolescent Well-Being"- Brief #34 (Washington, DC: familyfacts.org). Retrieved from:
http://www.familyfacts.org/briefs/34/family-and-adolescent-well-being
✳ The Heritage Foundation, "Parental Involvement and Children's Well-Being"- Brief #40 (Washington, DC: familyfacts.org). Retrieved from:
http://www.familyfacts.org/briefs/40/parental-involvement-and-childrens-well-being

The joy of marriage and family is time spent loving, laughing, playing, worshipping, praying, learning, and growing up together, and why anyone in their right mind would deprive themselves or other family members of these joys is incomprehensible. While there are times when we need to come apart before we come apart, prolonged absences are counterproductive to family solidarity and risks one or more family members slipping into a dysfunctional mode.

All too often, we cave into peer pressure, cultural and societal expectations, and attempts to curry the acceptance of others or to buy love. We have been brainwashed by the media and commercial entities who insist that having "things" produces happiness and gives us security, and we have allowed them to convince us that saving money for a rainy day is not necessary, and to turn us into a *trinket* and *techno-novelty* society. Theref6re, we invest insane hours at work to earn enough money to have things, or feverishly run from one activity to another hoping to achieve fulfillment or the illusive feeling of happiness. Then when we have exhausted ourselves, we realize how illusive happiness really is, that *enough* is never *enough*, and learn with perhaps some disappointment that possessing or having "things" does not provide nurturing love, security, nor long lasting happiness.

The quicker we realize that family comes first in the pecking order of life and society, the faster we will restore sanity in the home and within ourselves. Should we not reach for the moon and realize our fullest potential as individuals? Most definitely we should, but why not make it a family affair, and if this is not possible, then be content that it may take a little longer to reach our goals and accomplish our dreams. This goes against the grain of the American *instant-got-to-have-it-now* mindset, but to continue in this mindset is to jeopardize that which we hold most dear- our mate and our children.

There is also one word we don't like to use with our children or ourselves, and that is the word "No." Dare to be brave and allow the word "No" to build character. The next commercial or peer that dangles a new techno-gadget or flashy toy in front of you or your family, tell yourself or your family member, "No."

You may get this:

However...

Not only will saying "NO" build character, but it will also produce a strong sense of freedom from grief and enslavement to things. In the process, you, your mate or your children may develop withdrawal symptoms; if so, the following resource will help navigate raging currents:

⁎ Jill Rigby (2008), *Raising Unselfish Children in a Self-Absorbed World* (New York: Howard Books).

Responsible stewards of freedom *stay informed and engaged with what their children or grandchildren are taught in public, charter or private schools, and responsible parents take their rightful place as the primary educators of their children.* You may have heard the saying, "It takes a village to raise a child." In some cultures, this means that it takes a local village or community in concert with the immediate family to raise a child. However, true to the reconstructive lingo and utopian vision of Socialists, it means that it takes the government's compulsory education system, media, Hollywood, and socialistic institutions to raise a child, and parents or legal guardians are not considered a vital part of that process.

On a regular basis, your children are subjected to a battery of surveys, personality assessments, and other psychosocial tests aimed at readjusting and re-educating your children. These psychosocial instruments are designed to contradict and diminish the influence of traditional moral and ethical values instilled by the child's parents by using multiple-choice questions that force an either/or choice void of a clear distinction between right vs. wrong and leaves zero room for logical thinking. They are also used to measure if a child needs an attitude or behavioral re-adjustment treatment administered by a school counselor, medical professional or "special" class. More often than not, parents are denied access to these psychosocial survey and assessment results, which is a blatant disregard for parental authority. Signs that your child may have been subjected to these surveys or psychological tests are- an increased level of agitation and rebellion towards his or her parents, or the onset of illness or depression in a child who was perfectly healthy and happy before being submitted to a battery of conflicting questions. In other words, children are programmed as to what to think, not how to think.

We have already discussed at length the plans that American socialists have for our children. Therefore, to facilitate further understanding, the following resources reveal what the public and charter schools are teaching or not teaching, and other useful information:

* Big government takeover of your child's education:
  - → http://www.eagleforum.org/educate/marc_tucker/marc_tucker_le tter.html (Tucker's plan to prepare your children to be part of the national workforce, i.e., servants of the state)
  - → B. K. Eakman (2007), *Walking Targets* (Midnight Whistler Publishers)- a chronicle of public education's psychological child abuse
  - → Pamela Hoeffecker, *Outcome-Based Education: The State's Assault on our Children's Values* (Vital Issues Publishers, 1996).
  - → B. K. Eakman (1998), *Cloning of the American Mind* (Huntington Press Publishers)
* Parental rights to guide their own children without government interference or public education intrusion:
  - → https://www.rutherford.org/publications_resources/john_whitehe ads_commentary/do_parents_rights_end_at_the_schoolhouse_ga te/
  - → John Whitehead (1995), *State vs. Parents: Threats to Raising Your Child* (Moody Press)
  - → Steve Baldwin & Karen Holgate (2008), *From Crayons to Condoms* (Los Angeles, CA: WorldNetDaily). This resource contains a wealth of resources for parents.
* Legal assistance for parents and guardians:
  - → American Center for Law and Justice: www.aclj.org
  - → Alliance Defense Fund: www.alliancedefensefund.org
  - → Rutherford Institute: www.rutherford.org
  - → Liberty Legal Institute: www.libertylegal.org
* UN intrusion in the classroom and home:
  - → B. K. Eakman, *Educating for the New World Order* (Halcyon House, 1991)
  - → http://www.dickmorris.com/clinton-obama-un-to-tell-us-how-to-raise-our-children/
  - → http://www.eagleforum.org/column/2001/sept01/01-09-19.shtml
  - → http://www.eagleforum.org/un/2011/11-05-12.html (video on brainwashing children to earth-centered loyalty/worship in order to promote the socialist green agenda and create loyalty to the State)
  - → http://www.eagleforum.org/psr/1993/mar93/psrmar93.html
* Islamic indoctrination in the textbooks and charter schools:

165

- → American Textbook Council: www.historytextbooks.org
- → http://www.eagleforum.org/educate/2012/apr12/islamist-agenda.html
- → http://www.eagleforum.org/column/2012/apr12/12-04-04.html
- → http://www.onenewsnow.com/Perspectives/Default.aspx?id=1314254
- → http://www.coachisright.com/islamic-%E2%80%9Cvalues%E2%80%9D-are-seeping-into-charter-schools-and-via-the-discovery-channel-and-gulen-movement/#
* Sex education cloaked as family planning in K-12 by Planned Parenthood (pushing safe sex instead of abstinence):
  - → http://www.eagleforum.org/educate/2012/feb12/sex-standards.html
* Crisis of Competence- regarding political activism on campuses:
  - → http://www.nas.org/images/documents/A_Crisis_of_Competence.pdf
* Efforts to centralize and globalize daycare and pre-school programs:
  - → http://www.eagleforum.org/educate/2005/nov05/studies.html
  - → http://www.eagleforum.org/column/2001/may01/01-05-02.shtml
  - → http://www.eagleforum.org/educate/2002/apr02/pre-school.shtml
* Organizations that evaluate academic soundness of textbooks and curriculum:
  - → *Parents' Handbook for Successful Schools*, Texas Public Policy Foundation, P. O. Box 40519, San Antonio, TX 78229, www.texaspolicy.com
  - → The Textbook League: www.textbookleague.org
  - → Core Knowledge Foundation: www.coreknowledge.org
  - → Math textbooks: www.mathematicallycorrect.com
  - → Reading textbooks- The Phonics Store: www.readingstore.com
  - → American Values: www.americanvaluesforkids.org
* Book review of children's literature in schools and school libraries and literary standards- http://www.factsonfiction.org/
  - → http://www.classkc.org/
  - → http://www.eagleforum.org/educate/2007/feb07/bad-books.html
  - → http://www.eagleforum.org/educate/2003/sept03/book-list.shtml
  - → http://www.eagleforum.org/educate/2004/oct04/reading.html
* Safe Libraries: http://www.safelibraries.org/
* Pornography in the schools and what you can do:
  - → http://www.eagleforum.org/educate/2005/oct05/focus.html

→ http://www.eagleforum.org/educate/2006/mar06/court.html
http://www.eagleforum.org/educate/2000/oct00/library-porn.shtml
* Who decides what drugs are forced on children:
→ http://www.eagleforum.org/psr/2001/feb01/psrfeb01.shtml

The resources listed below are recommended as an aid for charting a course of action for your child's education, safety, and sanity:

* Alternate school choices:
→ Gateways to Better Education: www.gtbe.org
→ Discover Christian Schools: www.discoverchristianschools.com
→ Citizens for Excellence in Education: www.nace-cee.org
* Recommended classical reading for children:
→ http://www.eagleforum.org/educate/2003/sept03/book-list.shtml
→ http://www.ourdocuments.gov/content.php?flash=true&page=milestone
* John and Susan Yates (2011, reprint edition), *Raising Kids with Character that Lasts* (Grand Rapids, MI: Revell). Teaching children about choices and consequences is important.
* Recommended curriculum and resources for homeschooling or extra help for children:
→ http://www.abeka.com/HomeSchool/
→ http://www.markdown.com/education/homeschooling.html
→ http://www.homeschoolacademy.com/homeschool-learning-programs/christian-homeschooling/
→ http://thegraceacademy.org/tuition.php
→ http://www.familycenteredlearning.org
→ http://www.homeschool.com
→ http://www.homeedmag.com
→ Gateways to Better Education: www.gtbe.org
* Homeschooling support groups:
→ http://christian-homeschooling.meetup.com/
* Homeschooling Legal Defense:
→ http://hslda.org/athome/Home.aspx

Responsible stewards of freedom actively educate their families and the next generation to be responsible stewards of American freedom. Why are our children and young people in the crosshairs of American socialists? In John Dewey's own words, "You can't make

Socialists out of individualists—children who know how to think for themselves spoil the collective society which is coming...", so it is important to reprogram children to "progress" into a new world order. This has been transpiring for several decades in America, and we have lost several generations of children to the socialist machinery.

Recently there has been increased pressure from the UN and American Progressives to determine and dictate the curriculum for ages one to six because they clearly understand that character and trust are established at these ages. Socialists want to usurp parental influence and indoctrinate our children to hate America and the *Constitution* so that children can be molded to fit the amoral new world order and be blindly loyal to a global government. As the twig is bent, so leans the tree.

So, let's pull together, take the helm of our children's education, and impart to them an appreciation for American heroes who fought to secure our liberties and for the unchanging principles that undergird those liberties, and make sure our young people have access to educators who are supportive of traditional values, the American heritage, and American domestic families. Information that will help in this process:

- ✶ American Heritage Curriculum for different ages:
  - → http://homeschoolblogger.com/elcloud/743270/ (free)
  - → http://www.americanheritage.org/curriculum.html
  - → http://homeschoolcrew.com/785260/
  - → http://www.heritage.org/constitution/#!?utm_source=lfa&utm_medium=banner&utm_campaign=carousel (free)
- ✶ Heritage Foundation's Leadership for America guide:
  - → http://www.heritage.org/about/leadership-for-america
  - → http://www.heritage.org/about/internships-young-leaders/young-leaders-program
- ✶ Universities we can safely send our young people to:
  - → John Zmirak, *Choosing the Right College 2014-15: The Inside Scoop on Elite Schools and Outstanding Lesser-Known Institutions (10th ed.)*

Responsible stewards of freedom take personal responsibility and carefully consider the consequences of their decisions and actions and do not expect others to provide for their needs. Theodore Dalrymple stated that:

"It is a mistake, in my view, to assume that all people want to be free, in the sense of the American pioneers. I think they much prefer to be comfortable; as the establishment of welfare states almost everywhere ... has shown. [T]he greatest of all freedoms, the one that more people want more than any other, is...freedom from responsibility and consequences."[329]

And so, for generations our children and we have been shielded from the consequences of our choices and actions and failure to assume responsibility for our own welfare. The government continues to pick up the tab for our unwise choices and bad behavior at a high cost to taxpayers and our children's future. The irony is that some of our most applauded leaders knew the consequences of picking up the tab as demonstrated by FDR's statement that, "Continued dependence upon relief induces a spiritual and moral disintegration fundamentally destructive to the national fiber. To dole out relief in this way is to administer a narcotic, a subtle destroyer of the human spirit."

The tragedy is that FDR did not heed his own advice when he rammed an overreaching socialist welfare program down America's throat, which has enslaved Americans in welfarism's prison. Western civilization has declined into an *Age of Entitlement* in which humanity is viewed as depersonalized biological units divested of dignity, responsibility and freedom, and according to *extremist loons,* the State and environment determine their identity.

Have we not learned that whenever the government steps in to *rescue* people, the poor become poorer and the country becomes economically and morally weaker? Review the evidence presented in Chapter 8. Instead of creating more entitlement programs and more reasons to tax Americans such as the 2010 healthcare law, let's get our act together and become more self-reliant and less dependent on government aid, starting with our families, and regain the courage to say "NO" to government handouts. Think about this: "The American Dream is built on strong families—the building blocks of civil society, the incubators of personal responsibility. Unfortunately, the welfare state has severely damaged the institution of family."[330]

When Progressive politicians interfere with family self-reliance, poverty rates increase. For example, when the *War on Poverty* was launched in 1963, "93% of American children were born to married

169

parents. Today the number has dropped to 59%. In 2008, 1.7 million children were born outside marriage...to women who will have the hardest time going it alone" because they lack sufficient education and work experience to support a family with an absentee father.[331] "Single parents now comprise 70% of all poor families with children."[332]

The 1963 welfare program rapidly increased welfare spending, and the only time that it leveled off was when welfare reforms were implemented in 1981 and when TANF[333] was signed into law in 1996.[334] These two reforms required individuals to take personal responsibility, contribute to their own support, and be actively seeking employment. However, after spurts of success, leveling off welfare spending was reversed by Progressive politicians determined to inflate government welfare rolls with more dependents, so we now have a run-away government gravy train with no gravy. To add insult to injury, Progressive *loons* are continuing their assaults on traditional marriage in order to create yet another entitlement group ushered in by same sex-marriages.

Restoring strong domestic families with strong leadership from the husband and father is America's greatest weapon against poverty and enslavement to the State. This is supported by the following fact: "...the poverty rate for single parents with children was 35.6%. The rate for married couples with children was 6.4%."[335] When domestic families are functioning at their greatest potential, and there is order in the home, poverty, hunger and poor health are less prevalent.

Fathers who have unconditional love in full operation will always find a way to provide for their family and have a nest egg tucked away for a rainy day when illness or loss of income suddenly strikes. Responsible fathers and mothers will work any job to provide the necessities of life for their children, and when this level of responsible behavior is prevalent, even the older children are willing to contribute to the family doing odd jobs or part time work. In fact, remember that small family businesses marked the beginning of America's growth as a prosperous nation.

Below are a few resources that will help families avoid being at the mercy of government welfare-statism:

* Family economics:
  → R. C. Sproul, Jr. (2008), *Biblical Economics* (White Hall, WV: Tolle Lege Press)

→ Sound financial planning and advice:
Larry Olson, CFP and Erick Olson, CFP-
http://www.olsonadvisory.net/ (go to "Our Process")

→ Joyce Bone, *Millionaire Moms* (New York: Morgan James Publishing, LLC)- also see visit http://millionairemom.com/

→ Successful entrepreneurship:
http://www.entrepreneur.com/article/200730

→ Keeping more of your paycheck: http://www.fairtax.org/site/PageServer?pagename=HowFairTaxWorks

✶ Growing your own food in small spaces:
  → Edward Smith (2011), *The Vegetable Gardener's Container Bible* (North Adams, MA: Storey Publishers)

✶ Good nutrition and natural health remedies:
  → Joel Fuhrman, "Super Immunity" (free online fact sheet):
  http://www.drfuhrman.com/shop/pdf_product_factsheets/DrFuhrmans_Super_Immunity_factsheet.pdf

  → Joel Fuhrman (2011), *Eat to Live* (NY: Little, Brown & Co.)- obesity and toxins are major causes of disease and poor health— common sense steps to regain good health

  → Joel Fuhrman (2008, 2 vol.), *Eat for Health* (Gift of Health)

  → Joel Fuhrman (2006, Reprint ed.), *Disease Proof Your Child: Feeding Kids Right* (St. Martin's Griffin)

  → Janet Maccaro (2006), *Natural Health Remedies* (Lake Mary, FL: Siloam, a Strang Company)

There is a basic connection between individuals, families and a nation, and whatever the level of normalcy there is within families is reflected in a nation's government and social institutions. In *Commentaries on the Conflict of Laws*, Joseph Story points out that marriage is "the source of civility," therefore, the domestic family is the building block of society, not welfare programs, economics, cultural trends, the government, public education, or Hollywood. Once we have restored order in the home, the next logical step is to restore sanity in America's leadership, which we will dive into in Chapter 12.

21st Century Truth or Consequence Question: *What is my plan for restoring sanity in my home?*

Dig Deeper

1. Vern Sheridan Poythress (2011), *Redeeming Sociology: A God-centered Approach* (Wheaton, IL: Crossway).
2. John Loren & Paula Sanford (2009), *Restoring the Christian Family* (Lake Mary, FL: Charisma House, a Strang Company).
3. Movie: *Courageous* (Sony Pictures Home Entertainement, 2012)- available in DVD and Blu-ray.
4. Movie: *Facing the Giants* (Sony Pictures Home Entertainement, 2006)- available in DVD and Blu-ray.
5. Movie: *Fireproof* (Sony Pictures Home Entertainement, 2008)- available in DVD and Blu-ray.

CHAPTER 12
RESTORING SANITY IN AMERICA

"When the righteous are in authority, the people rejoice; But when a wicked man rules, the people groan."[336]

As we have learned in the previous chapter, America has been psychosocially herded into an *atomistic society* mindset whereby self-gratification trumps domestic family structure and stability, and then redirected into a groupthink mass easily controlled by big government and big corporations joined at the hip with the government through contracts and as acting agents of the government. As we plummet further into the abyss of an *atomistic society* and a groupthink mass, we will re-emerge as a totalitarian society unless "we the people" put the brakes on. We can stop this insanity by diligently working to restore order within our self and family. The skills we develop in that process will help us maintain a strong basis for decisions we make as we practice responsible citizenship locally and nationally.

What is our skill and engagement level as citizens?

☐ Do I know the American *Constitution* and *Declaration of Independence* well enough to spot when my God-given unalienable rights are violated or when the law of the land is being side-stepped or subverted by American socialists, lawmakers, judges, law enforcement or other government agents?

☐ Do I correctly distinguish between *unalienable rights* and *human rights*, or have I sold out to the socialistic version of *human rights* and demanded instant gratification at the expense of the unalienable rights of others?

☐ Do I consistently vote during local and national elections, and am I an informed and engaged voter by properly vetting the candidates in each election and being fully informed about issues on the ballot?

☐ Do I stay informed about current events and local, state and national laws, regulations or zoning laws to be voted on by my representatives, and do I communicate with my representatives when proposed legislation subverts the *Constitution* and jeopardizes my *unalienable rights*, including property rights?

☐ Do I hold my elected representatives accountable when I know they have strayed from doing what is morally and ethically right?

☐ Do I maintain a focus in one or two areas to increase effectiveness regarding my pro-active citizenship?

Responsible stewards of freedom are familiar with the language and original intent of the US Constitution, the Declaration of Independence, and the Bill of Rights, and understand that their responsibility does not end at the voting booth. One could decide to continue following the Progressive version of the constitution as an evolving document; however, this has proven to be destructive and self-defeating as our basic American liberties fade into the sunset. Responsible stewards have a firm grasp on their constitutional rights, and they know the *Constitution* well enough to know when their rights as enumerated in the *Bill of Rights* are being violated. For review, our basic constitutional freedoms or rights include the following (for more details, go to chart on page 42)

☑ Freedom to speak our mind, protest in peace, redress grievances with the government, and freedom from invasion of privacy

☑ Freedom to worship and pray without interference

☑ Freedom to keep and bear arms

☑ Freedom from military or other government enforcement agency entering our homes and occupying without our consent

☑ Freedom from warrantless searches (without probable cause) of person, home or property

☑ Freedom from being tried twice for the same crime

☑ Freedom from being forced to testify against one's self

☑ Freedom from government depriving us of our life, liberty, or property without following strict codes of conduct as in innocent until proven guilty

☑ Freedom from being jailed for unspecified charges and excessive bails or fines, and the right to a speedy and public trial

☑ Freedom to own and sell personal property or a business
☑ Freedom from property being taken for public use without just compensation

Because of rapid technological advances, America is quickly transitioning into a *Surveillance State* with identifiable *enemies of the State*. I realize this sounds conspiratorial or *Orwellian*, but let's consider a few facts regarding past and current events as they relate to freedom and rights of American citizens.

First, pre-emptive to Hitler's *Final Solution*[337] was the establishment of a census and profiling system called the Hollerith punch card machine created by IBM Corporation. Below is an IBM ad poster distributed in Germany in 1934 that advertised their punch card machine designed to centralize information for the German government. This was a profit venture for IBM Corporation and its subsidiaries; however, it was used by Hitler's regime as a way to identify friends and enemies of the State in Germany and German-occupied countries.

 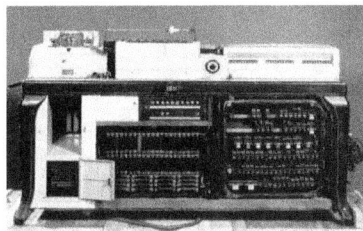

Figure 49: IBM poster- translated as, "See everything with Hollerith punch cards,"[338] and the Hollerith punch card machine[339]

By the time Hitler and Himmler were ready to activate their *Final Solution*, they had all the information they needed to round up their enemies and other *undesirable* citizens thanks to the Hollerith punch card system. When bread lines were long and anti-Semite sentiment was at an all-time high, IBM' autocratic chairman, Thomas J. Watson, capitalized on an opportunity to explode IBM's profit margin, using the 'ends justifies the means' philosophy and their "amoral corporate mantra: if it can be done, it should be done."[340]

IBM was founded in 1896 by German inventor living in America, Herman Hollerith, as a census tabulating company."[341] The IBM German subsidiary, Dehomag, in coordination with its parent company in

175

New York, custom designed the machine with special applications that included racial, religious, and economic profiles. They also serviced the machines (even the ones near concentration camps) and trained Nazi personnel on how to operate the machine for the Third Reich. Over 2,000 machines were distributed and utilized for Hitler's census gathering system, and these machines generated numbers tattooed on the arms of prisoners.[342] This punch card machine streamlined the process of identifying and locating Jews and *undesirables* in every city, making it possible for the SS to quickly swoop in unannounced and forcibly cease property, arrest people, and transport them to Ghettos, concentration camps, or gas chambers.

For more information and documented evidence regarding the Hollerith punch card machine and its use by the Third Reich, read Edwin Black's book, *IBM and the Holocaust* (warning— this book is verbally graphic). Black highlights the results when a big corporation ignores the human factor and becomes overtly involved with a tyrannical government solely to make a profit—the resulting human devastation was tragic, nightmarish and downright evil.

Now fast forward to 21st Century America. The U. S. Census forms have gradually morphed into racial and economic profiling forms. Its cousin, the American Community Survey (ACS) is a more invasive form that profiles you and occupants in your home regarding the house, vehicles, toilets, utilities, mental and physical status, education, ancestry or ethnicity, immigration status, home business, acreage, flood and hazard insurance, work status, welfare information, and income. Survey for each person is four pages long, so if a person is married and has three children he or she would have to fill out 20 pages of information—at this rate, the government ought to pay us to fill out these forms. Failure to fill out community survey forms comes with a hefty fine, and if a person provides inaccurate financial information by accident, and it is given to the IRS to check against tax forms, he or she could be audited and fined by the IRS if the information did not match on both forms.

Judges have ruled these forms as constitutional—no surprises there since socialist judges are complicit with the governments need to spy on American citizens and monitor their every move. The elephant in the room that few folks are not willing to acknowledge is this: When do the socialists plan to drop the other shoe and use this information against whom they consider *undesirable* citizens or *political enemies*, and which techno corporations and politicians are waiting in the wings to profit?

I have mentioned several chapters ago, 9/11 scared the American public into accepting invasive surveillance programs such as the TSA and their virtual strip search x-ray machines—the company that provided the equipment, Rapiscan, has as its chief lobbyist a recent former politician who benefits financially from the sales of their scanners.[343] It is not enough to invade our privacy at airports; they now have mobile x-ray units mounted in roving vans that can do a virtual strip search of us in our homes and vehicles without our knowledge; they also use surveillance drones in US airspace.[344] What part of right to privacy do *extremist loons* not understand, and are we going to continue allowing invasion of our privacy without probable cause?

"We the people" have allowed this to continue, and now we are on the verge of martial law being declared and becoming a totalitarian police state. Executive Order 12425, modified and signed by the President in 2009, gives Interpol (International Criminal Police Organization) immunity from American laws, thus making them an autonomous police agency on American soil. Interpol is not required to abide by the search and seizure provisions of the Fourth Amendment of the *U. S. Constitution*, and if they violate the rights of American citizens, they are exempt from prosecution. The FBI and other American law enforcement agencies share information with Interpol. Interpol also interfaces and shares information with the UN's International Criminal Court—none of this exchanged information is accessible to American citizens through the Freedom of Information Act (FOIA) thereby making it virtually impossible for American citizens to gather evidence if they have to defend themselves against charges from foreign police forces. Foreign intelligence agencies can now spy on American citizens, thereby moving us closer to being subject to a global police state without any recourse or defense should we be accused of a crime by foreign authorities.[345]

Second, there is another case of a government agency in coordination with large pharmaceutical companies not working for the welfare of people. The Texas Medical Board of Examiners, the FDA, NCI, and

PhRMA repeatedly harassed Dr. Stanislaw Burzynski through numerous legal maneuvers in an attempt to publically humiliate and ruin him so that a large pharmaceutical company could steal his cancer-treatment formula for their own profit. Dr. Burzynski had discovered a new drug, Antineoplaston, which was successful in treating various types of cancer, especially brain cancer. A significant percentage of people who had little or no chance of survival were cured, and his new drug had no life-threatening side effects.

Dr. Burzynski has endured harassment for over twenty years and is still Texas Medical Board's favorite target today despite the fact that Federal prosecutors conceded that his drug was saving lives. The FDA spent $60 million dollars of taxpayer's money to prosecute Dr. Burzynski, and out of four trials, none produced a guilty verdict, and the judge chastised the FDA. This is the most brazen example of government's failure to work for the welfare of people that I have ever seen in my entire life. It underscores the dangers of corporations becoming so big, powerful, and entrenched with the Federal government that it endangers the lives of American citizens. In addition, what is beyond inhumane is that cancer patients who were facing a death sentence were continually threatened with their only hope of a cure being denied them, and still children are dying. The only thing curbing this injustice toward patients was their petition to address grievances before Congress that resulted in Congressional investigations and hearings resulting in the exposure of the unholy alliance between the FDA, cancer research institutes, and big drug companies.

In some of the Phase 3 clinical test trial cases conducted by a pharmaceutical company not associated with Dr. Burzynshki, the company broke Dr. Burzynski's treatment protocol, changed the dosage and frequency schedule, and required patients to endure destructive and life-threatening radiation treatment before being allowed treatment with Antineoplaston. The man who led the charge against the FDA saw his own son die because they wanted him to have radiation before going into a "test" program with Dr. Burzynski. In this political-scientific bait and switch game, the patients were the ones who suffered. Unbelievable? View the documentary at: http://burzynskimovie.com/.

The FDA has attempted many times over the years to shut down health food stores and publications that offer natural means of healing and preventative healthcare. According to Dr. Passwater, drug company lobbyists keep the pressure on the FDA to close down natural health food stores, and they take turns occupying leadership positions in the FDA.[346] This is yet another example of a rogue government agency safeguarding the profit margins of large corporations and failing to look after the welfare of Americans. How many other cures have the FDA and big pharmaceutical companies hijacked and kept from American citizens or altered in such a way as to prolong treatment and costs?

Now can you just imagine what your quality of health care and longevity will be like if the 2010 healthcare plan remains in force as a law and when life and death decisions fall into the hands of government bureaucrats and their big corporate pals who will be the "chosen ones" or inexperienced non-medical personnel to serve on ethics panels?

"Try to think of health-care reform as a nice spring shower clearing the air."

Figures 50: Fruit Loon politician soliciting support for another entitlement program

Already, there are numerous testimonials to the fact that Medicare is denying some life-saving treatment for persons considered terminal or over 65 years old. We are beginning to understand why the Feds are so keen on forcing Americans to fill out their invasive questions about mental and health conditions in the American Community Survey. In addition, according to the 2010 healthcare plan of the current administration, Medicare is to deny life-saving treatment for persons 70 years and older.[347]

I have personally experienced medical professionals taking my 92 year old mother's age into account when they recommended treatments, strongly indicating that any costly treatment that would prolong her life would not be acceptable in the "opinion" of medical professionals. Excuse my mother for breathing, but God is the one who decides how long she lives, and not some socialist *loon* trying to play god. "And the LORD said, 'My Spirit shall not strive with man forever, for he is indeed flesh; yet his days shall be one hundred and twenty years.'"[348] There is nothing ethical about denying life-saving medical treatment for non-vegetative patients—it is a violation of the sanctity of human life and Hippocratic Oath to do no harm.

The previously mentioned true life scenarios are just a few examples of an overreaching government. If you are sufficiently outraged and want to know what you can do about it, below are a few recommendations. If you are not computer savvy—link with someone who is proficient at doing online searches. Web site addresses listed throughout this book must be entered exactly as listed—or type web addresses into the *Bing* search box, and it will get you close to the web site destination. Make sure you have a reliable security system on your computer such as VIPRE. Join other patriots and become a *proactive* citizen.

- ☑ Pray for guidance and wisdom, connect and fellowship with other like-minded Christians, and pray for our leaders.[349]
- ☑ Get your own house in order and take personal responsibility for the health, wealth, and welfare of yourself, your family, and/or your business, and don't expect Uncle Sam to bail you out.
- ☑ Save and store essentials for a rainy day.
- ☑ Be entrepreneurial and start your own business venture. Stop expecting the government to create jobs—all this accomplishes is growing government and not the economy, thus turning America into one large workforce and killing her entrepreneurial and inventive spirit. Do you really want a bunch of bureaucrats and wanna-be kings picking winners and losers in the jobs market?
- ☑ Be cautious about providing private information about you or your family's health and mental condition and refuse to answer invasive questions that are none of anyone's business.[350]
- ☑ Be focused- pick one or two areas that you are passionate about, become an expert, and concentrate your energies and actions to maximize effec-

tiveness and avoid spreading yourself too thin. Resist being manipulated, co-opted or centralized.

☑ Be aware of what is going on at the State and National level (use reliable news sources such as www.foxnews.com, OneNewsNow.com, www.wnd.com, or GBTV-The Blaze). Other sources regarding issues:
  → Heritage Foundation at www.heritage.org- access their Fact Sheets, Foundry.org, and Heritage Action
  → Eagle Forum- www.eagleforum.org/alert/bills/
  → Govtrack.com
  → InsiderOnline.org

☑ Shine the light on government secrecy in a way that does not jeopardize national security. Follow the money and discover the connections—assess the motive and power behind government programs and actions.

☑ Encourage elected representatives to decrease welfare dependency by supporting more welfare to work programs that actually work:
  → http://www.heritage.org/research/testimony/effective-work-programs

☑ Be pro-active at the local level. Attend town hall meetings, citizen's groups, budget and city/county council meetings, school board meetings, and any other government meeting open to citizens and speak up when appropriate.

☑ Be informed about local issues with organizations such as:
  → American Legislative Exchange Council- www.alec.org
  → State Policy Network- www.spn.org
  → Do an internet search of your city or county to see if there is an official web site that keeps citizens informed
  → Local newspapers and community publications (learn to read between the lines, detect bias, and research for yourself)

☑ Know your *Constitutional* rights and peacefully resist any violation of those rights (refuse to fill out surveys that ask for information not required by the constitution—the only information required by the constitution is name, age, and family position such as head of household, wife, children).

☑ When rights of American citizens are violated, persistently shout it from the rooftop—write editorials, use the media, the internet, and any other form of communication to inform people of any violation of our constitutional rights.

☑ Refuse to allow your children to be subjected to data mining in the public school system—be their front and rear guard and stand up for their rights to privacy, freedom of speech, and other constitutional rights, and teach children what their constitutional rights are so that they can ask for your help when their rights are violated

☑ Contact your elected representatives and respectfully state your grievances and encourage them to hold Congressional hearings and investigations into violators of your constitutional rights. Attend congressional hearings pertaining to your area of concern, and if you have evidence or pertinent information bearing on the case, be bold, speak out, and maintain peaceful and proper order at those hearings.

☑ Require a regular review of all major programs and encourage elected representatives to defund and dismantle any government agency that violates the *Constitution*, does not work to secure the safety and welfare of its citizens, or has become counterproductive, no longer necessary, or morphed into a rogue power.

☑ Respectfully demand that powers and responsibilities that rightfully belong to the States be transferred back to the States.

"The heads of rogue states are here."

Figure 51: Justice Department Loons' idea of social justice

☑ Object to unconstitutional federal laws and oppressive regulations, and demand that they be changed, defunded, repealed, challenged in the courts, and/or if necessary, amended in the *Constitution*.

☑ Stay informed about House and Senate bills coming up for votes and let your representatives know whether you support or oppose a bill. **Sign up with the following web site to stay informed and express your support or opposition: https://www.popvox.com/** (this is a Heritage Foundation web site).

☑ Link with others who have similar concerns and grievances that you do; organize and plan your strategy of action and swing into action (three holding a sign is better than one). Connect and work with non-violent groups that champion restoration and preservation of constitutional liberties such as the Tea Party.

☑ Require elected representatives to restore checks and balances between the Executive, Legislative, and Judicial branches of government.

☑ Respectfully demand that Congress override Executive Orders granting authority to a President that exceeds what is specified in the *Constitution* and/or threatens the rights and liberties of American citizens.

☑ Petition your elected representative to simplify and reduce Federal taxes, and repeal the 2010 healthcare tax law (www.FairTax.org)

Figure 52: IRS agent trying to explain three million-word plus Federal Tax Code and the 2010 Healthcare Tax Bill

Figure 53: Taxpayer's response to IRS agent's explanation

☑ Respectfully demand a balanced Federal budget and that 'earmarks and unrelated amendments to bills be stopped; require elected representatives to roll back overreaching government intervention, void unnecessary regulations, end automatic funding, and conduct aggressive oversight on how laws are carried out and how money is disbursed and spent.'[351] Here is a resource on how to *follow the money*:

→ http://www.followthemoney.org/

183

☑ Be alert and don't fall for a politician's empty promise and bag of tricks. Hold elected representatives accountable when they do not honor their oath to uphold the *Constitution* and defend the unalienable rights of Americans—vote the bums out and replace them with representatives who will limit government and repeal unconstitutional laws.

Figures 54: Politician promising voters 'to fundamentally transform America, meet all of your needs and wants, and not raise your taxes,' while thinking another thing

☑ Petition your elected officials to recall elected judges who refuse to stay within the boundaries of their duty, and who insist on legislating from the bench. Judges should uphold and abide by the Constitution. If need be in the case of activist judges who are legislating from the bench, request that they be impeached for not upholding and defending the *Constitution*. When judges overturn ballot initiatives that the people have voted on, judges are legislating from the bench and usurping the will of the people. Nineteen states permit recall of elected state officials, and twenty-nine permit recall of local officials.
  → http://www.ncsl.org/legislatures-elections/elections/recall-of-state-officials.aspx

184

→ http://en.wikipedia.org/wiki/Impeachment_investigations_of_United_S tates_federal_judges

☑ Be persistent and boldly speak the truth, exercise compassion, and walk out integrity until *extremist loons* and fence sitters either give up or decide to do what is right.

☑ Stop consenting to whatever the government wants to do, and don't let them turn you and your family into bobble-heads via the Delphi technique and welfare codependents. In working with socialist progressives, re-member that compromise is not an option, because it will always be more favorable toward the socialist agenda.

☑ Respectfully demand that your representatives not pass any bills they have not read and understood; require that they be extra cautious of house and senate bills longer than a hundred pages, and block any attempt to rush bills through the process without due consideration by "we the people" and our elected representatives.

Figure 55: Progressive strategy for getting bills passed without the consent of the people (2010 healthcare tax bill, for example)

185

☑ Become a local/county/state textbook reviewer and demand the use of textbooks that are not slanted in favor of socialism or any other anti-American ideology and that content be of high quality and based on truth. Write a textbook in your field of expertise or start your own publishing company to provide quality textbooks for our young people.

☑ If a local school system launches a PR campaign announcing their success, then do your homework and follow the money (i.e., where did they get their funding, where did the money go after it was awarded, and did you see your school taxes increase shortly before, during, or after the announced success).

☑ Be aware of what is going on in your neighborhood. If you are part of a Homeowner's Association or pay dues to an HOA, stand strong against being co-opted by city or county managers and Regional Urban Planners and herded into agreement with increased taxes and/or agendas that violate your property and privacy rights. Some zoning laws and rules are necessary to protect property owners, the value of their property, and the health of the community; however, anything beyond what is necessary should not be tolerated.

☑ Act locally- many organizations have already been successfully penetrated and leadership positions filled by Progressives, Muslim Brotherhood advocates and their supporters, and other anti-American, anti-Constitution groups. Concentrate efforts on the local level first. Locate strong, non-compromising conservative leaders who have a clean background and record and help them fill positions locally and nationally.

☑ Be willing to serve on school boards, city councils, county commissions, state and national leadership, and civic organizations.

☑ Remain vigilant about staying current and informed about local, state and national laws, regulations, codes, and zoning laws proposed, and then speak out and communicate with representatives and leaders when there appears to be a subversion of the law of the land and individual rights as outlined in the Constitution. Go to "Take Action" tab to let your voice be heard (remember to enter your zip code so that your Congressman and Senators know where you stand on each issue):
  → http://heritageaction.com/

☑ Keep an eye on the UN and petition your elected representatives to vote against any UN treaty that violates US sovereignty and our constitutional liberties, and encourage them to defund UN programs that give aid to our enemies and those nations that violate the unalienable rights of human beings. Read the following for UN's vision for Global Governance:
  → http://americanpolicy.org/wp-content/uploads/2011/05/
    Commonism.pdf

☑ Work diligently to keep AGENDA 21 programs, initiative, and NGOs out of your local city, county, and state laws and regulations.[352] Monitor NGOs that serve as the brain trust behind local, state and national leadership: such as the Council on Foreign Relations (CFR)—understand their connection with the UN and interconnections of persons. Also, for a list of UN accredited NGOs, retrieve the following information on how to root out AGENDA 21 initiatives at the local and state level:

→ http://www.sovereignty.net/p/ngo/ngomenu.htm
→ Henry Lamb, *The Rise of Global Governance* (Sovereignty International): http://www.sovereignty.net/store/gg-promo.html
→ Land use restrictions: http://www.sovereignty.net/p/land/index.html
→ http://americanpolicy.org/wp-content/uploads/2011/05/ICLEI-special-report-sust-develop.pdf
→ http://americanpolicy.org/kit/
→ http://americanpolicy.org/category/sustainable-development/
→ http://sovereignty.net/store/confront-A21-buy.html

☑ If necessary, seek legal help and reliable counsel when constitutional rights are violated. Consult battle-tested organizations such as the following:

→ Liberty Counsel- http://www.libertycounsel.org/
→ American Center for Law and Justice- http://aclj.org/

☑ Support and campaign for candidates with strong character, courage, morals and ethics. During the election season, work as a precinct volunteer and keep the voting system honest.

☑ Support and patronize small business:

→ http://www.markdown.com/shops

☑ New comers and other legal immigrants- re-examine why you came to America. If you came to America to be free, it is no longer expedient for you to sit on the sidelines and remain uninvolved in voting and other civic matters. Get informed and learn what it means to be a true American citizen and join us in this struggle to preserve our liberties.

For a more comprehensive understanding of the official law of the land as originally intended, review Chapters 1-3 and the resources listed in each chapter's *Dig Deeper* section. In addition, the following will help to firm up an American citizen's foundation on the *Constitution* and its related documents pertaining to the law of the land and our *unalienable rights*; these resources are appropriate for secondary school and college age students.

* www.blackstoneinstitute.org – Basic Blackstone
* Free online course: http://storiesofusa.com/free-us-constitution-course-from-hillsdale-college-starting-september-15th-2011/
* http://www.heritage.org/initiatives/first-principles
* Matthew Spalding, Edwin Meese, David Forte (2005), *The Heritage Guide to the Constitution* (Washington, DC: Regnery Publishing, Inc.).

Responsible stewards of freedom understand the difference between unalienable rights and human rights, and he or she makes a concerted effort to avoid treading on the liberties of others. By demanding *human rights* as determined by mere mortals who lack clear and stable moral and ethical values based in eternal truths and unchanging principles, we are allowing self-indulgence, lawlessness, and self-destructive behavior to rule the day . Balanced American freedom always honors the limits and boundaries of American liberties and respects the *unalienable rights* of everyone (see Appendix I).[353] *Unalienable rights* means the Creator endowed us with natural rights that cannot be justly taken away or transferred to another person or group; these *unalienable rights* include life, liberty, and the opportunity to pursue happiness.

Groups that are the greatest violators of the unalienable rights of others are *entitlement groups* or groups that demand to be classified as *entitlement groups*. Their demand is not based on justice, but is based on economics, or put another way, their desire to have taxpayers pay for poor judgments, mistakes, or the unfortunate results of immoral choices. It is a violation of taxpaying citizen's *unalienable rights* when they are forced to foot the bill out of their paycheck that does not rightfully belong to anyone else but the one who earned the money. The government is complicit by seeking ways to increase the welfare rolls by adding more entitlement groups, which continues to increase the size of government at taxpayer expense. So, American citizens need to state clearly to politicians and whiners—cut it out and stop stealing other people's money.

One of the key strategies that Socialist Progressives use to advance their agenda on a whole nation is to use women and children or races to advance their socialist causes and to gain mass acceptance for their utopian schemes. This is especially true in relation to what other nations and the UN expects of the United States and how they think American taxpayer's money should be redistributed. A prime example of this is found in the April 2011 Council on Foreign Relations (CFR) titled, "Family Planning and U. S. Foreign Policy."

Before getting into the weeds of CFR's family planning report, a brief explanation of who the CFR is needed. They were founded in 1921 as a think tank on foreign policy that originally served as advisors to Woodrow Wilson. Their main purpose was to influence and advise leaders in America regarding foreign policy, which means that they sought to redirect American policies and laws to advance and promote globalization at the expense of American sovereignty. As it turns out and with little surprise, the CFR holds no allegiance or loyalty to the American *Constitution* as originally intended, and is committed to advancing global interests over American interests at every opportunity. They wield tremendous influence over government leaders, the military and major social and economic institutions in America. CFR is the equivalent of a *shadow government*.[354]

Now back to CFR's international family planning report. As the UN's sustainable growth and development initiatives have just about worn out their welcome mat in America, CFR craftily merged these initiatives with family planning using women and babies as their new Trojan horse. As I reviewed CFR's report, I was struck by their feeble attempt to connect the dots between women, babies, sustainable development, economics, global security, and greenhouse emissions. Since I was in a meeting, I had to refrain from laughing out loud (LOL), because it took a number of mind-boggling verbal contortions to force a connection between these categories. As for the ludicrous connection between women, babies and greenhouse emissions, well, just think about how ridiculous that sounds (how much gas do babies have to emit before significantly affecting greenhouse emissions).

By page 18 of the report, I was already concluding that this was not about the welfare of women and children, but it was about money—full stop. BINGO—on page 25 of the chapter titled, "Moving Forward," point #2, there it was in bold print: **Increase U. S. funding for family planning**. In other words, CFR's international family planning report that was "made possible by the generous support of the United Nations Foundation," concluded that American taxpayer wealth needed to be

189

redistributed to countries that the CFR and UN deemed as worthy recipients. Why? So they can control American dollars by creating an international *entitlement group* and further centralize the UN's power base.[355] Abstinence is a whole lot cheaper (nickels and closed zippers work just fine), but then that wouldn't give *extremist loons* an excuse to steal other people's money to control another group of people so they can feel superior and powerful.

Ladies, here is a news flash—US and UN feminists, Planned Parenthood, and NOW do not have you and your children's best interest at heart. Wake up, shed victim mentality, take your rightful and honorable place with dignity as WOMEN, WIVES, MOTHERS, and ENTREPRENEURS, and refuse to allow yourselves and your daughters to be used as political pawns of *extremist loons*. Men, get your moral and ethical house in order, and stand boldly as MIGHTY MEN OF VALOR in the face of *loons* and tell them to keep their greedy paws out of your family treasury and stop using your wives and children in their nefarious schemes to enslave others.

Responsible stewards of freedom take the time and effort to do their own vetting of candidates and use sound judgment in their decision-making process. We all need to stop and ask ourselves, "Are my voting decisions based on a candidate's popularity, good looks, media news and ads, political pundits, promises to advance an issue to which I am partial, or Hollywood picks, or do I do my own research and set aside my personal agenda to make informed adult choices?" In 1876, President James A. Garfield issued a warning widely reported in the press at that time. He said:

> "Now, more than ever before, the people are responsible for the character of their Congress. If that body be ignorant, reckless, and corrupt, it is because the people tolerate ignorance, recklessness, and corruption. If it be intelligent, brave, and pure, it is because the people demand these high qualities to represent them in the national legislature."[356]

In 1832, Noah Webster stated in his American public school textbook, *History of the United States*:

> "When you become entitled to exercise the right of voting for public officers, let it be impressed on your mind that God commands you to choose for rulers, 'just men who will rule in the fear of God.' The

190

preservation of [our] government depends on the faithful discharge of this duty; if the citizens neglect their duty and place unprincipled men in office, the government will soon be corrupted; laws will be made, not for the public good so much as for selfish or local purposes; corrupt or incompetent men will be appointed to execute the laws; the public revenues will be squandered on unworthy men; and the rights of the citizens will be violated or disregarded."[357]

For a season, Americans heeded Webster's exhortation, but when the socialists took over America's public education system, the importance of principled leadership and the fear of God were excommunicated from the heart of America's youth. Now, 180 years later, we are overrun with unprincipled men and women in our leadership who will do anything to be elected or re-elected and who hold no allegiance to America's *Constitution*, God, or to the American people, and maintain the audacious attitude that they are above the law.

This decade of election cycles will be our last chance to right the course of American leadership by supporting existing principled leadership and voting out the rift raft and criminals. It is our last opportunity to clean House and seal the cracks by voting in new courageous leaders who have the integrity and fortitude of mind to do what is right in the sight of God and honor the oath of office to uphold the *Constitution* as was originally intended.

We can no longer rely on the media and national political parties to vet candidates for public office. Because we have essentially ended up with a one party system, that is, there is not much difference between today's Republicans, Democrats and Independents, you and I must take the initiative to do our own vetting. In the process of vetting, we can continue the 2010 election momentum by purging political parties of socialists and those who don't have the courage to stand firm and do what is right according to the *Constitution*.

"We the people" also have an historical opportunity to restore the Republican Party to its rightful place as the conservative party that stands on unchanging principles, honors its oath to uphold the rule of law, and refuses to pander to anti-American and self-centered corporate lobbyists and entitlement groups. It is past time to unseat all of the political, self-serving moneychangers from their high places and vote in uncompromising men and women of good and moral character who have the integrity and courage to champion truth at every turn and conduct themselves with honor and virtue. American citizen—the ball is now in our court, so let's roll up our sleeves and do the hard work of vetting political candidates and voting.

Instead of...

Pray, Be Proactive and...

Here is a checklist to get us started with the vetting process (you may add a few of your own items to this list):

☐ Do an internet or library search of candidate's name and gather as much information as possible about candidate's background, performances over time at debates, fund-raisers, rallies, and unrehearsed interviews and note the following:
  ▪ Personal character and virtue
  ▪ Any indications of manic depression, egotism, arrogance, compulsive lying, paranoia, delusions of grandeur, compulsion to control everyone and everything (all characteristics of a tyrannical personality)[358]
  ▪ Worldview or ideological leanings (beliefs and ideas influence decisions and actions)

- Position on moral and ethical issues, and if there is involvement in any illegal, immoral, or unethical activity
- Birthplace, residency, education, and work background
- Organizations to which he or she belongs
- Possible conflicts of interest
- Whether they support Israel
- What their positions are on UN treaties
- Social, religious, family, and community associations
- Political and/or governmental connections
- Decisions he or she made or opinions held about policies affecting Americans
- View State Sovereignty, American Sovereignty, and globalization
- How does candidate handles finances (sometimes IRS Income and/or Business Tax forms for major candidates are made public)
- Is candidate connected to a socialist, progressive, or jihadist group:
  - http://discoverthenetworks.org/
  - http://www.thegatewaypundit.com/2010/08/american-socialists-release-names-of-70-congressional-democrats-in-their-caucus/
  - http://en.wikipedia.org/wiki/Congressional_Progressive_Caucus
- Conduct and practices in the public and/or private sector
- Substance (does candidate demonstrate depth, logical thinking skills, and a strong moral compass that is founded in unchanging principles)
- Candidate's ability to articulate position on various issues (does candidate skirt the issues with vague responses or does candidate give clear, concise and logical responses)
- Level of support for domestic families and small businesses
- Stance on big government vs. small government
- Commitment to uphold the *Constitution* as originally intended
- Level of commitment to state and national security and sovereignty

☐ If candidate has held office, or is holding office, what is candidate's voting record, or, in the case of judges, what was candidates' decision on specific cases. Some voting records are available at:
- http://votesmart.org/
- http://www.govtrack.us
- City, county, and state elections office (a significant number of local governments have accessible web sites)

☐ Do an internet search for candidate's Campaign Disclosure Reports that candidates and elected officials are required to file and find out:
- Who candidate's major donors were to determine to whom the candidate or public official is potentially obligated such as big business, land

developers, unions, Hollywood celebrities, foreign power players, or other public officials are major supporters
- Is candidate a plant in your district from outsiders—check it out at: http://www.followthemoney.org/pvs/index.phtml?State=GA&c=0&CType=S&Committee=9759&Sector=0
☐ Throughout the election season, periodically check credible vetting websites such as: www.eagleforum.org/election/endorse.html
☐ Conduct your own interview with candidates and public officials by phone, email, or by personal appointment
☐ Determine if the words of a candidate or politician reveal party line lingo or if they truly are committed to following through and standing on principles when making decisions about issues. If candidate says they are going to do something when they get in office, ask HOW they specifically plan to accomplish their goal.
☐ Other information about vetting candidates, including scorecards on candidates and elected officials by organizations:
  - http://votesmart.org/
  - http://precinctproject.us/2011/04/vetting-candidates/
  - http://www.ehow.com/info_7827023_typical-vetting-questions-politician.html
  - http://www.cc.org/webform/congressional_scorecards (lists Congressional and Senate Scorecards)
  - http://voices.yahoo.com/the-importance-properly-vetting-political-candidates-10901265.html
  - http://www.columbian.com/news/2010/may/10/candidates-we-the-people-vancouver/
  - http://www.truthandpolitics.org/congress-scorecards.php
  - http://www.columbian.com/news/2010/may/10/candidates-we-the-people-vancouver/
  - http://www.plannedparenthoodaction.org/elections-politics/2010-elections-map.htm# (will show whether candidate is pro-life or pro-choice; thumbs down means they are pro-life)
☐ *Follow the money*- find out who, if anyone, is the financial power behind a candidate; this is important because it will affect how current and potential leaders vote. Start with the following resources to get up to speed on how to do this:
  - http://palinpromotions.blogspot.com/2011/12/how-to-vet-candidates-financial-records.html
  - http://www.followthemoney.org/
  - http://www.opensecrets.org/

- http://www.followthemoney.org/database/independentspending.pht ml
- http://www.followthemoney.org/database/IndustryTotals.phtml
- http://www.followthemoney.org/database/graphs/lobbyistlink/index. phtml
- http://www.followthemoney.org/database/top10000.phtml (this is a very revealing list of top campaign contributors—with the National Education Association union at the top followed by other union groups). Question: do we really want unions choosing our candidates?
- http://www.mrc.org/special-reports/special-report-george-soros-godfather-left

☐ Share what you learn on social media and blog sites and build your social network (such as your own personal web information, blog site or on Facebook)—be respectful and honest, and avoid spreading unfounded rumors. Back up what you share with evidence and primary sources.

You may have noticed that throughout this chapter I mentioned having a strong *character* and *moral compass* as important attributes for leadership. The reason is simple: leaders are easily manipulated and bought off by political or corporate power players when leaders have a dicey and indiscreet past (apart from brief moments of poor judgment), and do not have integrity and a moral compass to which they adhere. Even though the polls show that Americans will tolerate indiscretions and iffy character in candidates as long as candidates do what the people want, accepting less than the best tends to come back and haunt us. When a candidate or leader does not have the internal strength and security to stand for what is right and just according to the law of the land, American citizens literally pay for the compromise. It is time that "we the people" elect true *Statesmen* instead of settling for self-serving gophers. John Adams (1772) gave us a clear distinction between a statesman and a politician when he wrote in his diary that 'a politician will compromise to advance, but a true statesman will not compromise principles regardless of the cost.'[359]

This brings us full circle back to the original founding principles of this great nation. Until we restore America's Spirit of Liberty as established in the unchanging principles framed by God and contained within our *Constitution* and *Declaration of Independence*, we cannot hope to restore sanity. So let's dig deeper into restoring the Spirit of Liberty Tree in the next chapter.

195

21st Century Truth or Consequence Question: Am I willing to risk the liberties of my family for fleeting moments of pleasure, or am I ready to get in the trenches with other patriots and do the hard work of restoring and preserving our unalienable rights to life, liberty, and the opportunity to pursue happiness?

Whatever you do, PRAY and...

DON'T **EVER** GIVE UP!

Dig Deeper

1. Timothy Daughtry & Gary Castleman (2012), *Waking a Sleeping Giant* (New York, NY: Beaufort Books).
2. Edwin Feulner, Jr. (ed., 2000), *Leadership for America* (Dallas, TX: Spence Publishing Co.).
3. Edwin Black (2011), *IBM and the Holocaust* (Washington, DC: Dialog Press).
4. John Whitehead, *Freedom Wars* (Charlottesville, VA: Tri Press; Glass Onion Production [2010]).
5. David Barton (2003), *Restraining Judicial Activism* (Aledo, TX: WallBuilder Press).
6. David Barton (2000), *Keys to Good Government* (Aledo, TX: Wallbuilder Press).
7. Movie: *Mr. Smith Goes to Washington* (1939) (Columbia Classics).

CHAPTER 13
RESTORING THE SPIRIT OF LIBERTY TREE

"Blessed is the nation whose God is the LORD..."[360]

Let's pause for a moment and reflect on what really makes America unique and great. There is little doubt for people of sound mind that the American *Constitution* as originally intended played a significant role in securing a peaceful and free existence for individuals and families, and in facilitating equal opportunity to exercise individual ingenuity and entrepreneurship, thus paving the way for prosperity. Being disenchanted with the failure of socialism to follow through on its promises to provide for everyone's needs *and* wants, many Americans are re-acquainting themselves with the fact that there has been an unseen, yet tangible force behind securing, maintaining, and preserving liberty, thereby making prosperity a reality for those who sacrifice and invest personal sweat equity.

At age 14, I was hoeing weeds out of the family vegetable garden in Georgia one day, and I paused for a moment. As I surveyed the beauty of the trees gently pressed against the blue morning sky while nature's critters serenaded me, I realized that there could be only one explanation for this splendor of nature. There had to be Someone bigger and more powerful than anyone or anything who created all of what I surveyed. So who was this unseen, yet tangible force?

In the beginning of my faith journey, no one needed to tell me about the Creator of heaven and earth. There was already the *Law of Nature and Natural Order* written in my heart (or conscience) that witnessed to the fact that the universe, this world, nature, and humanity was not an accident, but was the intentional act of a loving Creator who designed, created, and put in order and motion all that was and is. I knew of no person, rock, star, pool of ooze, or amoeba capable of such an enormous undertaking, and it could not have been the result of an explosion, because with explosions, only death, destruction, and chaos exist. Even if part of creation was the result of an explosion, there had to be a Supreme Being capable of bringing order out of the explosion's chaos.

In response to the wonder of His creation, I sang "Oh What a Beautiful Morning," which was a song from the movie, *Oklahoma*. I had not yet learned any religious songs, so I offered up the one song that best expressed my appreciation and thanks to the One who put it all together and allowed me to be a small part of His creation. To this day, I continue to enjoy the wonder of His creative works. Here's a challenge: Try to explain how any of the following wonders of nature could have been an accident.

361

362

363

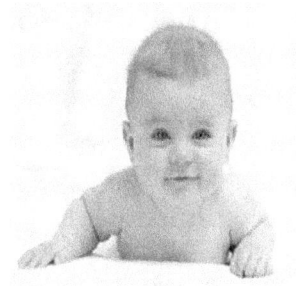

364   365

Each single human cell is a "complex structure that is…more compli-cated than a computer. The smallest of cells is composed of over fifty billion atoms arranged into one hundred different proteins, together with the staggering amount of information encoded in the DNA and RNA that govern its activities, nutrition, repair, and replication…" and "it takes all of the above to function."[366]

The human brain contains over fifty billion communication cells called neurons, three hundred billion glial, and a thousand synapses. Com-munication "amongst its billions of neurons" takes place instantly, and the "brain can store and manipulate almost infinite amounts of data."[367] "In less than a second, your brain can calculate the trajectory of a foot-ball thrown at thirty miles an hour toward you without warning."[368]

Sir Fred Hoyle, an English astronomer, wrote, "The chance that higher life forms might have emerged" through evolutionary means "is comparable with the chance that a tornado sweeping through a junk-yard might assemble a Boeing 747 from the materials therein."[369] The universe, this world, nature, and human life speak of Intelligent Design, purpose, and the work of a Supreme Being Who possesses power be-yond human comprehension or ability: "…since the creation of the world His invisible *attributes* are clearly seen, being understood by the things that are made, *even* His eternal power and Godhead so that they are without excuse."[370]

The Supreme Ruler of the Universe, Maker of Heaven and Earth speaks of God as being transcendent, that is over, above, and apart from His creation. However, He chooses to interact with creation by the power of His Spirit who works to synchronize and harmonize all of creation's dynamic moving parts. In the first five days of creation, God had set the stage for His final act of creation, which was to create man in His own image, which was described poetically in the last two verses of James Weldon Johnson's poem (1922), *The Creation*:

> "Up from the bed of the river
> God scooped the clay;
> And by the bank of the river
> He kneeled Him down;
> And there the great God Almighty
> Who lit the sun and fixed it in the sky,
> Who flung the stars to the most far corner of the night,
> Who rounded the earth in the middle of His hand;
> This Great God,
> Like a mammy bending over her baby,
> Kneeled down in the dust
> Toiling over a lump of clay
> Till He shaped it in His own image;
> Then into it He blew the breath of life,
> And man became a living soul."[371]

God made man in His own image, and when He breathed into man the *breath of life*, God exhibited His desire and intent to be in relationship with humanity, and to assign value and dignity to each individual person regardless of a person's stage of development before or after birth. God took this relationship with humanity further--after finishing His masterpiece, God did not abandon mankind, but chose to remain near and accessible.

> "God, who made the world and everything in it, since He is Lord of heaven and earth, does not dwell in temples made with hands. Nor is He worshiped with men's hands, as though He needed anything, since He gives to all life, breath, and all things. And He has made from one blood every nation of men to dwell on all the face of the earth, and has determined their pre-appointed times and the boundaries of their dwellings, so that they should seek the Lord, in the hope that they might grope for Him and find Him, though He is not far from each one of us; for in Him we live and move and have our being, as also some of your own poets have said, 'For we are also His offspring.'"[372]

> "For You formed my inward parts; You covered me in my mother's womb. I will praise You, for I am fearfully *and* wonderfully made; Marvelous are Your works, And *that* my soul knows very well. My

frame was not hidden from You, when I was made in secret, *and* skillfully wrought in the lowest parts of the earth. Your eyes saw my substance, being yet unformed. And in Your book they all were written, the days fashioned for me, when *as yet there were* none of them. How precious also are Your thoughts to me, O God! How great is the sum of them! *If* I should count them, they would be more in number than the sand; When I awake, I am still with You."[373]

"…they shall call his name Immanuel, which is translated, 'God with us.'"[374]

When we spend so much energy avoiding God and rejecting His guidance and will, it is a contradiction of our human spirit's nature that God has fashioned and by which God sustains us. C. S. Lewis expressed this tendency well when he shared his experience of, "the steady unrelenting approach of Him whom I so earnestly desired not to meet."[375]

During my lifelong faith journey and research, I can unreservedly state that there is a distinct difference between the God of the Bible and the essences and beings of other religions. None of the other religions offer to everyone, including *extremist loons,* a loving, personal relationship with a Supreme Being plus the added blessings of joy, lasting security, and a way to peace during dark and tragic times. Instead, other religions invoke fear or passivity, treat women with oppressive disrespect or cruelty require mind-numbing rituals, or even coercively demand a pound of flesh that may or may not earn a place in paradise.

In the Scriptures (Bible), God reveals Himself and communicates His desire, will, plan, and love directly to humanity. Our Creator consistently strives to be up close and personal and in touch with each person who willingly opens his or her heart to Him. After all, God demonstrated the depth of His love and mercy for us when He gave His only Son, Jesus Christ, to be our Savior, so that by faith in Christ, we could be reunited back into full fellowship with God. Apart from God and His Word, there are no other divine beings, gods, self, essences, or sacred texts that can open wide the door to such a dynamic personal, and loving relationship filled with purpose and meaning in this life or the next. Billy Graham put it this way: *"Without God, there is no point."*

Christianity has a larger percentage of adherents compared to any other single religion in the world.[376] The reason is simple: Christianity is not a crutch—it is a relationship. The Judeo-Christian God offers a living faith that meets the deepest need of the human heart; and fellowship with God is only a prayer away. Yep, that's right; no need to ring a bell five times, wave a wand, dip in a river, starve yourself, kill a chicken, lose your identity, climb a hundred steps, speak to a dead person, dance around in a frenzy, chant repetitive mantras, hug a tree, pay an entrance fee, howl at the moon, or blow yourself up. It is not my intention to be disrespectful, but let's face it—why do people make getting connected with God harder than it should be, only to discover the futility of human strivings? All that is necessary is to open our heart and mouth and speak to God, and He will answer. God is loving, forgiving, and accepting.

The Bible is the only sacred text that reveals the way of true liberty for individuals and humanity. The word *liberty* is totally absent in the Qur'an (Koran), and the word *freedom* is used only in the context of a slave earning his or her freedom or a slaves' freedom being bought by another master.

Liberty in the Hindu text, *Rig Veda*, is used three times in reference to quail and rivers but not in relation to humanity, and the path to true *freedom* is complicated and limited according to one's status within the Hindu caste system as determined by the person's previous life and current social or economic standing. The poor, or *untouchables*, have no freedom.

In Buddhism, individuals can never attain freedom or liberty in this lifetime while maintaining his or her individual identity. In other words, individuals must surrender individuality and freedom to become part of an impersonal state of being or essence (*Nirvana*) requiring multiple reincarnations until one 'gets it right.' For Buddhists, there are no endowed *unalienable rights* such as *life, liberty, and the pursuit of happiness* because mankind is, according to Buddha, without a soul having no more rights than any other life form, and life is simply cause and effect.

Now consider the following revelations and testimony from the Word of God:

202

"...I will <u>walk at liberty</u>, for I seek Your precepts."[377]

Jesus "...went into the synagogue on the Sabbath day, and stood up to read. And He was handed the book of the prophet Isaiah. And when He had opened the book, He found the place where it was written: 'The Spirit of the LORD is upon me, because He has anointed me to preach the gospel to the poor; He has sent me to heal the brokenhearted, <u>to proclaim liberty to the captives</u> and recovery of sight to the blind, <u>to set at liberty those who are oppressed</u>, to proclaim the acceptable year of the LORD.' Then He closed the book, and gave *it* back to the attendant and sat down. And the eyes of all who were in the synagogue were fixed on Him. And He began to say to them, 'Today this Scripture is fulfilled in your hearing.'"[378]

"Then Jesus said to those Jews who believed Him, 'If you abide in My word, you are My disciples indeed. And you shall know the truth, and <u>the truth shall make you free</u>...Therefore if the Son makes you free, you shall be free indeed.'"[379]

"For the law of the Spirit of life in Christ Jesus has made me free from the law of sin and death."[380]

"Now the Lord is the Spirit; and <u>where the Spirit of the Lord *is*, there *is* liberty</u>."[381]

"<u>Stand fast therefore in the liberty by which Christ has made us free</u>, and do not be entangled again with a yoke of bondage...<u>For you, brethren, have been called to liberty</u>; only <u>do not *use* liberty as an opportunity for the flesh, but through love serve one another</u>. For all the law is fulfilled in one word, *even* in this: 'You shall love your neighbor as yourself.'"[382]

"But he who looks into the perfect law of liberty and continues *in it*, and is not a forgetful hearer but a doer of the work, this one will be blessed in what he does."[383]

The benefit and blessing of being in relationship with God through Christ is liberty. As demonstrated in the previous "Stand fast..." scripture, not only did God reveal the way to liberty for you and I, He also defined its boundary and responsibility.

Equality is another blessing we have as beneficiaries of God's unconditional love and mercy. The second paragraph of the *Declaration of Independence* declares that, "We hold these truths to be self-evident, that all men are created equal." Based on transcendent truths of *nature and nature's God*, people are equal, which means that every human being has "a common human nature and the capacity for reason and liberty, but not possessing the same abilities, initiatives, and possessions."

In the world of Darwinists and humanists, humans are classified as a species of animals, and as such do not possess intrinsic value. In the Hindu caste system, there is no such thing as equality among persons, and according to Hinduism and Buddhism, human beings have no more value than a flower, animal, or rock, and as such every living and non-living thing is considered equal in value and is eventually absorbed into one great impersonal oneness. In other words, there is absolute oneness void of any creative variations (i.e., just meaningless sameness); in their view, there is nothing special or unique about being the "human animal," therefore, the value of human life is diminished, and existence is based on its usefulness to other parts of the world or State.

In numerous religions, women and female children come out on the losing end of life because they do not hold equal status with males, and are considered to be inferior and of lesser value than men. For instance, female children are aborted, killed (infanticide), or abandoned at birth in some countries such as China,[384] young women and female children in their preteens are enslaved in the sex trafficking trade, and among the Islamists, women exist to be slaves to men in this life and the next. At this point, on the behalf of humanity and as a woman, I have to pause and thank God for sending us the Great Equalizer and Redeemer, Jesus Christ. Read the following and let us reason together:

> "…He has made of one blood every nation to dwell on the earth…"[385]
> "There is neither Jew nor Greek, there is neither slave nor free, there is neither male nor female; for you are all one in Christ Jesus."[386]

> "For God so loved the world that he gave his only begotten Son, that whosoever believeth in him should not perish, but have everlasting life."[387]

God challenges each person to accept His gift of life. For those who chose to believe, the guiding principles of His word broke the chains of the human heart and mind thereby releasing humanity's full potential, and facilitating scientific, technological, and economic progress. God's mercy, grace, and love have been the driving forces behind America's uniqueness, greatness, and success, for from the beginning, "America was an act of faith"[388] and managed to survive and thrive against all odds. Following God's royal law of love, Christians have given of their lives, time and resources to aid the poor, the hungry, the homeless, the orphan, and the oppressed. For more in-depth understanding of Christianity's contributions to humanity and the stories behind America's uniqueness, read the following resources:

* ✶ Rodney Starks (2005), *Victory of Reason* (New York, NY: Random House, Inc.).
* ✶ Alvin Schmidt (2004), *How Christianity Changed the World* (Grand Rapids, MI: Zondervan Publishing House).

To spite the record of monumental achievements and contributions of Christianity over the past 100 years, and the trail of tears and devastation of anti-God and human-centered ideologies, there have been concentrated efforts to nullify and eliminate the influence of God and the Bible's unchanging principles from the public arena. These efforts have focused on assaulting freedom of religion and expression in America.

The ***first assault*** was the introduction of the socialist mandate to enforce its version of the *separation of church and state*. In 1947, the Supreme Court hijacked this phrase from Thomas Jefferson's writings and used it as a reason to limit religious expressions and influence in America's public or civic arena.[389] Again, in 1962, the Supreme Court went a step further by redefining the word "church" to mean "a public religious activity," which changed the meaning to, "public religious expressions must be kept separate from the public square."[390] The 1962 ruling has empowered anti-God forces and socialist *loons* to run rough shod over religious freedoms of Christians and Jews who dare to pray or recite biblical passages at public gatherings and events while allowing other religions free reign without interference.

But let's take a moment and throw this little red *extremist loon* caboose in reverse and consider the following facts overlooked by some and totally ignored by others:

1. The Supreme Court took Jefferson's phrase, Separation of church and state, out of context. Within the context, Jefferson never advo-

cated for a literal separation of church and state and never mentioned anything about keeping public religious expressions separate from the public square.

2. Jefferson was replying to the Danbury Baptists' concerns over the possibility that "one day the government might...wrongly believe that it did have the power to regulate public religious activities."[391]

3. Within the context of Jefferson's statement, he made it clear to the Danbury Baptists "that the 'wall of separation' was erected not to limit public religious expressions but rather to provide security against governmental interference with those expressions, whether private or public," thus affirming the original intent of the First Amendment of the *Constitution*.[392]

4. According to a Supreme Court ruling in 1878 (*Reynolds v. United States*), "The rightful purposes of civil government are for its officers to interfere [with religion only] when its principles break out into overt acts against peace and good order." Legitimate reasons to intrude would be with such religious acts as "human sacrifice," keeping a concubine, "incest, polygamy, injury to children, etc."[393]

5. The First Amendment states that, "Congress shall make no law respecting an establishment of religion or prohibiting the free exercise thereof." The phrase, *Separation of church and state,* is not in any of America's original governing documents, including the First Amendment or any other part of the *Constitution*.[394] Let's break this amendment down and review the original intent of each section:

   a. "Congress shall make no law respecting the establishment of religion..." is known as the Establishment Clause, which "prohibits the Federal government from establishing a single national denomination" or State religion.[395]

   b. "Congress shall make no law...prohibiting the free exercise thereof," is known as the Free Exercise Clause, which prohibits "the federal government from interfering with the people's public religious expressions and acknowledgements."[396]

The Founding Fathers fully intended for faith to have a central place in the private heart and public arena of America as expressed in George Washington's *Farewell Address,* when he stated:

"Of all the disposition and habits which lead to political prosperity, religion and morality are indispensable [inseparable] supports. In vain would that men claim the tribute of patriotism, who should labor to subvert these great pillars of human happiness—these firmest props of the duties of men and citizens. The mere politician, equally with the pious man, ought to respect and to cherish them."[397]

When faith and morality were excommunicated from the public arena in the early 1960s, teenage pregnancies increased by 700 percent, sexually transmitted diseases soared significantly, and public morality took a nosedive.[398] This is too high a price to pay for unrestrained, unprincipled freedom that lacks a stable moral compass.

The **second assault** was the criminalization of any communication, expression of thought, or action labeled as *intolerance*, which includes expressing or exercising a preference of one religious belief over another or making a distinction between religious belief systems.[399] The United Nations has set itself up as the enforcement agency to ensure everyone in the world complies, including the United States. The question is, will Americans rise up and peacefully protest and block any attempt to put American citizens under the ruling authority of the UN. To maintain freedom of religion in America, we are obligated to be vigilant and speak out against any attempts to subvert our constitutionally guaranteed liberties.

By now, there may be a nagging question burning in some people's mind, which is, "Why are *extremist loons* working so hard to eliminate or nullify Christianity and its influence from the public arena?" The answer is simple: God and His moral compass are the only things standing in the way of the utopian dreams of narcissistic nut cases seeking a seat at totalitarianism's head table and wanting the unrestrained freedom to act like barbarians. *Extremist loons* think they can become king of the world by equalizing everyone in the world.

It doesn't take a genius to understand the consequences of allowing self-centered, amoral, inhumane, and godless persons to occupy positions of power and influence, and consequences of continuing to install leaders who lack strong character, courage, and a fixed moral compass to guide their decisions and actions. The legacy of horrors left by Hitler, Marx, Lenin, Stalin, Mao Tse-tung, Sadam Hussein and other tyrannical nut cases is self-evident. The fact that the 20th century was the bloodiest time of human history should be a dead give-away regarding the utter failure of the reign of *self* on the throne of humanity and allowing moral ambivalence to be the rule of law. Our children today are reaping the consequences and cost of self-centeredness and excommunication of God from the Public Square and soul of America's youth.

Based on freedom of conscience and religion as guaranteed by our *Constitution,* I support a person's right to embrace whatever worldview or ideology he or she so chooses and to express those views freely. However, I draw the line at where worldviews are forced on Americans by enactment of laws, regulations, policies, coercion, and compulsory education that violate the moral conscience and liberties of those who embrace a different worldview.

Can Americans continue to tolerate and court anti-God, self-centered, and anti-human worldviews as *guiding standards* for our nation and families, knowing that such worldviews eventually digress into tyranny or totalitarianism? Bringing it closer to home, is destruction, death, starvation, slavery, and poverty the fate we want our families to suffer and the legacy we want to leave for our children and grandchildren? If your answer is "NO" to both questions, then we have no other choice but to restore the Spirit of Liberty Tree in America review page 18 and the foundation of its moral compass, the Scriptures, and stop pandering to Socialists, Progressives, Secular Humanists, Atheists, Darwinists, Pantheists, and any other self-centered ideologists.

Please don't panic. I am not suggesting we make Christianity a State religion, or passively go along with the creation of a centralized world religion. Based on past and current history, we have enough evidence to demonstrate the dangers of this. In a number of Islam's jihadist acts of genocide and mass suicide bombings, we have witnessed the Armageddon of religious extremism when a specific religion rises to the status of "State" religion and when world dominion becomes the central focus of that religion. No human being or religious group can handle unrestrained power resulting from a theocratic-type State or nation ('absolute power corrupts absolutely').

We also do not need to swing the pendulum to the opposite extreme by eliminating God and His timeless revelation from the Public Square. Granted, we cannot, for one moment, excuse past crimes perpetrated against humanity and allegedly committed in the name of God. However, *it is a mistake to attribute to God what a person willfully devised in his or her own mind apart from God's will and natural law.* Upon closer examination of historical records, unlawful and inhumane acts committed by religious zealots were the result of egocentric maniacs exalting his or her self as a god while forcing other members of their group to worship and serve them, and, in some cases, leading them toward mass suicide (Jim Jones and the Jonestown Massacre in Guyana is one example). This type personality is no different from other narcissistic megalomaniacs such as Hitler. The point is, there was never any evidence of God's grace and mercy in operation in such cases—just mad men acting out personal fantasies and delusions of grandeur and doing the bidding of demons.

One final question: If not the unchanging principles of the Bible, then what alternate moral and ethical system should we embrace as our moral compass, and will that alternate system endure, can it guarantee the greatest degree of liberty for individuals and families, and will it secure our safety as a sovereign nation? The only worldview that has the power to preserve a nation for the long-term, and has secured for Americans the greatest measure of liberty is the *Judeo-Christian* worldview as framed by God's direct revelation, the Bible. Therefore, "It is extremely important to our nation, in a political as well as religious view, that all possible...influence should be given to the Scriptures; for these furnish the best principles of civil liberty, and the most effectual support of republican government."[400]

The point is this: Societies who freely accept the redeeming work of Christ, the power of His Spirit, and His revealed truth have reaped healing, wholeness, liberty, sanity, civility, and stability. After extensive study and careful consideration, the Founding Fathers understood that in order to secure and preserve liberty for the long term, the unchanging principles of the Scriptures needed to be the main moral compass of individuals and the guiding standard for the rule of law and civil order in America. The capacity of a people to govern themselves is determined by the strength and stability of their character and principles. Listen to the voices of the past and present:

"The general principles on which the fathers achieved independence were...the general principles of Christianity...Our Constitution was made **only** for a moral and religious people. It is wholly inadequate to the government of any other."- John Adams, Second President of the United States[401]

"...reason and experience forbid us to expect that national morality can prevail in exclusion of religious principle."[402]- George Washington, First President of the United States.

"Our citizens should early understand that the genuine source of correct republican principles is the Bible, particularly the New Testament, or the Christian religion." [403]- Noah Webster (1778-1843), educator, and author of first American English language dictionary, *History of the United States*, and other textbooks.

"Men, in a word, must necessarily be controlled either by a power within them or a power without them, either by the Word of God or by the strong arm of man, either by the Bible or by the bayonet." [404]- Robert Winthrop, 1840s Speaker of the House of Representatives

"The only means of establishing and perpetuating our republican forms of government...is the...education of our youth in the principles of Christianity by means of the Bible."[405]- Benjamin Rush, signer of the *Declaration of Independence* and one of America's top educators.

"Our citizens should early understand that the genuine source of correct republican principles is the Bible, particularly the New Testament, or the Christian religion." [406]- Noah Webster (1778-1843), educator, and author of first American English language dictionary, *History of the United States*, and other textbooks.

"...belief in God has provided an absolute principle capable of grounding and integrating human values...it is the Judeo-Christian heritage which nurtures and replenishes the moral capital of our society."[407]- Guenter Lewy, 1990s professor of political science at the University of Massachusetts, and self-avowed agnostic defending the importance of Christianity to American society.

On Thursday, May 27, 1999, Darrell Scott, the father of Rachel Scott who was killed in the Columbine High School shootings in Littleton, Colorado, was invited to address the House Judiciary Committee's subcommittee. During that address, he read a poem he wrote:

> Your laws ignore our deepest needs,
> Your words are empty air.
> You've stripped away our heritage,

You've outlawed simple prayer.
Now gunshots fill our classrooms,
And precious children die.
You seek for answers everywhere,
And ask the question "Why?"
You regulate restrictive laws,
Through legislative creed.
And yet you fail to understand,
That God is what we need!

The next generation will reap what we have sown in our lifetime. Therefore, "We must shore up all the institutions of civil society…--families, churches, schools, and private associations--…so that they can sustain and cultivate the virtues and character required for republican government."[408] Moms, Dads, Grandparents, and Mentors- you are the guardians of America's next generation, so step up to the plate, grab ahold of the helm of America's ship and get back on course with God, for He and His revealed truths are the only true source of love, joy, peace, mercy, grace, provision, and freedom.

"BLESSED IS THE NATION WHOSE GOD IS THE LORD..." [409]

↓

21ˢᵗ Century Truth or Consequence Question: Am I teaching the next generation a worldview that produces purpose and abundant life now and in the hereafter and provides a sound moral and ethical foundation as defined by God that is consistent, stable, enduring and best supports and preserves their liberty?

Dig Deeper

1. Jerry Newcomb (2009), *The Book that Made America* (Ventura, CA: Nordskog Publishing).
2. David Barton (2007), *Separation of Church and State* (Aledo, TX: WallBuilder Press).

3. Robert Spencer (2007), *Religion of Peace: Why Christianity Is and Islam Isn't* (Washington, DC: Regnery Publishing, Inc.).
4. Dinesh D'Souza (2007), *What's so Great about Christianity* (Washington, DC: Regnery Publishing, Inc.).
5. Movie: *God's Outlaw: The Story of William Tyndale* (Vision Video: DVD, 2004).
6. Eric Metaxas (2010), *Bonhoeffer: Pastor, Martyr, Prophet, Spy* (Nashville, TN: Thomas Nelson).

APPENDIXES

APPENDIX A
Christian Socialism's Terminology

Collective salvation- voids the biblical doctrine of individual salvation through repentance and accepting Jesus Christ as one's Savior which comes by God's grace and not by human works, and substitutes it with a human-works salvation whereby each person's salvation depends on collective salvation (i.e., I cannot be saved unless I help save everyone else first).[410]

Ecumenism- is a movement seeking cultural, political and religious unity (i.e., One World Church) whereby all religions are considered valid and true, and ultimately evolving into a Socialist version of an earthly kingdom of God, emphasizing social justice and conformity to a unified worldview.[411] (See notes.)[412]

Liberal theology- (Postmodernism; Progressive theology) does not believe in absolute truth, but that each person constructs his or her own truth; advocates secular humanism, believes that all truth, values and religious beliefs are relative and equal, and its theology is fluid and shifts to whatever is trending politically and culturally at the time; its major emphasis is the social gospel.[413]

Liberation theology- is a humanistic secular gospel that melds scriptures with social and political ideology and emphasizes human solidarity with the poor and oppressed. As a product of historical social crisis, it requires the use of revisionary history and advocates revolutionary change by any means necessary; protests against poverty; seeks to equalize human conditions for everyone much in the same way as socialism does.[414]

Pluralism- rejects absolute truth, therefore, all religions are valid paths to salvation because they are based on subjective reasoning (i.e., truth is whatever each individual says it is, and everyone's truth has intrinsic value).

Social gospel- (Christian socialism) is defined by whatever social or economic crisis is occurring at the time and claims scriptural authority to justify the demand for equal wages and redistribution of wealth to solve economic problems or to provoke action regarding social injustices based on human rights of the poor at the expense of hard workers.[415] "Human rights" have evolved into human needs, desires, and demands that override the freedom of others. One prominent goal is to build an earthly 'Kingdom of God' (i.e., new world order or utopia).

Secular Humanism- believes that by nature, humanity is good and has no need for God or moral absolutes; there is no reality beyond the physical world, therefore, utopia is sought on earth; science, and human reasoning and experience determine what truth is, therefore, truth is relative.[416]

Social justice- is an equal claim to social and economic rights and power; ultimately, it requires an equal distribution of property and assets. Personal responsibility is replaced with human rights based on humanistic ideology and liberal theology. Winston Churchill describes it as '***equal sharing of misery.***'

Unitarianism- (originally 2nd century Monarchianism) is the group that formed the basis for liberal theology. They reject the Bible as God's revealed Word, deny God's transcendence and personhood and the divinity of Christ, and believe that "feelings" are a person's reality and that people are without sin and can obtain salvation without God's help. Their theology is fluid; currently, they are aligned with Eastern pantheism's New Age movement. [417]

APPENDIX B
Historical Eras & Philosophical Trends[418]

Pre-Modernity Era (Pre-1600):[419]

1) The nature of reality, values, and truth, and logic interconnect wherein:[420]
   a. God is supernatural and the First Cause and Creator of physical and spiritual realities
   b. God establishes His law (as revealed in the Bible) and the laws of nature; both are in sync with known scientific facts (not theory)
   c. Objective truth can be known; it agrees with reality; the Bible is God's self-revelation, therefore "the entirety of" His "word is truth"[421] which is inerrant and sufficient, and are expressed in statements of faith or doctrinal creeds (ex: Apostle's Creed)
   d. Values based on truth are real and objective, and are dependent on God's law and the supernatural
   e. Reconciliation and access to God is through His Son, the Lord Jesus Christ, by faith and not by human works (Judeo-Christian faith)[422]

2) Submerged in pagan, polytheistic and nature, Egyptian, Roman, Indo-European, African, and Greek religions, philosophers and religious persons devised various human-centered ideologies that were deceptive, illogical, pleasure seeking, or used as a means of controlling the masses (a majority of whom denied or opposed traditional, God-centered truth regarding reality and values). A few examples (some political philosophies are included and labeled as *pol.*):
   a. *Aristocracy*- ruling elite claiming to be best suited for ruling (*pol.*)
   b. *Atomists*- the only realities are matter, space, emptiness and atoms; there is no God, gods, or truth but in the human imagination (per Democritus)[423]
   c. *Democracy*- rule by majority; eventually digresses to anarchism or tyranny (*pol.*)
   d. *Epicureanism*- denied immortality; gods were not concerned with humanity, therefore they should not be worshipped;[424] for them, pleasure was good and pain was evil, so action bringing about the greatest pleasure for the greatest number of people was considered *right action* (i.e., *utilitarianism*)[425]
   e. *Ionians*- (first ancient Greek philosophers) belief that "might was right," were nature-centered in their worldview, believed in many gods (polytheistic), and were materialists and as such could be considered primitive scientists[426]

    f. ***Machiavellianism-*** ethics or morality were not a part of political process, and political organizations were social entities (*pol.*); Machiavelli was the first Socialist[427]

    g. ***Naturalism-*** nothing exists except time and space

    h. ***Oligarchy-*** rule by a few people, usually a select group of elites (*pol.*)

    i. ***Paganism and mysticism-*** gods or mystical beings devised by human imagination that were either of human, animal, nature (wind, fire, earth, etc.) or inanimate forms such as rocks and planets

    j. ***Pantheism-*** all is in God and God is in all

    k. ***Plato-*** truth is obtained by pure reason (*rationalism*), virtue is equated with human knowledge, and he devises an earthly political *utopia* (plutocracy) that later provided inspiration for socialism, Marxism, Communism, radical Islamism, Nazism, and Fascism[428]

    l. ***Polytheism-*** belief in many gods; the ancient Greeks regarded Christians as *atheists* because Christians and Jews did not believe in "many" gods but only believed in one God[429]

    m. ***Skepticism-*** argued against causality, agreed with relativism, truth was not obtainable, and only what was seen was real[430]

    n. ***Sophism-*** man is the measure of all things (*moral relativism* void of universal moral standards); an early form of secular humanism

    o. ***Tyranny-*** rule by one person controlling everyone else (*pol.*)

    p. ***Utopianism-*** Thomas More wrote *Utopia*, which advocates religious tolerance and works to abolish private property ownership (*pol.*)

3) In the 9th century, some medieval churches derailed from their original purpose by becoming centralized, nationalized and politicized (early signs of socialism in the church) wherein:

    a. Bible becomes a closed book to the masses because the ecclesiastical elite sought to maintain control over the people and State (Dark Ages)

    b. The gospel is diluted into a cheap salvation of works and indulgences

    c. *Nationalized* and *politicized* churches cease to function as the defenders and guardians of faith, family and freedom

4) From the 10th through the 15th, defenders of the Judeo-Christian faith rise up in opposition to the church oligarchy whereby they:

    a. Re-establish the sound teachings of God's truth, the supernatural reality of God's supremacy and His saving grace and realign faith to its proper place as coming before human understanding (Reformation)

    b. Rescue the Bible from the clutches of the church oligarchy and translate it into the people's language, thereby making scripture available to the masses (Wycliffe, Luther, and Tyndale were first translators)

Modernity Era (1600-1950):

1) Evangelical Protestant theologians maintain the interconnectivity of the nature of reality, values, and truth, and logic whereby Pre-modernity faith

traditions of Judeo-Christianity are preserved and maintained (see first point and its sub points under Pre-modern Era)[431]

2) Human-centered philosophers and theologians disconnect values and knowledge from supernatural reality, then human reasoning determines what knowledge and values are while logic aimlessly wanders between physical and psychological reality, values, and knowledge. Science and human reasoning become the source of truth and for many the Bible and God become irrelevant; first part of the Modernity Era was called the Enlightenment or Age of Reason. To discredit and dismantle traditional values and God's truth, psychological warfare is declared. The following ideologies included in this warfare:

a. *Anarchism*- belief that government is by nature oppressive; mob rule that eventually digresses into oppression of minority (*pol.*)

b. *Communitarianism*- is the philosophy that advocates the good of a community over individual liberty (Hegel)[432] (*pol.*)

c. *Critical theory*- changing society through social engineering; ideas are products of social processes; there is no **determinism**; originated at the Frankfurt School in Germany[433]

d. *Darwinism*- evolutionary theory further developed by Charles Darwin emphasizes survival of the fittest through struggle and competition, identifies humans as animal species and denies God as the Creator thereby digressing into a system that categorizes human races as inferior or superior in development and intellect.

e. *Deism*- an ideology derived from human reasoning that God created the universe but is detached from it and does not interfere or intervene in human affairs

f. *Determinism*- all events are caused by previous events or conditions; this leads to failure in taking responsibility for one's actions

g. *Dialectical or Historical Materialism*- Marxist theory of history whereby history is determined by economics and class struggle (feudalism vs. capitalism) (*pol.*); workers own means of production[434]

h. *Empiricism*- "knowledge results from sensory experience"[435]

i. *Evolution*- Lamarck theorized that an organism's desire for change caused it and its offspring to change over time[436]

j. *Existentialism*- meaning and ethics must come from individual experience; truth is subjective (Ex: 2+2=whatever you want it to equal)[437]

k. *Idealism*- ideas form the ultimate reality

l. *Logical Positivism (neo-positivism)*- a philosophy that combines Empiricism with rationalism that denies the validity of supernatural statements because they are not verifiable by observation, therefore, they are meaningless.

m. *Materialism*- only matter is real[438]

n. *Malthusianism*- Malthus merged the science of political economy with religion and advocated population control to advance society toward utopianism or the creation of a perfect society; this philosophy was used by Darwin as a basis for his natural selection theory of evolution and struggle for survival; according to Malthus, over population could be prevented by birth control, abortions, prostitution, and celibacy; he also supported the idea of eugenics; today, the Malthusian growth model is used as support for UN and Agenda 21's environmental *sustainable development or sustainable living* plans[439]

o. *Marxism/Communism*- free enterprise is abolished, and workers control means of production; private property is seized and held in common and redistributed as determined by centralized planners (*pol.*)[440]

p. *Naturalism*- argues against miracles because it cannot be explained by natural phenomena; for something to be true, it must be empirically verifiable; evolution is a naturalistic explanation of life by Spinoza, Hume, Kant, Positivists, and Darwin *and still remains unverifiable*; according to Kant, God is unknowable because His existence could not be proved scientifically or empirically[441]

q. *Nihilism*- belief in nothing; God is dead philosophy; scriptures no longer accepted as basis for morality, therefore there is no absolute truth; there is no purpose or allegiance; this leads to failure in taking responsibility for one's actions[442]

r. *Positivism*- "happiness is equated with pleasure; there is no objective good to be united with virtue;"[443] rejects supernatural and religion; August Comte is founder and coined the phrase "sociology"

s. *Pragmatism*- right or wrong is determined by its practical effects[444]

t. *Rationalism*- most reliable source of knowledge is human reason[445]

u. *Relativism*- there are no universal moral or ethical standards; developed by Nietzsche as a way to explain how good and evil are not subject to God's standards of morals and values, but humanity decides what is good or evil based on personal preferences[446]

v. *Romanticism*- intuition and emotion are sources of knowledge; advocated oneness with nature and spontaneity[447]

w. *Social Contracts*- originated by Rousseau; in his *Discourse on the Origin and Foundation of Inequality among Mankind*, he concludes that it is "an *abstract expression of the common good* that promotes liberty, equality, and fraternity"[448] (brotherhood); advocates for social rights and freedom (basis for *social justice* and *socialism*) (*pol.*)

x. *Social Darwinism*- is the application of Darwinian evolution to social contexts (including politics) with emphasis on the struggle for existence and survival of the fittest as applied to political and social policies (Ex: *Constitution* is a living organism, therefore, it constantly changes)

y. ***Socialism-*** according to Saint-Simon (father of socialism) change comes through a social understanding of society and advocates social ownership of the means of production and disperses the wealth for the common good and according to need thus voiding private ownership of property and businesses (*pol.*)[449]

z. ***Transcendental Idealism-*** a synthesis of empiricism and rationalism wherein Kant believed human action could become universal law; 'knowledge is limited to reality that is presented to the human mind'[450]

aa. ***Utilitarianism-*** the community determines what are right actions (i.e., "an action is right in so far as it promotes happiness...for the greatest number" of people in a community);[451] morality is subjective because "reason is a slave of the passions"; David Hume developed utilitarianism philosophy, and Immanuel Kant and Hegel used utilitarianism as a basis for their philosophy of idealism.[452]

bb. ***Utopianism-*** an envisioned, man-made perfect society socially engineered by those who think they know what is best for everyone else

Postmodernity Era (1950-Today):

1) Modern day Judeo-Christian conservatives continue to faithfully maintain interconnectivity of the nature of reality, values, and truth, and logic wherein:

   a. God's revealed truth continues to remain the foundation of faith, family and freedom

   b. Belief in the supernatural realm of God is still alive and well, and He is both present by His Holy Spirit, and the mysteries reserved for Him remain transcendent as He does in all of his fullness

2) Human reasoning defines truth, values, and reality, further subjecting truth to human interpretation whereby logic becomes irrelevant to the whole process of mental endeavors; truth and facts are reconstructed.[453] Philosophers and theologians throw out objective truth and logic under the bus, thereby replacing it with subjective human reasoning. If logic is applied, it is usually by the use of invalid or inductive arguments whereby an argument may be reasonable, but its conclusion is either "probably" true, or is both not true and not false, making the argument invalid.[454] Reality: *Only objective truth is subject to logic in order to come to right conclusions.*

   a. ***Deconstructionism-*** reader creates meaning of text (Derrida,)[455]

   b. ***Feminism-*** wisdom based in the Greek goddess, Sophia; applies female characteristics to deity; rejects the Bible's authority and views it as an oppressive patriarchal structure; devalues male leadership; calls for restoration of nature mysticism with a basis in female dominance; embraces liberation theology and applies a hermeneutic of suspicion to biblical interpretation[456]

c. ***Globalism***- centralized power and regulation by a world federation organization who writes and passes international laws and enforces or dictates them through either a global police structure or transnational non-government organizations (NGO) (also called *world federalism*)

d. ***Moralistic Relativism***- further development of Nietzsche's *relativism* of the Modernity Era into a situational ethics framework whereby each person decides what is right and wrong in each separate situation; it forms the basis of multiculturalism, diversity or cultural relativism and political correctness.

e. ***Neo-conservatism***- a political philosophy that favors big government, regulatory, monetary and legal interventionism, and is hostile to the influence of religion in the public arena[457]

f. ***Postmodern Utopianism***- the idea of socially engineering a perfect society becomes a global initiative to form a perfect world.

g. ***Post-structuralism***- no absolute truth; meaning is fluid (Derrida/Foucault)

h. ***Social Constructivism***- concerned with centrality of ideas and human thought and stresses a holistic and idealistic view of structures, thereby representing a postmodern version of *utopianism*[458]

i. ***Transhumanism (TH* or *H+)***- attempts 'to overcome death and create a utopia' through biological, chemical and technological manipulation and modification of the human body and mind. *Transhumanism* is rooted in the former philosophies of *naturalism, Darwinism, cosmic humanism* and *Progressivism* that seeks to sidestep God's authority, natural laws of creation, and redemptive plan for humanity. The ultimate goal of *Transhumanism* is to facilitate self-godhood and self-worship, to exercise total control over families and children, and to speed up the advancement toward a *new world order*. For example, prescribing *Ritalin* to school children and *Prozac* for adults without due consideration of natural and spiritual means of addressing difficult situations is a side effect of *Trans humanists* attempting to enforce their vision of a biochemically induced utopia.[459] Thomas More (1990) was original author of *Transhumanism* philosophy that melded together older humanistic and socialistic philosophies that makes man the center of the universe instead of God. Other advocates for *Transhumanism* include Nick Bostrom, Philip Hefner, Paul Tillich, UNESCO, James Ledford, and Ray Kurzweil.

APPENDIX C
A Social Creed for the 21st Century[460]

We Churches of the United States have a message of hope for a fearful time. Just as the churches responded to the harshness of early 20th Century industrialization with a prophetic "Social Creed" in 1908, so in our era of globalization we offer a vision of a society that shares more and consumes less,[461] seeks compassion over suspicion and equality over domination, and finds security in joined hands rather than massed arms. Inspired by Isaiah's vision of a "peaceable kingdom," we honor the dignity of every person and the intrinsic value of every creature, and pray and work for the day when none "labor in vain or bear children for calamity" (Isaiah 65:23). We do so as disciples of the One who came "that all may have life, and have it abundantly" (John 10:10), and stand in solidarity with Christians and with all who strive for justice around the globe.

In faith, responding to our Creator, we celebrate the full humanity of each woman, man, and child, all created in the divine image as individuals of infinite worth, by working for:
- Full civil, political and economic rights for women and men of all races
- Abolition of forced labor, human trafficking, and the exploitation of children
- Employment for all, at a family-sustaining living wage, with equal pay for comparable work
- The rights of workers to organize, and to share in workplace decisions and productivity growth
- Protection from dangerous working conditions, with time and benefits to enable full family life
- A system of criminal rehabilitation, based on restorative justice and an end to the death penalty

In the love incarnate in Jesus, despite the world's sufferings and evils, we honor the deep connections within our human family and seek to awaken a new spirit of community, by working for:
- Abatement of hunger and poverty, and enactment of policies benefiting the most vulnerable
- High quality public education for all and universal, affordable and accessible healthcare
- An effective program of social security during sickness, disability and old age

- Tax and budget policies that reduce disparities between rich and poor, strengthen democracy, and provide greater opportunity for everyone within the common good
- Just immigration policies that protect family unity, safeguard workers' rights, require employer accountability, and foster international cooperation
- Sustainable communities marked by affordable housing, access to good jobs, and public safety
- Public service as a high vocation, with real limits on the power of private interests in politics

In hope sustained by the Holy Spirit, we pledge to be peacemakers in the world and stewards of God's good creation, by working for:
- Adoption of simpler lifestyles for those who have enough; grace over greed in economic life
- Access for all to clean air and water and healthy food, through wise care of land and technology
- Sustainable use of earth's resources, promoting alternative energy sources and public transportation with binding covenants to reduce global warming and protect populations most affected
- Equitable global trade and aid that protects local economies, cultures and livelihoods
- Peacemaking through multilateral diplomacy rather than unilateral force, the abolition of torture, and a strengthening of the United Nations and the rule of international law
- Nuclear disarmament and redirection of military spending to more peaceful and productive uses
- Cooperation and dialogue for peace and environmental justice among the world's religions

We — individual Christians and churches — commit ourselves to a culture of peace and freedom that embraces non-violence, nurtures character, treasures the environment, and builds community, rooted in a spirituality of inner growth with outward action. We make this commitment together — as members of Christ's body, led by the one Spirit — trusting in the God who makes all things new.

APPENDIX D

Five Philosophical Schools of History[462]

Cyclical History- history occurs in a circular pattern like nature's seasons and tends to be pessimistic; common view held by ancient and oriental worlds; and reappears in Nietzsche's eternal recurrence philosophy and Toynbee's civilization's rise and fall cycles of history. This school is "widely diffused in China, India, the Middle East and the Graeco-Roman world,"[463] is prevalent in ancient and modern day paganism, pantheism, New Age movement and Cosmic Humanism, and usually breeds passivity and prefers despotism to feudalism.

Linear History- straight-line pattern having a purpose and destiny; commonly observed by Judeo-Christians wherein human history began at Creation, God intervenes in human affairs, and is characteristically optimistic about human purpose and destiny. This school prefers liberty rather than socialism or tyrannical forms of government.

Progressive History- traditional Christians preserve the straight-line pattern, but a majority of British and French philosophers and historians set the linear pattern aside during the *Enlightenment*. Humanity determines its own material destiny in this life without God's input and with no view of an after-life; individuals determine morality, therefore, absolute morality becomes irrelevant. This school is optimistic about the present and near future, but fatalistic about the end of life, and prefers a Socialist type government. The value of life is viewed materialistically or communally (Socialistically). This pattern laid the groundwork for sociology which was systemized by French theorists such as August Comte.

Cultural History (Historicism)- totally abandons the linear pattern of history, and history becomes "the story of the growth of various cultures."[464] This was a German and Italian reaction to *Enlightenment's* Progressive history. This school sought to classify various human races based on Malthusianism and Darwinism, generating class and race struggles with particular emphasis on survival of the fittest and preservation of superior races.

Historical Materialism (Marxism)- mixed and matched Progressive history with cultural history, thereby producing an "historical process created by man as he *labors* to satisfy his basic needs."[465] This school is deeply entrenched in Hegel's philosophies of idealism and communitarianism, is fluid and unstable, and is materialistically focused. Main adherents are Secular Humanists, Progressives, liberals, Socialists, liberation theologians, Communists, Marxists, and Fascists.

APPENDIX E
Categories of Federal Means-Tested Spending on
Welfare and Government Dependence Budget[466]

Programs Used to Calculate Index Values

I. Housing
  Mortgage credit
  Housing assistance
  Community development block grants
  Urban development action grants
  Subsidized housing programs

II. Health and Welfare
  Health care services
  Health research and training
  Consumer and occupational health
    and safety
  Unemployment compensation
  Food and nutrition assistance
  Other income security
  Disease control (preventive health
    care services)
  Health resources and services
  Substance abuse and mental health
    services
  Grants to states for Medicaid
  Child nutrition programs
  Food stamp programs
  Family support payments to states
  Social services block grants
  Children and families service
    programs
  Training and employment services
  Unemployment trust fund

III. Retirement
  Medicare
  Social Security
  General retirement and disability
    insurance

IV. Education
  Federal higher education
  State higher education

V. Rural and Agricultural Services
  Farm income stabilization
  Agricultural research and services
  Community development
  Area and regional development
  Disaster relief and insurance
  Rural community advancement
    program
  Homeland Security disaster relief

Source: The Heritage Foundation

Table 2 • SR-104 ☎ heritage.org

APPENDIX F
Three Sets of Meanings for Educational Buzzwords

(Berit Kjos: http://www.crossroad.to/charts/NewMeanings.html- chart used by permission.)

	TRADITIONAL EXPECTED MEANING	TRANSITION WHAT PARENTS ARE TOLD	NEW UN/NEA PARADIGM ACTUAL MEANING WITHIN THE CONTEXT
Outcome-Based Education (OBE)	Educating according to planned results or "outcomes"	A systemic plan to prepare *all* students to meet high standards	UN education **management system** based on international standards using incentives such as finances to ensure local schools prepares students to meet its ***affective*** (feeling-based, not factual) standards. **Mastery Learning** is the delivery system (**see below**)
Mastery Learning	Students must learn the facts required in subjects such as math, grammar, history, etc.	Students will be given time needed to master the new standards	Psychological strategies for conditioning students to new beliefs, values and ways of thinking. Failure to meet attitudinal (not factual) standards means more drilling until students demonstrate the "right" responses
Local Control	Elected school board officials represent local parents.	Local schools choose and manage their own learning programs.	The lowest level of a new centralized bureaucracy whereby a selected panel of supportive citizens makes sure students learn what national standards and tests require.
Values Clarification	Help students clarify traditional American values.	Help students clarify and communicate their own values.	Facilitated dialogue used to replace old paradigm of beliefs and values with moral relativism and self-made choices, and transition paradigm is replaced with new global beliefs and values, faith is shattered, modesty destroyed, child is desensitized to evil, and frees children to follow their feelings.
Logical/ Critical Thinking	Rational, factual study and analysis.	Teaching students to think for themselves.	Criticizes and challenges traditional beliefs, values and authorities; uses ridicule, intimidation and rejection to conform children to the new paradigm.

	TRADITIONAL	TRANSITION	NEW UN/NEA PARADIGM
World Class Standards	New standards needed for global challenges	"High standards" needed for work in a global economy	Low standards for literacy, comprehension, and factual knowledge. High standards for beliefs, attitudes, and group thinking needed to prepare human capital for global workforce
Higher Order Thinking Skills	Factual, rational thinking.	Apply, analyze, synthesize, evaluate.	Analyzing, synthesizing, and applying information based on politically correct sets of opinions and facts.
Conflict Resolution	Resolving conflicts.	Learning to settle disputes peacefully.	Learning to synthesize beliefs and trade old absolute beliefs and values for compromise positions and a new set of absolutes.
Consensus Building	Agreement through facilitated group discussion.	Seeking mutual understanding on a given subject.	Reaching a predetermined outcome through facilitated dialogue that involves labeling, intimidating, ridiculing, or ignoring any form of dissent.
Whole Language	The writer or speaker's normal, intended meaning.	Learning to read and write in a relevant, meaningful context.	Student gives his own expression and meaning to text, rather than learning to extract meaning of author. Accuracy and literacy fade in this process of standardizing human capital.
Co-operative learning	Students working together.	Preparing for work with people whose cultural values differ from yours.	Vital to global standards in education and workplace. Faster students help slow students instead of moving ahead. All must practice *unity* and *tolerance* for other ways and values.
Multicultural Education	Learning about other cultures.	Learning to respect and appreciate "all" cultures & lifestyles	*Becoming* a multicultural person, open to the pluralistic beliefs and lifestyles of *all* except those who cling to Judeo-Christian values.
Drug or Sex Education	Warning students to avoid drugs and premarital sex.	Teaching facts and values needed for healthy lifestyles.	Classroom encounter groups that discuss options under guidance of non-judgmental teacher. Unthinkable acts become alluring possibilities.

APPENDIX G
UN Principles of Smart Growth[467]

[Shaded text in *italics* is what UN NGO planners intend for urbanites, families and private property owners based on UN Agenda 21 and socialists goals.]

Box #8: Principles of Smart Growth

Mix Land Uses: Smart growth supports the integration of mixed land uses into communities as a critical component of achieving better places to live. *[Although mixed use sounds convenient, the intent is to restrict movement of population and discourage ownership of automobiles.]*

Take Advantage of Compact Building Design: Smart growth provides a means for communities to incorporate more compact building design in lieu of conventional land consumptive development. *[This is a capacity-building scheme whose goal is to move people into small multi-family habitats and restrict private property ownership.]*[468]

Create a Range of Housing Opportunities and Choices: Providing quality housing for people of all income levels is an integral component in any smart growth strategy. *[Equal housing for everyone regardless of personal investment or sweat equity.]*[469]

Create Walkable Neighborhoods: Walkable communities are desirable places to live, work, learn, worship and play and therefore a key component of smart growth. *[Restrict car ownership and force mass transportation systems on people thus increasing the statistical probability of assaults and robberies.]*

Foster Distinctive, Attractive Communities with a Strong Sense of Place: Smart growth encourages communities to create a vision and set standards for development and construction that respond to community values of architectural beauty and distinctiveness, as well as expanded choices in housing and transportation. *[Local community residents are manipulated into a consensus of pre-determined architectural plans thus removing quality of construction out of local control; transportation and housing choices are pre-determined, therefore choices will be limited for the common good.]*

Preserve Open Space, Farmland, Natural Beauty and Critical Environmental Areas: Open space preservation supports smart growth goals by bolstering local economies, preserving critical environmental areas, improving our communities' quality of life, and guiding new growth into existing communities. *[All economic and residential growth will be restricted to urban areas, and zoning laws will be implemented to severely restrict human intrusion into open spaces and natural habitats of animals and plants. Farmland development is restricted to co-operative farming programs run by the UN who determines quality and distribution of food produced by co-operatives.]*

Strengthen and Direct Development Towards Existing Communities: Smart growth directs development towards existing communities already served by infrastructure, seeking to utilize the resources that existing neighborhoods offer, and conserves open space and irreplaceable natural resources on the urban fringe. *[Plans to move more rural and suburban area people into already crowded cities and restrict economic growth or business entrepreneurship.]*

Provide a Variety of Transportation Choices: Providing people with more choices in housing, shopping, communities, and transportation is a key aim of smart growth. *[This is an illogical interpretation of smart growth plans, because when land use and movement of people is restricted to a densely populated urban area (city), choices are naturally limited.]*

Make Development Decisions Predictable, Fair and Cost Effective: For a community to be successful in implementing smart growth, it must be embraced by the private sector. *[Government bureaucracies and their NGOs have a major part in city planning; they work for the common good of their respective district, county, state, region, or federal population and are in sync with Agenda 21 plans; private sector is promised payback if it goes along with pre-determined plans. After following UN guidelines and cost-cutting measures, venture to guess what the level of quality, endurance, functionality and cost will be for local taxpayers. Tax, spend, and borrow is the UN's financial policy; "State" bank owned municipal bonds temporarily fund projects, and local community assets serve as collateral in case local community cannot pay back loans.]*

Encourage Community and Stakeholder Collaboration: Growth can create great places to live, work and play—if it responds to a community's own sense of how and where it wants to grow. *[Brings in planners and non-governmental organizations (district, county, regional, state, and sometimes federal NGOs) from outside the community to establish a solid support base for a pre-determined plan for local community in order to push for consensus and then claim to law makers that the pre-determined plan had the consensus of the local community.]*[470]

230

APPENDIX H
UN Environment Program (UNEP)
List of Unsustainable Activities

I agree that some of these activities are unsustainable if done in excess. "The Global Biodiversity Assessment directed by the United Nations Environment Programme (UNEP) calls for urgent action to reverse the effects of unsustainable human activities on global biodiversity including but not limited to the following":[471]

337 Ski Runs	749 Logging Activities
350 Grazing of Livestock: cows, sheep, goats, horses	728 Fossil Fuels - Used for driving various kinds of machines
351 Disturbance of the Soil Surface - Page 350 Large hoofed animals, compaction of soil, reducing filtration	755 Dams, Reservoirs, Straightening Rivers
351 Fencing of Pastures or Paddocks	757 Power Line Construction 763 Economic systems that fail to set a proper value on the environment
728 Agriculture	763 Inappropriate Social Structures
728 Modern Farm Production Systems	763 Weaknesses in Legal and Institutional Systems
728 Chemical Fertilizers	*766, 838 Modern attitudes toward nature - Judeo-Christian-Islamic religions*
728 Herbicides	
728 Building Materials	*767, 782 Private Property*
730 Industrial Activities	771 Population Growth - Human Population Density
730 Human-Made caves of brick and mortar, concrete and steel	773 Consumerism
730 Paved and Tarred roads, highways, rails (page 351)	774 Fragmentation of Habitat - cemeteries, derelict lands, rubbish tips, etc.
730 Railroads	774 Sewers, Drain Systems, Pipelines
730 Floor and Wall Tiles	783 Land use that serves human needs
733 Aquaculture	969 Fisheries
733 Technology Improvements	970 Golf Courses
733 Farmlands, Rangelands	970 Scuba Diving
733 Pastures, Rangelands	728 Synthetic drugs
733 Pastures	990 Fragmentation - Agricultural development, Forestry Urbanization (impervious surfaces)
733 Fish Ponds	
733 Plantations	
738 Modern Hunting	
738 Harvesting of Timber	

Appendix I
1 Corinthians 13

A good starting point for walking within the boundaries of freedom is I Corinthians 13 and the Ten Commandments.

"Though I speak with the tongues of men and of angels, but have not love, I have become sounding brass or a clanging cymbal.

And though I have *the gift of* prophecy, and understand all mysteries and all knowledge, and though I have all faith, so that I could remove mountains, but have not love, I am nothing.

And though I bestow all my goods to feed *the poor,* and though I give my body to be burned, but have not love, it profits me nothing.

Love suffers long *and* is kind; love does not envy; love does not parade itself, is not puffed up;

does not behave rudely, does not seek its own, is not provoked, thinks no evil;

does not rejoice in iniquity, but rejoices in the truth;

bears all things, believes all things, hopes all things, endures all things.

Love never fails. But whether *there are* prophecies, they will fail; whether *there are* tongues, they will cease; whether *there is* knowledge, it will vanish away.

For we know in part and we prophesy in part.

But when that which is perfect has come, then that which is in part will be done away.

When I was a child, I spoke as a child, I understood as a child, I thought as a child; but when I became a man, I put away childish things.

For now we see in a mirror, dimly, but then face to face. Now I know in part, but then I shall know just as I also am known.

And now abide faith, hope, love, these three; but the greatest of these *is* love."[472]

"For God so loved the world that he gave his only begotten Son, that whosoever believeth in him should not perish, but have everlasting life." John 3:16 (KJV)

Ten Commandments

1. "I *am* the LORD your God, who brought you out of the land of Egypt, out of the house of bondage. "You shall have no other gods before Me.
2. "You shall not make for yourself a carved image—any likeness *of anything* that *is* in heaven above, or that *is* in the earth beneath, or that *is* in the water under the earth; you shall not bow down to them nor serve them. For I, the LORD your God, *am* a jealous God, visiting the iniquity of the fathers upon the children to the third and fourth *generations* of those who hate Me, but showing mercy to thousands, to those who love Me and keep My commandments.
3. "You shall not take the name of the LORD your God in vain, for the LORD will not hold *him* guiltless who takes His name in vain.
4. "Remember the Sabbath day, to keep it holy. Six days you shall labor and do all your work, but the seventh day *is* the Sabbath of the LORD your God. *In it* you shall do no work: you, nor your son, nor your daughter, nor your male servant, nor your female servant, nor your cattle, nor your stranger who *is* within your gates. For *in* six days the LORD made the heavens and the earth, the sea, and all that *is* in them, and rested the seventh day. Therefore, the LORD blessed the Sabbath day and hallowed it.
5. "Honor your father and your mother, that your days may be long upon the land which the LORD your God is giving you.
6. "You shall not murder.
7. "You shall not commit adultery.
8. "You shall not steal.
9. "You shall not bear false witness against your neighbor.
10. "You shall not covet your neighbor's house; you shall not covet your neighbor's wife, nor his male servant, nor his female servant, nor his ox, nor his donkey, nor anything that *is* your neighbor's."[473]

Appendix J
Socialist/Progressive Terminology

Terms used by Socialists that sound good on the surface, however, it is important that we ask folks how they define these terms and what they mean.

- abatement of poverty
- Brotherhood of the kingdom
- central jurisdiction/control
- change
- civil rights
- coalition
- collaborative learning
- collective bargaining
- collective salvation
- collectivism
- common good
- communal life/education
- communitarian
- commune or community
- complete justice
- consensus
- cooperative learning
- critical thinking (not logical)
- cultural literacy (politically correct perspective)
- death of God
- Delphi technique
- diversity
- democracy/democratic (minus the "republic" component)
- dynamic growth
- Earth worship (pantheism)
- Economic/political rights for everyone as protected by new governing structures (big government)
- Ecumenism/ecumenical unity
- emerging church
- entitlements
- environmental justice
- equal distribution
- equitable division of the products of industry
- equality (uncritical equality)
- eugenics
- evolving/evolution
- fairness (but not for Christians or conservatives)
- Fatherland
- federal council/federation
- feminism
- for the better good
- government intervention/regulation
- global family
- globalism
- global justice
- global solidarity
- global spirituality (New Age)
- guerilla gardening (use of private property w/o owner's permission)
- golden rule as supreme law of society (replacing biblical basis for morality with "feelings" morality)
- grace over greed (anti-free market enterprise)
- group consensus
- guided imagery
- hold all things in common
- human brotherhood or brotherhood of man
- human capital/resource
- human rights (feelings-based)
- human species (equating humans with animals)
- inner God-self
- Internationalism
- it takes a village to raise a child
- Kingdom of God

235

- equitable global trade
- liberal
- liberty
- lifelong learning (brainwashing)
- magic gathering
- myth/stories (liberal claims about the Bible)
- moral relativism
- mother earth (Gaia- earth goddess)
- multiculturalism
- nationalism
- natural selection
- "new" (usually means a repackaged old ideology)
- new social/world order
- open minded (to everything but absolute truth and unchanging principles)
- open borders (weakening of national security)
- open society
- oneness with the planet
- outcome-based education
- peaceable kingdom (earthly utopia)
- pluralism
- population control (eugenics/abortion)
- populist
- progressive
- public service as a high vocation (undermining private businesses and increase size of government)
- redirection of military spending
- redistribution/redirection
- regulation (social and economic)
- relationships of mutuality
- reparation
- restorative justice
- revenue enhancement (increasing taxes)
- serving the greater good/whole
- shared responsibility/values
- shared sacrifice/vision
- social capital (assets and property controlled and redistributed for the common good)
- social conferences
- social contract
- social control
- Social Darwinism
- social gospel/social justice
- social revolution
- solidarity
- spiritual evolution
- spontaneous order (opposite of natural order)
- stakeholders
- sustainable growth/development
- sustainable communities w/ affordable housing (government owned properties)
- synergy (a type of group dependence cancelling individual initiative or thought)
- Third Wave (new world order)
- tolerance
- transition or transformation
- TQM (total quality management-continual assessment used to control groups or individuals)
- unconditional submission
- undocumented worker (i.e., illegal alien/immigrant)
- unifying spiritual blend
- unilateralism
- union or trade unions
- unity, oneness
- universal programs such as universal healthcare and education
- universalism/universal values
- utilitarian
- utopia
- WCC/NCC
- work-based learning/school-to-work programs (social engineering students to serve the State)
- workers party

Appendix K
Principles of Fact Checking

1. Always use credible primary sources whenever possible to fact check; and distinguish between primary vs. secondary sources of information.

   a. *Primary sources* are original works directly generated by the source, and information contemporary to an event. Abraham Lincoln's *Gettysburg Address* is an example of a primary source document. Other examples of primary sources are:

      1) professional research and information sites such as local, state or government web sites or publications (city, county, state or nation profiles, statistics, policy statements or information, demographics, census, etc.)

      2) specialized dictionaries and encyclopedias (topics are by experts on the subject written about); be alert for any ideological bias or slant and always verify information with another credible source

      3) official web sites or information brochures of organizations, original historical and official documents (such as city records and court documents)

      4) diaries, letters, speeches by original speaker, autobiographies (written by the sources themselves), memoirs or first-hand eye-witness accounts

      5) older newspapers (when accurate reporting was considered a plus as opposed to today's media propaganda mill)

   b. *Secondary sources* would include second-person accounts, blogs, and viewpoint or opinion pieces and are usually interpretive by nature; for example, an article written about Abraham *Lincoln's Gettysburg Address*. Wikipedia is not a primary source because information given is not always by writers who have the expertise, experience or education to adequately address the topic, and information on Wikipedia can be altered or edited by anyone; therefore, it would not be considered a credible primary source of information. Always check accuracy of secondary sources by checking footnotes/endnotes if provided, or using primary sources to confirm accuracy of secondary source information. Other secondary sources include:

      1) newspaper, magazine and some journal articles

      2) general encyclopedias that present an overview of subjects

      3) textbooks writing about events outside the historical and geographical context of the authors

      4) creative non-fiction

2. Determine the credibility of the author or organization providing the information. Some useful questions to ask are:
   a. Do authors or organizations use credible primary sources, first-hand or eyewitness account information or other credible experts to support their statements? Do they have sufficient expertise, education, or research or practical experience to address the topic or subject matter about which they are writing or speaking?
   b. Do they list their sources of information by providing footnotes, endnotes or verbal acknowledgements of their sources of information?
   c. Is an opinion or viewpoint backed by truthful facts, or are the facts misleading, inaccurate or distorted?
3. Determine the worldview background of authors and organizations to assess whether they are prone to distort information or use rhetoric for the purpose of manipulating the reader or viewer. Also check the worldviews and educational background of those who sit on the boards of organizations (their bios are usually available).
4. When gathering information, do not hesitate to use the *Freedom of Information Act (FOIA)* in requesting information that government agencies prefer not to provide. City, county, state, and federal government agencies are considered non-profit organizations and are required to provide information to American citizens upon request unless the information would jeopardize national security.
5. Verify information gathered with two or three other sources of information or firsthand eyewitnesses, using primary sources as the first line of verification whenever possible.
6. Due to the volume of rumors floating around in cyberspace, it is important to check for accuracies--be skeptical of so-called fact-checking web sites that claim to be non-partisan when in truth they are biased.

Develop the habit of using trustworthy resources to fact check. (P.S. Contrary to popular belief, .org web sites are not always trustworthy.)

Appendix L
Proclamation 5018 -- Year of the Bible, 1983

February 3, 1983

By the President of the United States of America

A Proclamation

Of the many influences that have shaped the United States of America into a distinctive Nation and people, none may be said to be more fundamental and enduring than the Bible.

Deep religious beliefs stemming from the Old and New Testaments of the Bible inspired many of the early settlers of our country, providing them with the strength, character, convictions, and faith necessary to withstand great hardship and danger in this new and rugged land. These shared beliefs helped forge a sense of common purpose among the widely dispersed colonies -- a sense of community, which laid the foundation for the spirit of nationhood that was to develop in later decades.

The Bible and its teachings helped form the basis for the Founding Fathers' abiding belief in the inalienable rights of the individual, rights which they found implicit in the Bible's teachings of the inherent worth and dignity of each individual. This same sense of man patterned the convictions of those who framed the English system of law inherited by our own Nation, as well as the ideals set forth in the Declaration of Independence and the Constitution.

For centuries, the Bible's emphasis on compassion and love for our neighbor has inspired institutional and governmental expressions of benevolent outreach such as private charity, the establishment of schools and hospitals, and the abolition of slavery.

Many of our greatest national leaders -- among them Presidents Washington, Jackson, Lincoln, and Wilson -- have recognized the influence of the Bible on our country's development. The plainspoken Andrew Jackson referred to the Bible as no less than ``the rock on which our Republic rests.'' Today our beloved America and, indeed, the world, are facing a decade of enormous challenge. As a people, we may well be tested as we have seldom, if ever, been tested before. We will need resources of spirit even more than resources of technology, education, and armaments. There could be no more fitting moment than now to reflect with gratitude, humility, and urgency upon the wisdom revealed to us in the writing that Abraham Lincoln called ``the best gift God has ever given to man . . . But for it we could not know right from wrong."

The Congress of the United States, in recognition of the unique contribution of the Bible in shaping the history and character of this Nation, and so many of its citizens, has by Senate Joint Resolution 165 authorized and requested the President to designate the year 1983 as the ``Year of the Bible."

Now, Therefore, I, Ronald Reagan, President of the United States of America, in recognition of the contributions and influence of the Bible on our Republic and our people, do hereby proclaim 1983 the Year of the Bible in the United States. I encourage all citizens, each in their way, to reexamine and rediscover its priceless and timeless message.

In Witness Whereof, I have hereunto set my hand this third day of February, in the year of our Lord nineteen hundred and eighty-three, and of the Independence of the United States of America the two hundred and seventh.

Ronald Reagan

[Filed with the Office of the Federal Register, 10:10 a.m., February 3, 1983][474]

ENDNOTES

[1] K.I.S.S.- keep it simple silly

[2] Galatians 5:13, *New King James Version,* hereafter listed as *NKJV.*

[3] 2 Chronicles 7:14, *NKJV.*

[4] 2 Corinthians 3:17, *NKJV.*

[5] Matthew 5:14, paraphrased.

[6] Because the extreme left intentionally uses name changing as a way to cloak their real intentions or to hide their agendas, the terms socialism, liberalism and progressivism are used interchangeably since they represent the same ideological theme, which is collectivism, big government, and centralized power.

[7] Endowed and unalienable rights are those given by God, not man. When man doles out rights, man can take them away.

[8] Matthew 12:33, *NKJV.*

[9] Image and information retrieved from http://oldcomputers.net/osborne.html, on December 20, 2011. No copyright information posted on web site.

[10] *2001: Space Odyssey* was a 1968 sci-fi movie in which an egocentric malfunctioning computer named HAL took control of a spaceship bound for Jupiter and disconnected life support system of the crew. Dave, the sole surviving astronaut, managed to disconnect HAL.

[11] Psalm 37:25, *NKJV.*

[12] Galatians 5:13, *NKJV.*

[13] The committee completed the final draft of the *Articles of Confederation* on November 15, 1777, ratified on March 1, 1781, and remained in effect until March 4, 1789. Retrieved January 6, 2012 from Library of Congress web site:
http://www.loc.gov/rr/program/bib/ourdocs/articles.html. For further information go to:
http://www.loc.gov/teachers/classroommaterials/presentationsandactivities/
presentations/timeline/newnatn/confed/confed.html.

[14] W. Cleon Skousen, *The 5,000 Year Leap: A Miracle that Changed the World* (Malta, IN: National Center for Constitutional Studies, 2006), pp. 10-18.

[15] Sandra Reid, *America: Land of Principles and Promises* (Mesa, AZ: Heritage Academy, 2011), p. 51.

[16] Ibid., pp. 51-52.

[17] Ibid., p. 58.

[18] Jean Leon Gerome Ferris, *The Mayflower Compact 1620* (Cleveland, OH: Foundation Press, 1932). Retrieved January 19, 2012 from Library of Congress Prints and Photographs Online Catalog at web site: http://www.loc.gov/pictures/item/99471902/

[19] Reid, p. 61.

[20] Ibid., pp. 61-62.

[21] Painting by Jennie A. Brownscombe (1914). Retrieved January 6, 2012: http://www.clipartpal.com/clipart_pd/holiday/thanksgiving/thanksgiving_10061.html.

[22] Reid, pp. 63-64.

[23] Ibid., p. 64.

[24] Ibid., p. 64.

[25] Key Principle: Read history as recorded in original historical documents or texts by historians who have the integrity to stay true to the original historical facts and state their source, and not to the Humanism's revisionist or reconstructed version of history slanted to further the socialist political agenda that purposely stirs up class warfare to enslave the people.

[26] Mark A. Beliles and Stephen K. McDowell (1989), *America's Providential History* (Charlottesville, VA: Providence Foundation (2010).

251

[27] Reid., pp. 149-150.

[28] Larry Schweikart and Michael Allen (2004), *A Patriot's History of the United States* (New York: Sentinel, Penguin Group, 2007), p. 86

[29] Exodus 12, *NKJV*.

[30] Polytheism is the worship of multiple gods.

[31] E. C. Wines, *Commentaries on the Laws of the Ancient Hebrews: With an Introductory Essay on Civil Society and Government* (Powder Spring, GA: American Vision Press, 2009; originally published by the Presbyterian Board of Publication, Philadelphia, 1853), p. 344.

[32] Exodus 18:14-26, *NKJV*.

[33] Exodus 32, *NKJV*.

[34] Exodus 20:7-17 and 28, *NKJV*.

[35] Deuteronomy 1:13, *NKJV*.

[36] Exodus 18:21, *NKJV*.

[37] Joshua 1:12-15, *NKJV*. See also the book of Judges (OT).

[38] Exodus and Deuteronomy are foundational books supporting these principles. See section on "Fundamental Principles" in E. C. Wines *Hebrew Republic* online at: http://www.amprpress.com/fundamental_principles.htm.

[39] Beliles and McDowell, p. 23-24.

[40] Last line of America's Pledge of Allegiance.

[41] Proverbs 1:5, *NKJV*.

[42] Preamble of the *U. S. Constitution of the United States of America*.

[43] According to Schweikart and Allen (pp. 116-117), after completing the *U.S. Constitution* in 1787, the meaning of federalism was reversed, declaring that Congressional laws are 'the supreme law of the land.'" This placed the power to print money, raise armies, and regulate foreign and interstate commerce into the hands of the Federal government.

[44] Schweikart and Allen, p. 94.

[45] Ibid., p. 94..

[46] David Gibbs, Jr. and David Gibbs III, *Understanding the Constitution* (Seminole, FL: Christian Law Association, 2006 by Gibbs Law Firm, P.A.), pp. 4-9.

[47] Skousen, *The 5,000 Year Leap...*, pp. 32-33.

[48] Beliles and McDowell, 102-111.

[49] David Barton, *Original Intent: The Courts, the Constitution, & Religion* (Aledo, TX: WallBuilder Press, 2000), p. 100.

[50] Ibid., p. 79 quoting from *The Code of 1650, Being a Compilation of the Earliest Laws and Orders of the General Court of Connecticut* (Hartford: Silus Andrus, 1822), p. 2.

[51] Barton, pp. 107-108.

[52] Ibid., pp. 213-214.

[53] Ibid., p. 226.

[54] See Romans 3:20-24, Matthew 5:17-20, John 3:16-17, Ephesians 2:8, John 15:13, Isaiah 61:1-3, and Luke 4:18, *NKJV*.

[55] Hebrews 8, 9:11-15, and John 14:26-27, *NKJV*.

[56] Deuteronomy 6:5-9, Leviticus 19:18, Matthew 22:36-40, Mark 12:29-31, and Romans 13:19, *NKJV*.

[57] James 2:1-8, *NKJV*.

[58] In this context, "state" means government or a governing structure.

[59] Reid, p. 212. Consent to approve meant that the Congressional delegates worked toward consensus rather than being forced to compromise (i.e., allowing common agreements on sound principles rather than forcing a single person's will over another regarding issues). Stated briefly- principles trumped issues.

[60] The Heritage Foundation, *We Still Hold these Truths: A Leader's Guide* (Washington, DC: The Heritage Foundation, 2010), pp. 19-24.

[61] Ibid., p. 25.

[62] Ibid., pp. 26-27.

[63] Ibid., pp. 31-33.

[64] Ibid., p. 43.

[65] Ibid., pp. 53-55.

[66] Ibid., p. 55 and 71.

[67] Ibid., pp. 71-72.

[68] Skousen, *The 5,000 Year Leap...*, pp. 22-23.

[69] Reid, p. 213.

[70] Skousen, *The 5,000 Year Leap...*, p. 25.

[71] Ibid., pp. 23-25.

[72] Ibid., pp. 154-158.

[73] Ibid., pp. 154-158.

[74] The Heritage Foundation, p. 72.

[75] Ibid., p. 66.

[76] Proverbs 22:6, *NKJV*.

[77] Vladimir Lenin, *The State of Revolution*-Chap. 5. Retrieved January 29, 2012: http://www.marxists.org/archive/lenin/works/1917/staterev/ch05.htm#s2.

[78] Bucknell University (Lewisburg, PA). Retrieved April 9, 2012: http://www.departments.bucknell.edu/russian/const/1977toc.html

[79] Archibald Roosevelt's Introduction to Zygmundo Dobbs (ed.), *The Great Deceit* (Veritas Foundation Staff Study, 1964).

[80] Ronald Pestritto and William Atto, *American Progressivism* (Lanham, MD: Lexington Books, a division of Rowman & Littlefield Publishers, Inc., 2008), p. 2.

[81] Skousen, *The 5,000 Year Leap...*, p. 156.

[82] Alister E. McGrath (ed.), *The Blackwell Encyclopedia of Christian Thought* (Oxford, UK: Basil Blackwell Ltd., 1993), pp. 360-361.

[83] Oxford Dictionaries Catherine Soanes; Angus Stevenson (2010-10-19). Oxford Dictionary of English, 2nd Edition (Kindle Location 141354-141355). Oxford University Press. Kindle Edition.

[84] Noyes, John Humphrey (2011-03-30). History of American Socialisms (Kindle Locations 376-377). Kindle Edition, public domain copy originally published in 1870.

[85] Ibid., Kindle Location 409.

[86] Ibid., Kindle Location 328.

[87] Ibid., Kindle Locations 7571 and 7575.

[88] Ibid., Kindle locations 7699 and 7701-7702.

[89] Oxford Dictionaries, Kindle Locations 760834-760835.

[90] John A. Stormer (1992), *None Dare Call It Treason...25 Years Later* (Florissant, MO: Liberty Bell Press), pp. 58-60.

[91] Federal Mediation and Conciliation Service, *A Timeline of Events in American Labor Relations*. Retrieved 3 February 2012: http://www.fmcs.gov/internet/itemDetail.asp?categoryID=21&itemID=15810

[92] Eugenics is the study of improving the human population through controlled breeding by scientific and medical means; the intent is to weed out unfit and genetically inferior members of society.

[93] George Bernard Shaw, Lecture to the Eugenics Education Society, Reported in *The Daily Express*, March 4, 1910.

[94] As expressed by Margaret Sanger, *The Pivot of Society* (New York: Brentano's Publishers, 1922); see also *Woman and the New Race* (New York: Truth Publishing Company, 1920, printed by Brentano's). Free copies of books available on Google ebooks.

[95] Oxford Dictionaries; Kindle Location 299875).

[96] Stormer, p. 64.

[97] Ibid., p. 60.

[98] Retrieved January 29, 2012: http://dlib.nyu.edu/findingaids/html/tamwag/iss.html, para. 1

[99] Stormer, p. 60

[100] John Taylor Gatto (2003), *The Underground History of American Education: A School Teacher's Intimate Investigation into the Prison of Modern Schooling* (New York: The Oxford Village Press), pp. 142-144.

[101] Gatto, p. 133.

[102] Murray N. Rothbard, *Education: Free and Compulsory* (Auburn, AL: The Ludwig Von Mises Institute, 1999), p. 34-35.

[103] Zygmundo Dobbs (1969), *Keynes at Harvard: Economic Deception as a Political Credo* (Austin, TX: A Veritas Study, Perry Press, 2009), preface. Retrieved February 4, 2012: http://keynesatharvard.org/book/KeynesatHarvard-Note.html.

[104] Gatto, p. 13.

[105] John A. Hardon, *John Dewey: Radical Social Educator* (Montreal, Quebec, Canada: The Catholic Educational Review, October, 1952). Retrieved February 4, 2012: http://www.ewtn.com/library/HOMESCHL/JNDEWEY2.HTM

[106] John Taylor Gatto, p. 67.

[107] Rothbard, p. vi.

[108] Ibid., p. 5.

[109] Rothbard quoting George Harris, *Inequality and Progress* (Boston: Houghton, Mifflin, 1898), pp. 74-75, and 88.

[110] Dennis Laurence Cuddy, Ph.D., *Chronology of Education with Quotable Quotes* (Highland City, FL: Pro Family Forum, Inc., 1993).

[111] George S. Counts (1932), *Dare the School Build a New Social Order* (New York: The John Day Company), pp. 3, 9, 28, and 45-46 . Retrieved February 9, 2012: http://www.undoctrination.info/Books/education/Counts,%20George%20%20 Dare%20the%20School%20Build%20a%20New%20Social%20Order%20(1932).pdf. (Cannot access using this url address, therefore, use search engine to access free online pdf of book).

[112] *Critical theory*- an atheistic alternative philosophy of metaphysics and self-determination with emphasis on the study of social, historical, and ideological influences on human structures; and is rooted in Hegelian dialectics and the ideology of Sigmund Freud, Max Weber, and Friedrich Nietzsche (see http://www.encyclopedia.com/topic/Critical_theory.aspx).

[113] "Frankfurt School." International Encyclopedia of the Social Sciences. 2008. Retrieved February 11, 2012: http://www.encyclopedia.com/doc/1G2-3045300855.html.

[114] John A. Stormer (1999), *None Dare Call It Education* (Florissant, MO: Liberty Bell Press), pp. 39-40.

[115] BTW- by the way

[116] Diane Ravitch, *The Language Police: How Pressure Groups Restrict What Students Learn* (New York: Knopf, 2003).

[117] Jeff Riggenbach (2009), *Why American History is not what they Say: An Introduction to Revisionism* (Auburn, AL: Ludwig von Mises Institute).

[118] "Beard, Charles A." International Encyclopedia of the Social Sciences. 1968. *Encyclopedia.com*. (February 11, 2012). http://www.encyclopedia.com/doc/1G2-3045000094.html.

[119] Charles A. Beard, *The Supreme Court and the Constitution* (New York, The Macmillan Company, 1912).

[120] Stormer, *None Dare Call it Education*, p. 71.

[121] Ibid, p. 73.

[122] Retrieved February 14, 2012:
http://www.usgovernmentdebt.us/year_spending_1910USbn_11bs1n_40#usgs302
http://www.usgovernmentdebt.us/year_spending_2010USbn_11bs1n_40#usgs302
http://www.usgovernmentdebt.us/year_spending_2007USbn_11bs1n_40#usgs302

[123] U.S. Department of Education, Institute of Education Sciences, National Center for Education Statistics, National Assessment of Educational Progress, *Reading Report Card*. Retrieved February 14, 2012:
http://nationsreportcard.gov/reading_2007/r0001.asp (November 2, 2007).

[124] Eagle Forum, "Through Grade Inflation, B+ is the New Average," *Education Reporter* (Number 282; July 2009). Retrieved February 14, 2012:
http://www.eagleforum.org/educate/2009/july09/grade-inflation.html

[125] Dinkes, R., Kemp, J., and Baum, K. (2009). *Indicators of School Crime and Safety: 2009* (NCES 2010–012/NCJ 228478). National Center for Education Statistics, Institute of Education Sciences, U.S. Department of Education, and Bureau of Justice Statistics, Office of Justice Programs, U.S. Department of Justice, Washington, D.C., p. 7. Retrieved February 14, 2012:
http://bjs.ojp.usdoj.gov/content/pub/pdf/iscs09.pdf

[126] CBS Cleveland (February 13, 2012), "Cincinnati High School Paying Students to Come to School" (Cincinnati: CBS Local Media, 2012). Retrieved February 15, 2012:
http://cleveland.cbslocal.com/2012/02/13/cincinnati-high-school-paying-students-to-come-to-school

[127] Retrieved February 14, 2012:
http://www.usgovernmentdebt.us/year_spending_1910USbn_11bs1n_40#usgs302
http://www.usgovernmentdebt.us/year_spending_2010USbn_11bs1n_40#usgs302

[128] OWS- Occupy Wall Street

[129] Proverbs 11:29a, *NKJV.*

[130] Reinhold Niebuhr (1892-1971) described himself as a Christian Marxist and constructed a theology of justice. Sinclair Ferguson and David Wright, *New Dictionary of Theology* (Leicester, England: Universities and College Christian Fellowship, 1988), pp. 469-470.

[131] Noyes, Kindle location 7699.

[132] Zygmund Dobbs (ed.), *The Great Deceit:* (Austin, TX: A Veritas Study, Perry Press, 2009), p. 265.

[133] God's revealed truths are in the Old and New Testament (i.e., the Bible).

[134] W. W. Bartley, III, *The Collected Works of F. A. Hayek (Vol. I): The Fatal Conceit- The Errors of Socialism* (Chicago: IL: University of Chicago Press; copyright 1988 F. A. Hayek).

[135] Edward Bellamy, *Looking Backward* (New York: Houghton, Mifflin & Co., 1888 copyright by Ticknor and Company).

[136] Ibid.

[137] Ibid.

[138] Leviticus 19:13; Isaiah 65:21-22; Jeremiah 22:13; 1 Timothy 5:18; James 5:4; *NKJV.*

[139] 2 Corinthians 9:7-8; Proverbs 31:10-20; Leviticus 19:9-15; *NKJV.*

[140] Proverbs 10:4; Ruth 2; *NKJV.*

[141] Proverbs 6:6-11; 13:4; 24:30-34; Ephesians 4:28; 2 Thessalonians 3:10-12; *NKJV.*

[142] Psalm 24:1; Malachi 3:10; *NKJV.*

[143] Elwell, "Social Gospel," p. 1027.

[144] Conservapedia (2011), "Robert Malthus" article retrieved February 29, 2012 from:
http://www.conservapedia.com/Robert_Malthus

[145] Elwell, p. 1028 and Allister, p. 604.

[146] Allister, "Rauschenbusch, Walter" article, p. 542.

[147] Gene TeSelle (8-20-07), "The Social Creed after a Hundred Years: Time for a New Social Awakening" & Christian T. Iosso (9-27-04), "Celebrating the Social Creed of 1908, and considering a new one for 2008". See Appendix C for new social creed for 21st century. Retrieved March 1, 2012 from: http://www.witherspoonsociety.org/2004/social_creed.htm. Website dedicated to expressing the "A union of The Witherspoon Society and Voices of Sophia; (see top banner of their website). According to feminist theologians, Sophia means wisdom and is the female version of God, and Jesus is the liberator of women and returns women to participatory reign with God (McGrath, p. 225, second column).

[148] McGrath, "Social Questions" article, p. 606.

[149] More about the UN Agenda 21 will be covered in another chapter (Loonyville).

[150] Me-Church.org (2010), retrieved March 1, 2012 from: http://www.me-church.org/

[151] David Noebel (2nd Edition, 2006), *Understanding the Times* (Manitou Spring, CO: Summit Ministries: Summit Press), pp. 82-83. Emerging church leaders go to great lengths to defend postmodernism and seek a pluralistic melding of modernity (traditional biblical worldviews) with postmodernity (worldview in opposition to traditional biblical worldviews) through the process of conflict resolution, using psychosocial philosophies as the mediator between the two. In a word, compromise is required of those who embrace biblical truth; "shared vision" and storytelling, along with a twist of social justice and liberation, are tools used in this melding process. Christians are once again required to accept skepticism of biblical truth and move further down the path of accepting postmodernism's denial of the Bible's inerrancy (see http://www.next-wave.org/ mar01/shields2.htm). The recommended book on this web site, *The Fifth Element*, is a training manual in groupthink processes that translates into group collectivism, an old, worn out and culturally repackaged mind manipulation tactic of socialists.

[152] Documentary: Vision Video (2005), *Hanged on a Twisted Cross*. This is a video presentation about Dietrich Bonhoeffer's life that gives an accurate account of the various responses by the church to Hitler's rise to power and regime, and demonstrates that compromise and thirst for power by the church never works when dealing with a megalomaniac. Note that Dietrich Bonhoeffer brought together a group called the Confessing Church who were devoted to upholding the Christ-centered gospel and opposed the vile treatment of the Jews. The insidiousness of Hitler's horrific acts against the Jews and social misfits was that he used liberal churches to deceive church leaders, falsely claiming that the Jews killed Jesus. Just a little research would have produced the truth—the Romans crucified Jesus (opposite of the Jewish method, which is stoning). When we dig deeper, we also discover that the sins of humanity nailed Jesus to the cross, and by His sacrificial act, He redeemed us and made a way for us to be reconciled to God through Christ, for "For God so loved the world" (you and I) "that He gave His only begotten son, that whosoever believes in Him should not perish, but have everlasting life." (John 3:16).

[153] *Worldview*- how we individually **or** corporately explain our beliefs, ideas, values and morals about seen and unseen realities in relation to God, humanity and the world; how we explain the meaning of life.

[154] 1 Peter 5:8, *NKJV*.

[155] John Dewey wrote the Humanist Manifesto I and admits in his work, *A Common Faith,* that he maintains the term "religious" regarding such topics as natural, "human relations, welfare, and progress." (New Haven, CT: Yale University Press, 1934 and 1962, p. 84). See 501 (c) (3) tax-exempt information for the Council for Secular Humanism Inc., retrieved March 1, 2012 at: http://www.taxexemptworld.com/organization.asp?tn=506577

[156] Craig Vincent Mitchell (2007), *Charts of Philosophies and Philosophers* (Grand Rapids, MI: Zondervan), Chart 118.

[157] Ibid.

[158] Ibid, Chart 114, 117 and 200.

[159] Ibid, Charts 114 and 118.

[160] John 16:13, *NKJV*.

[161] Rauschenbusch, p. 5.

[162] Ephesians 4:14-15, *NKJV*. This quote is not referring to all philosophy, but to false philosophy or that which is intentionally misleading, deceptive, and illogical.

[163] Philippians 2:5-11 and John 18:36, *NKJV*.

[164] Lord Acton's quote regarding absolute power.

[165] 1 John 2:16, *NKJV*.

[166] William B. Bean, "The Illness of Charles Darwin" (American Journal of Medicine, Volume 65, Issue 4, October 1978), Pages 573.

[167] Jerry Bergman (2011), *The Dark Side of Darwin* (Green Forest, AZ: Master Books), p. 97-98.

[168] Infanticide- infant homicide

[169] See Chapter 7- Races of Man in Darwin's, *Descent of Man*.

[170] Retrieved March 15, 2012: http://www.dianedew.com/sanger.htm.

[171] Bergman, p. 18.

[172] Kelley Ross, *Fallacies of Moralistic Relativism* (2011), retrieved March 11, 2012: http://www.friesian.com/poly-1b.htm.

[173] Kelley Ross, retrieved March 11, 2012: http://www.friesian.com/poly-2.htm.

[174] Justified mass murder- justified in the eyes of those ordering and/or committing mass murder when there is no justification for such heinous acts.

[175] Bourgeois morality- morality of the well-to-do middle class.

[176] "Houston Stewart Chamberlain." Encyclopedia of World Biography. 2004. Retrieved March 12, 2012 from Encyclopedia.com: http://www.encyclopedia.com/doc/1G2-3404701223.html

[177] R. J. Rummel, *Death by Government* (Brunswick, NJ: Transaction Publishers, 1994), Table 1.3. Retrieved February 12, 2012: http://www.hawaii.edu/powerkills/NAZIS.TAB1.3.GIF. If you read further into Rummel's book, be aware that he advocates social justice based on secular humanism; he also pushes for a world federation organization and presents it as democratic, but it is Democratic Socialism, not a democratic republic. Remember what was mentioned earlier—that democracy paves the road to socialism and socialism is the precursor to some form of tyranny like Marxism, Communism or Fascism.

[178] Ethnic cleansing is another word for genocide.

[179] Ibid.

[180] Noebel, *Understanding the Times*, p. 81

[181] NASA, *Visible Earth: Earth's City Lights (Korean peninsula)* (NASA Public Domain satellite picture, 2003).

[182] Marlin Maddoux, Public Education Against America (New Kensington, Penn.: Whitaker House, 2006), pp. 141-142.

[183] Galatians 2:4, *NKJV*.

[184] Romans 8:35, 29, *NKJV*.

[185] Genesis 1:1-2:15; John 1:1-4, *NKJV*.

[186] McDurmon, *God versus Socialism*, p. 210.

[187] See Woodrow Wilson's writings: *The New Freedom* and *Constitutional Government in the United States* (New York: Columbia University Press, 1908).

[188] Woodrow Wilson, *The New Freedom*, with an introduction by William Leuchtenburg (Englewood Cliffs: Prentice-Hall, Inc., 1961), p. 42.

[189] David Kennedy, "Can the West Lead Us to a Better Place," *Stanford Magazine,* May/June 2008 (Stanford Alumni Association, 2011). Retrieved March 19, 2012: http://www.stanfordalumni.org/news/magazine/2008/mayjun/features/west.html

[190] U.S. Debt Clock.org, retrieved February 5, 2016. This means that each American citizen would have to pay the government $58, 854 to bail out Uncle Sam.

[191] Pestritto and Atto (eds.), *American Progressivism,* Chapter 9: The Socializing of Property (by Rauschenbusch).

[192] Go to the following web site for more in-depth information: http://keynesatharvard.org/book/KeynesatHarvard-ch03.html

[193] Pestritto and Atto (eds.), Chapter 16: The Study of Administration," by Woodrow Wilson.

[194] Domestic Extremism Lexicon accessible at: http://www.fas.org/irp/eprint/lexicon.pdf

[195] The White House Office of the Press Secretary, *Executive Order – National Defense Resources Preparedness* (Washington, DC: March 16, 2012). Retrieved March 20, 2012: http://www.whitehouse.gov/the-press-office/2012/03/16/executive-order-national-defense-resources-preparedness.

[196] Wafa Sultan (2009), *The God Who Hates: The Courageous Woman Who Inflamed the Muslim World Speaks Out against the Evils of Islam* (New York: Saint Martin's Press), Kindle Location 2770.

[197] 2 Timothy 1:7, *NKJV.*

[198] Hegemonic Economics- usually applied on the international level, but has been applied in America whereby a centralized power controls the nation's economy (federal government's control of state economies, for example).

[199] Robert Murphy, *Study Guide: Murray Rothbard's Man, Economy, and State with Power and Market, 2nd ed.* (Auburn, AL: Ludwig von Mises Institute, 2006), p. 243.

[200] Matthew Spalding, *We Still Hold these Truths,* p. 200.

[201] The Heritage Foundation, *We Still Hold these Truths: A Leader's Guide* (Washington, DC: The Heritage Foundation, 2010), pp. 19-24.

[202] Franklin Roosevelt's Annual Message to Congress January 1944.

[203] Retrieved February 14, 2012:
http://www.usgovernmentdebt.us/year_spending_1910USbn_11bs1n_40#usgs302
http://www.usgovernmentdebt.us/year_spending_2010USbn_11bs1n_40#usgs302
http://www.usgovernmentdebt.us/year_spending_2007USbn_11bs1n_40#usgs302

[204] Terry Miller and Kim Holmes *2009 and 2012 Index of Economic Freedom* (The Heritage Foundation and Dow Jones & Company, Inc., 2009/2012). For more detailed information go to: http://www.heritage.org/index/country/unitedstates.

[205] 2 Thessalonians 3:10b, *NKJV.*

[206] Karl Marx (1848), *The Communist Manifesto,* Frederick Engels, ed. (Lawrence, KS: Digireads.com Publishing, 2009), Kindle Location 954-955.

[207] Proverbs 20:13, *NKJV.*

[208] David Wiesman & Samuel Arenberg (Analysts), *Common Characteristics of the Government* (Washington, DC: U. S. Office of Personnel Management , 2010), p. 11. The 2.11 million federal staff figure does not include USPS and independent government corporations.

[209] Retrieved March 24, 2012: http://nbcpolitics.msnbc.msn.com/_news/2011/12/28/ 9776509-for-2012-a-curb-on-federal-hiring (web page inactive as of February 5, 2016).

[210] William Beach & Patrick Tyrrell, *The 2012 Index of Dependence on Government (A Report of the Heritage Center for Data Analysis),* (Washington, DC: The Heritage Foundation, SR 104 February 8, 2012), pp. 15-16.

[211] Heritage Foundation, "Welfare Reform: The Next Steps" (Washington, DC: Heritage Foundation's Leadership for America, March 17, 2011).

[212] Beach & Tyrrell, Chart 2, p. 3. Government dependence includes welfare and subsidy recipients. Statistical, budget, and spending figures used by Beach and Tyrrell originated from federal government's Office of Management and Budget, Fiscal Year 2012, and their historical tables.

[213] Ibid., p. 25.

[214] Ibid, Chart 1, p. 2.

[215] Ibid., Chart 14, p. 29 and p. 13.

[216] Ibid., Chart 1, p. 2.

[217] Romans 13:1-7, *NKJV*.

[218] Burton Folsom, Jr. (2008), *New Deal or Raw Deal: How FDR's Economic has Damaged America* (New York, NY: Simon and Schuster), pp. 63-69.

[219] Affordable Housing Institute (2012), "History of US public housing: Part 3"; retrieved March 28, 2012: http://affordablehousinginstitute.org/blogs/us/2008/10/history-of-us-public-housing-part-3-the-slum-clearance-era.html

[220] Oxford Dictionary, Kindle Locations 760836-760837.

[221] Mark Levin, *Ameritopia* (New York, NY: Simon and Schuster).

[222] Rummel, http://www.hawaii.edu/powerkills/TJP.CHAP4.HTM.

[223] Mark Levin (2009), *Liberty and Tyranny* (New York, NY: Simon and Schuster), pp. 16-17

[224] Retrieved February 5, 2016: https://betterworldcampaign.org/us-un-partnership/fy17-funding-request/

[225] One World Guide, "Aid Sources and Statistics" (London, UK: OneWorld UK). Retrieve March 26, 2012: http://uk.oneworld.net/guides/aid#Statistics.

[226] Marc Perrusquia, "Memphis Habitat homeowners lead nation in bankruptcy, losing homes," article in *The Commercial Appeal* December 7, 2003 (Memphis, TN: Scripps Newspaper Group online, 2012), para. 2.

[227] Retrieved February 6, 2012: http://www.businessinsider.com/dems-double-down-with-flawed-strategy-on-ows-2011-10

[228] Richard Cloward and Frances Piven, "The Weight of the Poor: A Strategy to End Poverty": *The Nation*, May 2, 1966 (New York, NY: The Nation Co., L.P.).

[229] EPA Historical Publication (Spring 1992), "The Guardian: Origins of the EPA" (Washington, DC: United States Environmental Protection Agency). Retrieved April 1, 2012: http://www.epa.gov/aboutepa/history/publications/print/origins.html

[230] Proverbs 16:25, *NKJV*.

[231] Green New Deal Group, *A Green New Deal* (London, UK: New Economics Foundation, 2007), p. 35. Retrieved March 26, 2012: http://www.neweconomics.org/publications/green-new-deal

[232] GSCEC is a Chinese company in China. Robert Johnson (June 28, 2011), "The San Francisco Bridge that's Being Built in China is almost Done" (Business Insider, Inc., 2012). Retrieved April 1, 2012:
http://articles.businessinsider.com/2011-06-28/news/30088661_1_chinese-workers-unemployed-workers-unemployment-compensation
http://www.telegraph.co.uk/news/worldnews/asia/china/8602786/New-San-Francisco-bridge-built-in-China-to-be-shipped-to-US.html

[233] Brett Schaefer (September 29, 2010), " President Klaus Highlights UN's Limits" (Washington, DC: The Foundry: The Heritage Foundation), para. 3. Retrieved April 2, 2012: http://blog.heritage.org/2010/09/29/president-klaus-highlights-un%e2%80%99s-limits/

[234] Tim Jackson (March 2009), *Prosperity without Growth: A Transition to a Sustainable Economy* (London, UK: Sustainable Development Commission), p. 5.
With a little persistent "binging", a free pdf copy can be obtained online.

[235] See article at: http://www.infowars.com/un-wants-world-tax-to-help-the-poor/ print/. Read UN Secretariat report: United Nations Secretary-General's High-Level Panel on Global Sustainability (2012). Resilient people, resilient planet: A future worth choosing, Overview, New York: United Nations.

[236] UN Secretariat report: United Nations Secretary-General's High-Level Panel on Global Sustainability (2012). Resilient people, resilient planet: A future worth choosing, Overview, New York: United Nations.

[237] United Nations Department of Public Information (UNDPI), *Basic Facts about the United Nations* (New York: United Nations Department of Public Information, 2011), p. 168.

[238] Ibid, p. 169.

[239] Ibid.

[240] Ibid., pp. xvii-xviii.

[241] For more in-depth information go to: http://www.un.org/law/ilc/index.html

[242] David Ehrlich, "The ICC: International Justice or Global Government?" *The Foundry,* March 4, 2010 (Washington, DC: The Heritage Foundation).

[243] Ted Bromund, "Why the U.S. Should Be Concerned About the Domestic Effects of the U.N. Arms Trade Treaty" WebMemo, No. 3430, December 11, 2011 (Washington, DC: The Heritage Foundation). Retrieved April 5, 2012: http://report.heritage.org/wm3430

[244] Steven Groves, "Accession to U.N. Convention on the Law of the Sea Would Expose the U.S. to Baseless Climate Change Lawsuits," *Backgrounder,* No. 2660, March 12, 2012; and "U.N. Convention on the Law of the Sea Erodes U.S. Sovereignty over U.S. Extended Continental Shelf," *Backgrounder,* No. 2561, June 8, 2011 (Washington, DC: The Heritage Foundation). Retrieved April 5, 2012: http://thf_media.s3.amazonaws.com/2012/pdf/bg2660.pdf http://thf_media.s3.amazonaws.com/2011/pdf/bg2561.pdf

[245] Ibid., p. 157.

[246] Berit Kjos, *Brave New Schools*, see Chapters 2 and 5.

[247] UNESCO, *UNESCO at the Dawn of the 21st Century 1988-1999* (France: UNESCO, 1999), p. 211.

[248] UNEP, *Concept Paper for the Task Force on Sustainable Lifestyles* (UN Environmental Protection, 2007), pp. 5 and 7-8. Retrieved April 4, 2012: esa.un.org/marrakechprocess/pdf/TFSL_ConceptPaper.pdf

[249] Berit Kjos, "Can't we all Share One Religion," *Forcing Change, Vol. 6, Issue 3, March 2012*, p. 1. Retrieved March 3: http://www.forcingchange.org/files/ 1874178/uploaded/Volume%206,%20Issue%203.pdf

[250] Berit Kjos, *Brave New Schools* (Harvest House Publishers, 1995), p. 88,

[251] United Nations, *Agenda 21* (United Nations, 2009). Document can be purchased at: http://www.un.org/esa/dsd/agenda21/

[252] Visit the following web site for suggestions as to how to give the international NGO their walking papers by terminating city contracts with the ICLEI: http://www.freedomadvocates.org/articles/sustainable_development/kick_iclei_out%21_20100 410407/

[253] Stephen Poole (August 17, 2011), "Benefit Corporations: Expansion of the Public-Private Fascist State, Part 4" (Freedomadvocates.org, August 11, 2011). Retrieved March 28, 2012: http://www.freedomadvocates.org/articles/illegitimate_government/benefit_corporations%3a_e xpansion_of_the_public-private_fascist_state%2c_part_4_20110817449/

[254] Freedomadvocates.org slide #10, "UN Agenda 21: Global to Local: Understanding and Countering Agenda 21/Sustainable Development/Smart Growth."

[255] UN environmental *extremist loons* consider humans as a species (true to their Darwinian ideology), therefore humans would be considered an invasive species in many environmental situations.

[256] Brett Schaefer, " The History of the Bloated U.N. Budget: How the U.S. Can Rein It In," *Backgrounder,* No. 2767, April 2, 2012; and "U.S. Must Ensure that U.N. Accounting Gimmicks Result in Real Cuts to Bloated U.N. Budget No. 2642, January 20, 2012 (Washington, DC: The Heritage Foundation).

[257] Brett Schaefer (February 3, 2010), "Time to Rein in the UN's Budget," *Backgrounder #2368* (Washington, DC: The Heritage Foundation). Available online: http://s3.amazonaws.com/thf_media/2010/pdf/bg_2368.pdf

[258] Freedom Advocates (2012). Retrieved March 13, 2012: http://www.freedomadvocates.org/components/com_joomgallery/img_pictures/cartoons_1/cart oon_21_20090513_1296507653.jpg[/IMG].

[259] Report of Habitat: the United Nations Conference on Human Settlements, convened in Vancouver, Canada, 31 May - 11 June, 1976 (Nairobi, Kenya: UN-Habitat; electronic version, 2006), last paragraph of Preamble and paragraph II.10.

[260] http://www.govtrack.us/congress/bills/111/s510 and http://foodfreedom.wordpress.com/2010/05/10/food-safety-the-worst-of-both-bills-hr-2749-and-s-510/

[261] Mike Opelka, "Is the Soros-Sponsored 'Agenda 21' a Hidden Plan for World Government? (Yes, Only it Is Not Hidden)," *The Blaze,* June 14, 2011.

[262] Juliett Jowit, "UN says Eat less Meat to Curb Global Warming," *The Observer*, September 6, 2008 (Guardian News and Media Limited, 2012). Retrieved April 5, 2012: http://www.guardian.co.uk/environment/2008/sep/07/food.foodanddrink

[263] Utilitarianism- actions are right if they are for the common good; egalitarianism- belief that all people are equal with the added twist of believing that everyone should benefit equally regardless of personal investment or effort.

[264] Berit Kjos, "The Transformation of America" (original author granted permission for use of chart). Retrieved February 29, 2012: http://www.crossroad.to/charts/postmodernity.html

[265] Berit Kjos, *Brave New Schools*, Chapter 2.

[266] Berit Kjos, "Postmodern Emphasis in Schools and Culture" (Kjos Ministries, No copyright listed, author granted public domain use of information posted on web site). Retrieved February 29, 2012: http://www.crossroad.to/charts/emphasis.html

[267] For more insight into *sustainable history* and *Transhumanism (H+)* go to: http://sustainablehistory.com/key-concepts.html#32 and /key-quotes.html

[268] Gary Kah (1998), *The New World Religion* (Noblesville, IN: Hope International Publishing, Inc.), pp. 188-189.

[269] Michael Carl, "Muslims: Wipe Christianity from the Face of the Earth," (WND.com, Inc.). Retrieved July 8, 2012: http://mobile.wnd.com/2012/07/muslim-group-wipe-christianity-from-face-of-earth/?cat_orig=world

[270] Stephen Pools, "Benefit Corporations: Expansion of the Public-Private Fascist State, Part 4" (Freedom Advocates online, 2012). Retrieved January 11, 2012: http://www.freedomadvocates.org/articles/illegitimate_government/benefit_corporations%3a_e xpansion_of_the_public-private_fascist_state%2c_part_4_20110817449/

[271] Psalm 51:6, *NKJV.*

[272] Karl Marx (1848), *The Communist Manifesto*, p. 63.

[273] Dean Halverson, *The Compact Guide to World Religions*, p. 241.

[274] Ibid.

[275] Andy Andrews (2011), *How to Kill 11 Million People* (Nashville, TN: Thomas Nelson, Inc.), p. 21.

[276] Noah Webster (2009-03-24). American Dictionary of the English Language - 1828 Noah Webster Dictionary (Kindle Locations 86654-86655). Misbach Enterprises. Kindle Edition.

[277] 1 Corinthians 13:6, *NKJV*.

[278] Andy Andrews, p. 32.

[279] Erwin Lutzer (2010), *When a Nation Forgets God* (Chicago: IL: Moody Publishers), Kindle Locations 889-899.

[280] Joel McDurmon, *Biblical Logic in Theory and Practice* (Powder Springs, GA: American Vision Press), p. 22.

[281] Ibid, p. 23.

[282] Grant Jeffrey (1996), *The Signature of God* (New York, NY: Inspirational Press).

[283] For insight into reframing the debate tactic according to Progressives, read the following book: George Lakoff & Elisabeth Wheling (2012), *The Little Blue Book: The Essential Guide to Thinking and Talking Democratic* (New York: Free Press).

[284] Erwin Lutzer, Kindle Location 859.

[285] Okay, so I made up a word, i.e., *delphied*. It simply means that the *Delphi techniques* has been used to manipulate a person or a group.

[286] Brannon Howse, *Grave Influence*, p. 99.

[287] B. K. Eakman (2011), *How to Counter Group Manipulation Tactics* (Raleigh, NC: Midnight Whistler Publishers), pp. 6-7.

[288] Ibid.

[289] Ibid., p. 11.

[290] Ephesians 6:11-18 and 2 Corinthians 10:3-5, *NKJV*.

[291] Proverbs 20:7b, *NKJV*.

[292] Genesis 1:26, *NKJV*.

[293] Nancy Pearcey (2005), *Total Truth: Liberating Christianity from it Cultural Captivity* (Wheaton, IL: Good News Publishers/Crossway Books), Kindle Location 2879-2884.

[294] Ibid, Kindle Locations 2884-2885.

[295] Genesis 2:24, Matthew 19:5, *NKJV*.

[296] Genesis 1:28; Malachi 4:6; Ephesians 5:21-33, *NKJV*.

[297] Carle Zimmerman (1947) and James Kurth (editor), *Family and Civilization* (Wilmington, DE: ISI Books, 2008).

[298] Malachi 2:14, *NKJV*.

[299] Ephesians 5:22-33 and 6:1-4, *NKJV*.

[300] Zimmerman, p. 200.

[301] Matthew 19:6, *NKJV*.

[302] Zimmerman, p. 232.

[303] Ibid., p. 235.

[304] Ibid., p. 27.

[305] Ibid., p. 223.

[306] Zimmerman, p. 229.

[307] Deuteronomy 5:16-21, *NKJV*.

[308] Zimmerman, p. 235.

[309] Ibid., p. 210.

[310] Ibid., p. 27.

[311] Ibid., p. 239.

[312] Ibid., p. 33.

[313] Ibid., p. 245.

[314] Ibid., p. 246.

[315] Ibid., p. 244.

[316] Ibid., pp. 250-251.

[317] Ibid., p. 255.

[318] Retrieved May 26, 2012: http://familyfacts.org/charts/150/the-proportion-of-married-adults-has-decreased

[319] Retrieved May 26, 2012: http://www.cdc.gov/nchs/fastats/divorce.htm.

[320] Retrieved May 26, 2012: http://www.familyfacts.org/charts/110/nearly-12-percent-of-couples-living-together-are-unmarried

[321] Retrieved May 26, 2012: http://familyfacts.org/charts/140/despite-recent-decline-two-thirds-of-children-live-with-married-parents-#

[322] Paula Goodwin, William Mosher, & Anjani Chandra, *Marriage and cohabitation in the United States: A statistical portrait based on Cycle 6 (2002) of the National Survey of Family Growth*- Vital Health Stat 23(28) (Washington, DC: National Center for Health Statistics, 2010), p. 3. Retrieved May 26, 2012: http://www.cdc.gov/nchs/data/series/sr_23/sr23_028.pdf

[323] Retrieved May 26, 2012: http://familyfacts.org/charts/207/unwed-childbearing-has-increased-dramatically-regardless-of-mothers-age

[324] Zimmerman, p. 224.

[325] The Heritage Foundation, "Cohabitation vs. Marriage"- No. 9" (familyfacts.org, 2012), para. 1. Retrieved May 26, 2012: http://thf_media.s3.amazonaws.com/familyfacts/briefs/FF_Brief_9.pdf

[326] Ibid., p. 4.

[327] Bradford Wilcox, etal., "Why Marriage Matters" (New York: Institute for American Values, 2005), p. 2. Retrieved May 26, 2012: http://www.americanvalues.org/pdfs/wmmexsumm.pdf

[328] The Heritage Foundation, "Family Environment and Children's Prospects for Marriage"- No. 39" (familyfacts.org, 2012), para. 1. Retrieved May 26, 2012:
http://www.familyfacts.org/briefs/39/family-environment-and-childrens-prospects-for-marriage

[329] B. K. Eakman (2010), *A Common Sense Platform for the 21st Century* (Raleigh, NC: Midnight Whistler Publishers), p. 19 quoting from Theodore Dalrymple, "Do we all want freedom?" Axess Magazine, Oct. 17, 2010.

[330] The Heritage Foundation, "Saving the American Dream: The Heritage Foundation 2011 Annual Report" (Washington, DC: The Heritage Foundation), p. 24.

[331] The Heritage Foundation, "Married Fathers: America's Greatest Weapon Against Child Poverty"- WebMemo #2934, June 16, 2010 (Washington, DC: The Heritage Foundation), para. 6. Retrieved from http://report.heritage.org/wm2934.

[332] Ibid., para. 7.

[333] TANF is Temporary Assistance for Needy Families.

[334] Heritage, "Saving the American Dream," p. 25.

[335] Heritage, "Married Fathers...",

[336] Proverbs 29:2, *NKJV.*

[337] *Final Solution*- the extermination of the Jewish race, those considered unfit to be a part of the human race and those who opposed Hitler.

[338] Adbranch.com, "How IBM Automated the Nazi Death Machine" (A Dehomag (IBM German Subsidiary) poster, circa 1934). Retrieved June 13, 2012 from:
http://www.adbranch.com/tag/punch-cards/

[339] Retrieved June 14, 2012 at:
http://merahza.files.wordpress.com/2009/05/hollerith.jpg?w=300&h=211

[340] Edwin Black (2011), *IBM and the Holocaust* (Washington, DC: Dialog Press), p. 7.

[341] Ibid., p. 9

[342] Ibid.

[343] Read the following article: http://www.nowpublic.com/world/full-body-scanner-lobby-michael-chertoff-rapiscan-2552674.html

[344] Review the following article: http://www.foxnews.com/politics/2012/06/14/lawmakers-erect-challenges-to-drones-in-us-airspace/

[345] John Whitehead, *The Freedom Wars* (Charlottesville, VA: Tri Press; Glass Onion Productions [2010]), see Chapter 9.

[346] http://www.drpasswater.com/nutrition_library/Nov_05/
Murray_FDA_part_1_final.html
http://www.drpasswater.com/nutrition_library/Nov_05/Murray_FDA_Struggle_final.html

[347] Read the following:
→ http://www.therightscoop.com/shock-brain-surgeon-confirms-obamacare-rations-care-has-death-panels/
→ http://familysecuritymatters.org/publications/id.3790/pub_detail.asp
→ http://www.americanthinker.com/2012/02/unequal_protection_under_the_healthcare_law.html

[348] Genesis 6:3, *NKJV*.

[349] 1 Timothy 2:2 and 2 Chronicles 7:14, *NKJV*.

[350] Review the following:
http://cnsnews.com/news/article/57-billion-taxpayer-money-spent-so-far-encourage-use-electronic-health-records

[351] Heritage.org/solutions, "Solutions for America: Get to Work- Get Control of Government," November 3, 2010 (Washington, DC: Heritage Foundation, 2010).

[352] Review the following article:
→ http://cnsnews.com/news/article/un-global-environmental-program-gets-boost-rio20-conference
→ http://www.foxnews.com/world/2012/06/12/un-climate-organization-wants-immunities-against-charges-conflict-interest/
→ http://www.foxnews.com/world/2012/06/01/rio-20-conference-negotiators-producing-mammoth-messy-and-expensive-grab-bag/

[353] Galatians 5:13-14, *NKJV*.

[354] For more information see the following: www.cfr.org
→ http://nwoobserver.wordpress.com/2009/11/24/the-council-on-foreign-relations-cfr-and-the-new-world-order/
→ http://nwoobserver.wordpress.com/2009/11/15/the-council-on-foreign-relations/#more-6119
→ http://nwoobserver.wordpress.com/2009/08/27/the-council-on-foreign-relations-to-govern-the-world-by-means-of-david-rockefeller%c2%b4s-studies-program/

[355] Isobel Coleman & Gayle Tzemach Lemmon, "Family Planning and U. S. Foreign Policy" (New York, NY: Council on Foreign Relations, Inc., 2011).

[356] President James Garfield, "A Century of Congress," Atlantic, July 1877, 63, 64 as quoted by Andy Andrews (2011), *How Do You Kill 11 Million People*, p. 61.

[357] David Barton (2000), *Keys to Good Government* (Aledo, TX: WallBuilder Press), p. 7. (During the time of Noah Webster, "men" was a generic term for men and women.)

[358] Jablow Hershman & Julian Lieb, *A Brotherhood of Tyrants* (Amherst, NY: Prometheus Books, 1994).

[359] Ibid., p. 13.

[360] Psalm 33:12a, *NKJV*.

[361] Psalm 65:5-6 & Genesis 1:9-10, *NKJV*. Colorado Mountains, retrieved June 24, 2012: http://www.free-extras.com/images/colorado_mountain-12097.htm

[362] Genesis 1:24-25, *NKJV*. Zebra Mom with Baby, retrieved June 24, 2012: http://www.bing.com/images/search?q=Zebra+with+Baby&view=detail&id=620A72649A7BA4CB310F3961E9AC042B3AEFBB8A

363 Genesis 1:30-31 & Matthew 6:25-27, *NKJV*. Hummingbird retrieved June 24, 2012: http://www.bing.com/images/search?q=photos+of+hummingbirds+and+flowers&view=detail&id=BB91F8B3488BCB0D513259F45F849C2EF1F86448&first=351

364 Baby retrieved June 25, 2012: http://www.bing.com/images/search?q=Cute+Black+Babies&view=detail&id=8894BC03D9B2BEDE4811D36647F17E019D8292C4&first=281

365 Genesis 1:26-28, *NKJV*. Baby retrieved June 24, 2012: http://www.bing.com/images/search?q=photos+of+baby&view=detail&id=1DD4B0F16DAB4F0D67A0EF1A4170F82561D3E1DB

366 Grant Jeffrey (1997), *The Handwriting of God* (New York, NY: Inspirational Press), p. 517.

367 Ibid., p. 518-519.

368 Grant Jeffrey (1996), *The Signature of God* (New York, NY: Inspirational Press), p. 128.

369 Grant., *The Handwriting of God*, p. 519.

370 Romans 1:20, *NKJV*.

371 Poetry-Archive.com (2002) retrieved June 25, 2012: http://www.poetry-archive.com/j/the_creation.html

372 Acts 17:24-28, *NKJV*.

373 Psalm 139:13-18, *NKJV*.

374 Matthew 1:23, *NKJV*.

375 C. S. Lewis, *Surprised by Joy* (Orlando, FL: Harcourt, Inc., C. S. Lewis PTE Limited, 1995), p. 228.

376 Go to the following website for details: http://www.adherents.com/Religions_By_Adherents.html

377 Psalm 119:45, *NKJV*.

378 Luke 4:16b-21, *NKJV*.

379 John 8:31-32, and 36, *NKJV*.

380 Romans 8:2, *NKJV*.

381 2 Corinthians 3:17, *NKJV*.

382 Galatians 5:1, and 13-14, *NKJV*.

383 James 1:25, *NKJV*.

384 Retrieved June 30, 2012: http://www.state.gov/j/drl/rls/hrrpt/2008/eap/119037.htm

385 Acts 17:26a, *NKJV*.

386 Galatians 3:28, *NKJV*.

387 John 3:16, *NKJV*.

388 Richard John Neuhaus, "Faith" in Edwin Feulner, Jr.'s (2000), *Leadership for America* (Dallas, TX: Spence Publishing Company), p. 236.

389 See Supreme Court Case: *Everson v. Board of Education*, 330 U.S. 1, 18 (1947).

390 David Barton (2007), *Separation of Church and State* (Aledo, TX: WallBuilder Press), p. 14.

391 Ibid., p. 12.

392 Ibid., pp. 12-13.

393 Ibid., p. 13.

394 Ibid., p. 6.

395 Ibid., p. 7.

396 Ibid.

397 Ibid., p. 11.

398 Ibid., p. 17 (Barton quotes statistics from The National Campaign to Prevent Teen Pregnancy, the Department of Health and Human Serves, and the Center for Disease Control.)

[399] Retrieved June 23, 2012; see Article 2:2 of the following document, which was included as Appendix C of the July-August 2010 International Religious Freedom Report; original document is from: UN General Assembly, *Declaration on the Elimination of All Forms of Intolerance and of Discrimination Based on Religion or Belief*, 25 November 1981, A/RES/36/55, available at: http://www.unhcr.org/refworld/docid/3b00f02e40.html [accessed 23 June 2012]

[400] Jerry Newcombe, *The Book That Made America* (Nordskog Publishing, Inc., Kindle Edition), Kindle Locations 267-269.

[401] David Barton, *Separation of Church and State*, p. 4 & 9.

[402] Ibid., p. 11.

[403] Ibid., p. 8.

[404] Ibid., p. 10.

[405] David Barton (2000), *Keys to Good Government* (Aledo, TX: WallBuilder Press), p. 10.

[406] Ibid., p. 8.

[407] Guenter Lewy, *Why America Needs Religion* (Grand Rapids, MI: William B. Eerdmans Publishing Company, 1996), p. 135 & 141.

[408] Matthew Spalding, *We Still Hold these Truths*, p. 232.

[409] Psalm 33:12a, *NKJV*.

[410] Ephesians 2:8-9; John 3:16; *NKJV*.

[411] Edgar C Bundy, *Collectivism in the Churches: A documented account of the political activities of the Federal, National, and World Councils of Churches* (Wheaton, Illinois: Church League of America, 1957), page 97.

[412] Ibid. Major ecumenical organizations include the World Council of Churches (WCC), National Council of Churches (NCC was formerly called the Federal Council of Churches until communist infiltration of the organization prompted a name change), World Bishops Council (World Federation of Churches); and Ecumenical Advocacy Alliance (EAA of the UN).

[413] Sinclair Ferguson and David F. Wright, "Liberalism and Conservatism in Theology" article in *New Dictionary of Theology* (Leicester, England: Universities and Colleges Christian Fellowship, 1988; published by Intervarsity Press in Downers Grove, IL), pp. 384-385.

[414] Alister E. McGrath (ed.), "Liberation Theology" and "Marxism" in *The Blackwell Encyclopedia of Christian Thought* (Oxford, UK: Basil Blackwell, Ltd., 1993).

[415] Walter A. Elwell (ed.), "Social Gospel" article by N. A. Magnuson, *Evangelical Dictionary of Theology* (Grand Rapids, MI: Baker Books, 1984), pp. 1027-1029.

[416] Donald C. Halverson, *The Compact Guide to World Religions* (Minneapolis, MN: Bethany House Publishers, International Students, Inc., 1996), pp. 185-187.

[417] Fritz Ridenour (2001), *So What's the Difference* (Ventura, CA: Regal Books), pp. 205-207. Unitarians are included because their worldview connects with secular humanism in the *Humanist Manifest I*, and many early American Socialists were members of this group. Currently they have distanced themselves from Secular Humanists and embraced neo-paganism to add a "spiritual" component to their worldview.

[418] Theology is included because it has had a connection with philosophy throughout human history. This is a brief overview and not an exhaustive survey, highlighting areas that have impacted faith, family, and freedom the most.

[419] Modernity- is a modern way of thinking, and the new way of thinking may or may not agree with established truth

[420] The nature of reality (metaphysics), the nature of values/ethics (axiology), the nature of truth (epistemology), the nature of being (ontology).

[421] Psalm 119:160 and John 17:17, *NKJV*.

[422] Ephesians 2:8-9, *NKJV*.

[423] John Marshall (1891), *A Short History of Greek Philosophy* (London, England: Percival and Co.; Public Domain, Kindle Edition, 2009), p. 47.

[424] Ibid., Chart 185.

[425] Norman Geisler and Paul Feinberg, *Introduction to Philosophy: A Christian Perspective* (Grand Rapids, MI: Baker Books, 1980), p. 389.

[426] Frederick Copelston (1946), *A History of Philosophy, Vol. 1: Greek and Roman* (New York: Doubleday, a division of Bantam, Doubleday and Dell Publishing Groups), p. 19-20.

[427] Wayne Mayhall, *Philosophers* (Boca Raton, FL: Quick Study- BarCharts, Inc., 2010), Early Modern Philosophers- Niccolo Machiavelli, p. 2. (quickstudy.com)

[428] Mark R. Levin (2012), *Ameritopia* (New York: Threshold Editions, a Division of Simon and Schuster, Inc.), pp. 23-24. Utopia theme was prevalent in Plato's *The Republic.*

[429] Alister McGrath (2004), *The Twilight of Atheism* (New York: Doubleday), p. 8.

[430] Mitchell, Chart 186.

[431] Ibid., Chart 144. The nature of reality (metaphysics), the nature of values (axiology), the nature of truth (epistemology), the nature of being (ontology).

[432] Ibid., *Philosophy*, Section 2: History of Political Philosophy

[433] SparksCharts, *Philosophy*, Section 3: Modern Philosophy- Marxism

[434] Ibid., Section 3: Modern Philosophy- Marxism

[435] Mitchell (2007), Chart 29.

[436] Mayhall, Modern Philosophers- Jean-Baptiste Lamarck, p. 3.

[437] Ibid.

[438] Ibid., Section 2: Modern Philosophy- Materialism.

[439] Geoffrey Gilbert, introduction to Malthus T.R. 1798. *An essay on the principle of population.* Oxford World's Classics reprint. Viii.

[440] Ibid.

[441] Mitchell, Chart 132.

[442] Ibid., Section 3: Modern Philosophy- Existentialism

[443] Ibid, Chart 50.

[444] SparkCharts, *Philosophy* (USA: SparksNotes, LLC, 2002; Barnes and Noble Publication), Section1: Overview of Philosophy- Ethics.

[445] Ibid.

[446] Ibid., Section 1: Overview of Philosophy- Ethics.

[447] Mayhall, Philosophical Movements, p. 3. (quickstudy.com)

[448] SparkCharts, *Western Civilization* (USA: SparksNotes, LLC, 2002; Barnes and Noble Publication), Section 4: Enlightenment.

[449] Mayhall, Modern Philosophers- Comte de Saint-Simon, p. 3. (quickstudy.com)

[450] SparkCharts, *Philosophy*, Section 3: Modern Philosophy- Immanual Kant

[451] Oxford Dictionary, Kindle location 760752-760755.

[452] Mitchell (2007), Charts 205 and 161.

[453] Ibid., Chart 147.

[454] Geisler and Feinberg, pp. 57-58. In philosophy or theology, subjective means lacking a truth value.

[455] Mayhall, Modern Philosophers- Jacques Derrida, p. 6.

[456] Ferguson & Wright (editors), "Feminist Theology," pp. 255-256.

[457] "Neo-conservatism" retrieved March 15, 2012:
http://www.conservapedia.com/Neoconservatism

[458] Mayhall, *Political Science: International Relations* (Boca Raton, FL: Quick Study- BarCharts, Inc., 2010), Social Constructivism, p. 3.

[459] Thomas Horn (2011), *Pandemonium's Engine* (Crane, MO: Defender). Specific article by Cris Putnam, "Chapter 5—Christian Transhumanism: Pandemonium's Latest Ploy."

[460] NCC, "A Social Creed for the 21st Century," (Approved by the General Assembly of the National Council of Churches USA and Church World Service on November 7, 2007). Retrieved March 23, 2012: http://www.ncccusa.org/news/ga2007.socialcreed.html
[461] Underlining is added to highlight Socialist language.
[462] David Bebbington (1990), *Patterns in History* (Vancouver, Canada: Regents College Publishing), pp. 17-20.
[463] Ibid., p. 21.
[464] Ibid., p. 19.
[465] Ibid., p. 20.
[466] William Beach & Patrick Tyrrell, *The 2012 Index of Dependence on Government (A Report of the Heritage Center for Data Analysis),* (Washington, DC: The Heritage Foundation, SR 104 February 8, 2012), p. 23.
[467] World Urban Forum III (June, 2006), *Our Future: Sustainable Cities- Turning Ideas in Action* (Vancouver, CAN: UN-Habitat). www.un-habitat.org
[468] United Nations Department of Public Information, *Basic Facts about the United Nations,* p. 166.
[469] Ibid.
[470] During a "citizen's" planning session in a small city, I sat next to a regional NGO employee, a non-resident of our city, who did not hesitate to express what she wanted for our city. It was not appropriate for a non-resident to voice her wants for our city, especially if she would not reap the results of her wants if implemented. How in the world was this responding to a community's own sense of how and where it wants to grow?
[471] Freedom Advocates, "What is Unsustainable." Page numbers reference the 1142 page UNEP Global Biodiversity Assessment 1995. Retrieved February 27, 2012: http://www.freedomadvocates.org/articles/sustainable_development/what_is_%22unsustainable%22?_2003022414/
[472] 1 Corinthians 13:1-13, *NKJV.*
[473] Exodus 20:2-27, *NKJV.*
[474] Retrieved June 19, 2012 from: http://www.reagan.utexas.edu/archives/speeches/1983/20383b.htm

Restoring Faith, Family & Freedom, LLC
191 Sequoyah Place
Dahlonega, GA 30533

www.elisewhitworth.com
elisewhitworth@gmail.com

www.ingramcontent.com/pod-product-compliance
Lightning Source LLC
Chambersburg PA
CBHW062132280526
45788CB00001B/137